McPHEE GRIBBLE/PENGUIN BOOKS

AN ABORIGINAL MOTHER
TELLS OF THE OLD AND THE NE

Elsie Roughsey was born in 1923, a member of the Lardil tribe of
Aborigines from Mornington Island, or Goonana as they know it, in the
southern Gulf of Carpentaria. Her parents called her Labumore after the
fruit of a native plant. From the age of eight she was raised in a mission
dormitory, an institution which aimed to educate and condition Aboriginal children into the European way of life. During the war years the
missionaries were evacuated from the island, and Elsie rejoined her
parents to live in the bush and on the beaches, travelling between the
many camps of her people and gathering the native foods of their land.

The missionaries returned in 1946, and Elsie married the author-artist,
Dick Roughsey. Elsie is now the mother of six – a daughter and five sons.
During her adult life she has worked as a nursing assistant, teacher aid and
has been involved in voluntary community work. She has also actively
participated in the revival of Aboriginal culture on the island.

Dr Paul Memmott has had a close association with the people of
Mornington Island over the last ten years. He is now principal of a
research consultancy practice closely allied to the Aboriginal Data
Archive at the University of Queensland. Specializing in Aboriginal
projects, it aims at facilitating information exchange between black and
white Australians.

After completing a B.A.Dip.Ed. at Sydney University in 1976 Robyn
Horsman was posted as a teacher to Mornington Island, where she, over
two and a half years, assisted in establishing the secondary department of
the State School. She formed a close bond with the Island community,
and with the Roughsey family. She now works as a research assistant in
the Aboriginal Data Archive.

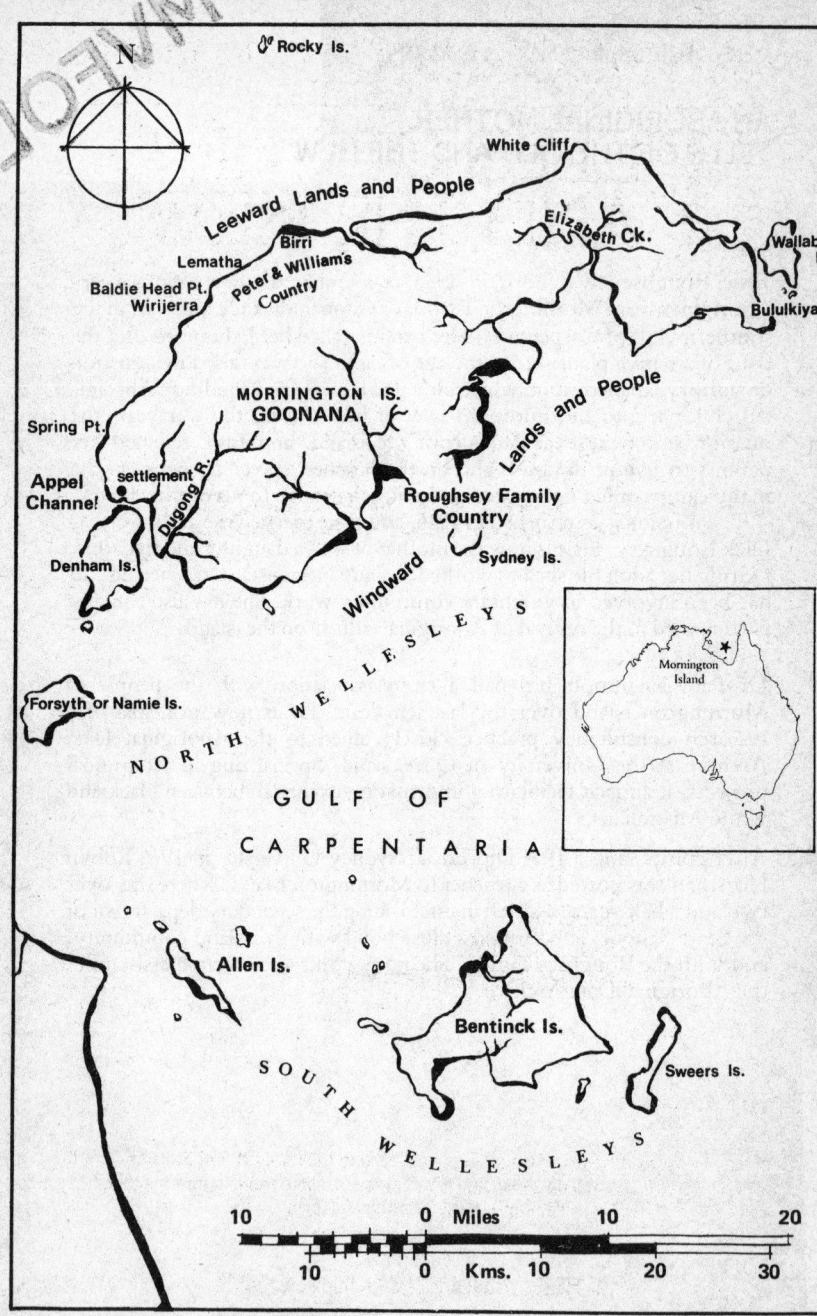

AN ABORIGINAL MOTHER

TELLS OF THE OLD AND THE NEW

LABUMORE: ELSIE ROUGHSEY

edited by
PAUL MEMMOTT
AND ROBYN HORSMAN

This work has been produced with the support and assistance of the Aboriginal Arts Board and published with the assistance of the Literature Board of the Australia Council

McPHEE GRIBBLE/PENGUIN BOOKS

McPhee Gribble Publishers Pty Ltd
66 Cecil Street
Fitzroy, Victoria, 3065, Australia

Penguin Books Australia Ltd,
487 Maroondah Highway, P.O. Box 257
Ringwood, Victoria, 3134, Australia
Penguin Books Ltd,
Harmondsworth, Middlesex, England
Penguin Books,
40 West 23rd Street, New York, N.Y. 10010, U.S.A.
Penguin Books Canada Ltd,
2801 John Street, Markham, Ontario, Canada
Penguin Books (N.Z.) Ltd,
182-190 Wairau Road, Auckland 10, New Zealand

First published by McPhee Gribble Publishers
in association with Penguin Books Australia, 1984
Reprinted 1984, 1986
Copyright © Elsie Roughsey, 1984

Typeset in Bembo by Bookset, Melbourne
Made and printed in Australia by
The Dominion Press–Hedges & Bell

National Library of Australia
Cataloguing-in-Publication data

Roughsey, Elsie, 1923–.
An aboriginal mother tells of the old and the new.

ISBN 0 14 007244 6.

1. Roughsey, Elsie, 1923– . [2]. Aborigines,
Australian – Biography. I. Title.

994'.0049915

Contents

cont . . .

Preface

Elsie Roughsey's book represents many things. It is a self-study of the forces shaping an Aboriginal life and an Aboriginal mind in a period of acute and often traumatic cultural change, and may be interpreted as a product of that cultural change. The work contrasts many aspects of Aboriginal and mission values, particularly through Elsie's discussion of religion, power, leadership, crime and punishment, employment, education, love and marriage, from both a traditional and contemporary perspective. It is partly an autobiography, partly a family history, partly a tribal history and partly a mission history. It is a philosophic statement on Aboriginal identity.

The reader will be aware of an apparent contradiction in Elsie's discussion of cultural change; for example, her emotional responses to the childhood days in the mission dormitory, and the philosophic statements about the future of her people at the conclusion of the book. These contradictions do not reflect a flaw in her argument, but rather, reflect the complex array of dilemmas that the people of Mornington have faced over the past seventy-five years, where the process of irreversible change has been marked by conflicting moral and material values. Elsie has no clear solution for her people's future, but she does provide a valuable insight into their thoughts and feelings concerning their changing cultural identity.

Elsie's style of relating her thoughts and experiences is in itself a unique cultural expression. Today oral histories are becoming more and more common in Aboriginal publications, but there have not yet been many histories or autobiographies written by Aboriginal authors who have experienced a traditional bush lifestyle and the system of beliefs, values and day to day activities that are part of that lifestyle. Elsie's dual perceptions of the bush and mission life of her people are a key feature of the book; as is her obvious deep concern for other Aboriginal Australians, their past, present and future.

Above all, however, Elsie's work is a valid and powerful literary work in its own right.

We feel privileged to have had the opportunity to work closely with Elsie Roughsey and her manuscript.

Paul Memmott and Robyn Horsman
May 1983

Acknowledgements

The editors and the author are appreciative of the assistance received from the Commonwealth Government through the Aboriginal Arts Board of the Australia Council, and in particular, of the enthusiasm of the Arts Board Project Officer, Elaine Godden. Thanks also go to Hilary McPhee of McPhee Gribble Publishers for her confidence in, and support for the project. To Diana Eades, linguist in the Department of Anthropology, University of Queensland, goes much appreciation for her valuable advice about a variety of dilemmas we faced and the ethical aspects of the editing style.

We are also grateful for the assistance of Mick Walker, Robyn Davidson and Steve Mark.

I am making a doll out of cotton tree.

I'm a full blood Aboriginal, born 1923, on Goonana mission, Mornington Island. Goonana is the name of my native home, far up in the North, in the Gulf of Carpentaria, Queensland.

Thinking back those many years, from eight year old, when I was a child, now a full grown up woman with human sense of grown up person, I can see way, way back of my childhood days, thinking of the many of my good laws, customs and culture. Those days were so wonderful. Everybody was happy, full of laughs and fun. Laws were so strictly kept and obeyed. Everybody lived as one real people. Lardil, my people, lived a fine life with all they had.

I feel proud of myself. I was a child belonged of old parents that never went to school or hardly knew of the white man ways. But I must not say they did not know of the white man laws and rules. Of course they knew, but to keep away from them. They were happy to live and roam where they belonged to, out bush, where they were much happier and contented to be amongst themselves. All their effects they put in were hunting, dancing, gathering for tribal meetings, gathering together for great feast of eating all kinds of food, whether they were land or sea food. They never were selfish or mean, nasty or greedy. They lived to share whatever they had, and that's why they were great people of that time . . . splendid race.

Finally . . . crept in a white man, with all its different hard life, with the laws of Government, that drove away all our good ways of living. I wondered so much about all this.

So one day, I desired to put my time to write a book of my childhood to this present days, recalling back the things of my tribal people. Their laws and rules, culture-customs were so much better than the present times. I can look back

. . . most of the things I saw, heard . . . and was able to do them also with my people, and kept them. All the laughs and fun were ended among the people. Then sad, quiet, frightness, shyness came and made everything change rather different. Goonana life was passing out, out of our life altogether. Mission people settled in, in a different style.

The tribals' walk about was now on its way to a different search, now to come to face the new way to live and know of a European way of life. It seemed a bit different to come and understand. They were happy but not too sure to trust a white person. But above all this, what the European came to give was not the life they should depend on, for the coming years to really hold it. Their background life was so important that they really held with firmness and could not destroy their ways of life. They knew if they grabbed the life of another race firmly, their tribal life could have been wrecked, worthless, unwanted and altogether forgotten. But the tribal man knew what belonged to him . . . worth his life with freedom, with all he had to make him healthy, to hunt, to be brave, to love and care for all and live as one real people and live on the land as real Lardil people, on Goonana. Today, race has been mixed. The life has changed and there is sadness and happiness here. So our choice is mixed background and forward step together and make it one, and live as one real people for the days that are to come.

After so many waste of years, hardly doing much at all, thoughts came again and again. I must now write a book of my country life. My Lardil people must be brought forward, of all they did, of all they had and did, all their laws, customs, their culture, their tribal band of race of one people, were so well completed, formed . . . living much better than many Aboriginals from other places of the world.

My people never were myall, as most people consider we were. But I can honestly say they were very clever people . . . how they went about among their own people with their fine tribal laws and customs. I can look back when I was told by my father and Uncle Gully Peters about when Mr Hall was killed . . . how my grandfather Peter, that's my dad's father, he said, 'Never kill a white man, because that fellow got plenty more people like him, to come here and kill us all.' Then you wonder how on earth he knew about more white people . . . were more than a black man. Although, my grandfather must have had his own belief or feeling of such thing can be done at anytime when the case needed, because my grandfather's people never saw a white man before . . . although they knew they were the only people on Mornington Island, or Goonana was then at the time.

My people had so many wonderful beliefs. They were not wild tribes but lived contented roaming the island with all its wonderful ways of life. We were told they never been savages at all, but lived calm isolated people, people of the tribe of their own country. Some people do say my people are savages. That's when a white man wants to come here. But they are not. They are fine people . . . if they only come and look closely at our country and life.

Now looking in the year I was small, it's quite a long, long way back. Only now I am able to understand it all. When I was a child, I hardly knew anyone. I cannot ever explain really of my life. To me, I just got along the way things went. Memories were nothing to remember anything at all to me. But now my memories are wonderful. I just can see it all today, as if it happened just last year or fortnight ago.

It struck my minds very much, when I helped my husband collecting materials for the *Moon and Rainbow*. Reading through it, there were more of my laws, customs, cultures and legends . . . were not there. So I thought it would be a fine idea that I should write a book of some of the customs we had . . . and were finally ruined, and forgotten by my people, when the white man came and made us to throw it aside, because then their belief was another thing that stepped in. And all our real tribal relationship and friendship were never to be seen again, or used. I can say it really ruined the Lardils, living everything that was too good to be destroyed. I can write now that most of the way we lived with, are yet still now known to the world.

In the outer parts of the world, people of other states and continents do not know of my people really. Lardil customs, laws, culture and its legends will never be known to the people who never saw the tribes of Goonana people, the Lardil. They have so many things that are interesting . . . are still not known so far. Only very few have been told, or given to a white man.

I'm sure the world should know what was not mentioned, because other people can live by us if they only know the good laws of one time we had.

14 August 1972

Some old women sitting around the camp. *Ed. note:* Elsie's mother is on the far left.

These people were long before I was born so I don't know who they are.

Childhood days

When I was born, my mother and her friends made a rough circle of wind break for my arrival, and so my mother could be kept warm and find her baby without harm. No razor or scissors were used to cut the cord, but they used shells or bottles or perhaps their teeth. The time I came was when they started using piece of broken bottle. I really cannot explain that, but I was well looked after. Cure for my navel to stop it from bleeding was an ash from the fireplace. It also was used for drying up the bleeding. Even white pipe clay, that was also used for my mother's health.

My parents were young couples but they did not speak English. They spoke languages, and most of their talks and yarns were signs and signals. Most times, when I was growing up, I lived in the bush. Wherever my parents went, they took me. But truth to say, when I write this book, I have not a slightest idea of my dear mother. Was I with her when I grew a bit older? Oh, how I'd love to know it all . . . when I could take notice of who was my father or mother.

When I was eight years old, I lived with my father and his relatives. I never saw much of my mother or at least I really could not look back from eight year downwards, from the time I suckled from my mother's breast. It's too hard for me to trace back. I think my minds were too dim to understand. But anyway I still lived to grow up. The time I was a little girl, my mother was most of the time with her relatives. My mother, she was from the South side of Mornington Island. My father was from the North side of the island. So it was so hard for me to see them both together living as man and woman should. Living amongst my people, I hardly knew of them. I cannot explain how everything went.

I shall never, never tell any stories of all those times, only the day I noticed myself with my sister May William, other two friends Vera Barney and Gertie Gammon . . . how we walked along the shores of our island, going to the mission, singing, talking, laughing and playing as we went along. In the mission we stood around the place wondering what's going on. Hardly anyone was moving around. Few girls and boys were in school, but I had no idea of schools yet. We played around the yard until someone gave us girls a damper for tea, and we left and went back to our camps to our people.

Everyday we four walked into the mission yard. We had three meals a day, no school, no work but just went around the place. There was no one who could come and talk to us and tell us why we were in, or no one ever mentioned to us and told or explained who was our relation by sister, auntie, uncle or other relatives, or friends. Everything was quiet . . . nothing like that we grew to learn to understand. Everything was so dull. It seems we all did not understand each other, or there was no need to, or no one could help us to know who was the nearest relation to us to keep us company. Everything went the white man way . . . quiet and lonely, also friendless. All the orders we got from the white man and his wife. After getting our damper for tea about five o'clock, we went home, back to our wind break roughly made . . . no house, but amongst scrubs, grass and trees. As I mentioned before about my parents, I do not know, but they could have been my father's parents who looked after me at the time. All I can say . . . I was contented with who I stayed with.

Each day it happened, until there was that time when the missionaries desired to have us put in the dormitory to stay with the other children and go to school.

My big sister and brother were already in the dormitory, but we all did not know each other as families. We were only ordinary to one another, like the rest of the boys and girls who were there. I wonder why?

It's because our parents were scattered people, or it's because the missionaries and my people did not understand each other when talking to each other to find who this child belongs to, and how family comes together, so they can help the children who have been taken away from their loved ones to the mission dormitory.

I even cannot think back whether my father or mother brought me in to the dormitory, or I was just taken in. I did not like being in the dormitory. I just had to live that life like the rest of them. There was now no father and mother to be near. I often felt sad to know my parents were no where near me. I had no one to take care of me. I did what was shown to me by the missionary lady. Things were so quiet each day. It was so awful.

Well, I was a sad little girl, hardly knew anyone. Times went by. I came to have a bit of sense to understand some things of the new life I now had to face. I began to play around on my own, still dim with sense. Very little I can pick up. Still don't know about sister Julie and brother Ginger. Father came in to visit his children. Father would call out Elsie, May, Julie and Ginger to come over to him. So we would all come to Dad, not realising we were his children.

So Dad would say, 'This is for you, you . . .' and so on until he had given us all he brought to give us.

Then we all look at each other not knowing we are brother and sisters. We say Good bye or Good night to Father, and he goes back home to his camp. Each day was the same to us to see our parents, until we became to know we were in family circle. So as Dad goes away to bush it's sad for me to know I've got no father and mother to come and see me.

But it was really a very difficult life to go through. No parents near to love us and to take care for us. My mother, I really did not know her. Living in the dormitory, I thought I only had father, but I had no idea of having mother. Mother was nothing I have known or understood. If mother's love and care . . . was nothing I knew of.

But as I grew up, I started to go to school, worked in the gardens digging holes for the plants to be planted, watering gardens with fruit trees, vegetables of all kinds. We girls were very busy. Hot days were not meant for us to stand or sit under shady trees, but get up on your feet to go on working, until the job was finished.

I can remember working the garden . . . was so hot, so hot that while carrying water to water the plants, me and my mate would run along the hot sand, to try and get to a place where it was cool for our feet, not a shoe on, to keep the heat off. But in those days, shoes were not known to us. Working in the sun was too bad . . . often wished we could go down to the sea for bathe, but just could not. The times were so strict you could not be allowed to bathe in the sea, that you even weren't allowed to get out of the fenced yard of the mission. We had to go on each day the same, work in the sun.

We had so many vegetables here such as cabbages, radish, sweet turnips, beetroots, shallots, melons, pumpkins, rock melons, sugar canes, green peas, snake beans, cowpeas, bananas, custard apples, oranges, lemons, mangoes, limes, sweet corns and many others. The garden was so beautiful and plentiful. We girls and boys worked so hard to prepare the soil, and mixed the soil for all the plants that had to be seed sowed, and then replanted the young plants in different beds of ground. But all that work was in the days when it was so hot.

I can remember how we had to hoe up the ground for potatoes to make potato rows, while the rain was pouring down. Others planted the vines. Others cut the length of the vine for the other girls to carry to the ones that were planting. It was a rushing job to do while the rain fell. Although it was hard to work, but we were always happy to see the work that had been done during the rain.

During very cold weather all the work had to be continued. No warm clothes were given to us to keep ourselves warm. Oh, it was too bad, but that was the way we lived and worked, because the days were not as what is today. You get too much comfort now. Everything is so good. We are just satisfied . . . how now to live, no gardening, not too many hard work, as my life time. Today, where we had gardens and fruit trees, there is now mess of grass, and it is all turned out to be just play ground for school children. Now we all buy fruits that come from Mount Isa. We have so many beautiful soil here to grow all kinds, for farming and cattle grazing, but not much equipment for the work.

After morning Service on a week day, we go to school. We had all Aboriginal teachers, besides Mrs Wilson. I think Mr Wilson had to be with the men working things out. With him were other Staffs who worked together in every way with the Aboriginal men. There were many work to be done. Going to school, I liked it, because it meant not too much going in the garden to work. I liked school. I had many good funs and laughs with my friends.

When caught by the teacher for playing instead of going on with lessons, you are called, 'Hands out', . . . and there is a hard whack on the hand, whether by strap, board or ruler. Getting smack each day really meant nothing to us. As children would think . . . it's the way you must take it. Although, I did not know the laws and rules of a white man, I knew we must do what always happened each day, year in, year out. I really understood the life of being in the dormitories. As I became older, I found it was hard for everything to be fenced and locked up in the dormitory. But that's how it went.

For breakfast we would have flour porridge with sugar and fresh cow's milk. For midday lunch . . . rice mixed with meat and vegetables of different sorts. Supper . . . damper, jam or other times bullock's fat that had been melted. Bush fruits and roots were all collected to be eaten at each day meals, also pineapple, oranges, lemon, tomatoes, paw paws, melons, rock melons, mangoes, coconuts. These even went to go along with our meals.

So in those days, we had to be supported also by our folks, who came in to sell all they could bring in to the mission. This is how we were able to eat different foods to give us health. Also dugong, turtle, fish, crabs and oysters were brought in to us for extra feed. So at the same time, each children who had been in the mission, we had our own parents to give us more food such as wild honey, panja, nail fruit, water lilies . . . these grow in lagoon or swamps, and are dug from the ground . . . fish, oyster, flying foxes, goanna, swamp turtles and many other kinds of roots that were good food to eat, different wild fruits from the bush that had been plucked and brought in for the children. This is how our old folk had to do . . . sell some to the missionary lady, and got whatever they wanted, such as dresses, flour, tea, sugar, hooks, line, tobacco, potatoes, matches, cotton and needle, pins and other stuff that was in the mission store to buy. Well, this is how everybody worked together to keep up the extra food to keep their children going. So it was a good idea, and that's why we children never had sores, colds, head ache or any sorts of body trouble. We were healthy as we grew up.

I learnt to wash my iron plate, not with water and soap, but rubbing it on the wet sand until it shined clean, then to dry it out. I rubbed it on the dry sand to get it nice and dry, then put it away for the next meal. By doing that, I see now that was the only way to be clean. Although, some people now would say, 'Gee that's a dirty way to have our plates washed' . . . but that's how it went. You may wonder why these missionaries did not show us the right way to be clean by washing with soap and water and dry with dry clean cloth.

But anyway, we did not get affected with germs or sickness. We were healthy and strong and never sick at all at anytime, only once a year, when mosquito were bad at nights on a certain season of the year. I suppose the fever we had was caused by too many mosquito. That could have affected us with fever, because that was the only sickness we had only once a while in a year. Whooping cough we had once that made us so sick. That's the only bad times we ever felt the way of being sick. Many sickness was not in my childhood days, as I can see today, where there are all kinds. Bad sickness is amongst my people, even school children, toddlers and infants are affected by strange sickness, that many of them are flown over to Mount Isa and other places.

Now at these present time you may have cold, sick, sore throats, cold in the chest, also at back, for days and days or for a year. When you get better from one sickness, all of a sudden, you fall in another accident. Perhaps another worser one. You never be free from sickness of any sort.

11

Some sickness can almost live in a person's body. Some are lucky, who always keep themselves from being sick or keep away from those who often get sick, or from germs.

You wonder why most of these children have all kinds of trouble, especially bodily harm. Something is wrong somewhere in their body. You think not much bush food to eat . . . except the white man's tin stuff, too much tea and sugar, flour and many other food and no chance to go bush? I think that can harm them, because their parents and grandparents lived most of their life roaming bush, and many huntings were done by them.

Well, going back . . . when I got used to the mission I was about eight year old, because I was much taller to be eight year old, but that must have been the right age of that time to bring children up to the school dormitory . . . when I could understand few things.

But when I grew up in dormitory, I really did not understand many things. All I knew . . . the rules. Not all things as I should have learnt, but rules.

To get up early in the morning, the missionary lady or one of her children comes with the keys and opens the padlock, and we all rush out of the dormitory, just to be free, free as the Summer's bird . . . then wash our faces, grab a stick and bucket and go down the well and pump out water from the well to fill a large tank for the day's drink, for all the boys and girls and the Adults who had job to do in the mission, while the boys go out to bush and bring wood to cook all our meals. We do these jobs every morning, before we have our breakfast. We never sit around.

We have white flour porridge every, every morning for breakfast, with fresh cow's milk and sugar mixed. Also, we have to drink the cow's milk raw. I never liked fresh milk raw. I used to vomit. I never liked the taste. But at noon, when it's supper time we drink boiled cow's milk and that tastes much better. Then after breakfast we get into line, about five or six rows of us all, both boys and girls. Mrs Wilson pokes her head out of the window from the mission house, to see if our plates are clean . . . stack them all on the table, then get buckets, fill them with water for to wash our hands, face and legs and head, then comb our hair, get into line when the church bell rings for Service.

School is over. We have a midday meal, and are locked up in the dormitory to have a rest.

I can remember being locked up in the dormitory. I hated to lie down and go to sleep. I would lie down on the ground and chat away to my next mate lying beside me. It was a verandah part of the dormitory on ground earth. The gate of the door way was fastened with plain wire to the mission house . . . where no one can get out during resting hour at midday.

To keep us in . . . from the missionary house at one end there is a long plain wire that connected to the door or gate of our dormitory door. To lock us up, they pull a strand of this long wire to the end of the catch and hook it on. To let us free, they take the end of the wire off the catch, from the mission house, and bring it forward to release the gate. That's how we were really tied down, by that way. The way we were treated, it was like the early settlers, negroes who left their home and parents and had to be caged in a cage wire and put on ships to other places. I was told that. They were put in cages for USA. We were not far off the line. The way we were treated was the same.

Although things were hard, but I cannot understand why all these things had to be done in a hard way. I think in those days they had to keep us together, so we may not do the things what the missionaries thought we might do. But today, I still just can't understand why it all meant . . . to be so tough with us.

At two o'clock, we are let out and back to school again. Three hours time, when the school is over we have to go down to the garden and water the young plants, and fill the water tank again, while the boys carry wood for the meals to be cooked. Sometimes we carry seaweeds from the beach to be put around the young plants. When there is a big job to do in the garden, boys, girls, men and women all work together, also for tilling up the grounds for different plants to be planted.

In the night, when I had to be locked with padlock on to

13

the door by the lady in the dormitory, I had to be put in bed with some one. Well, it was so dark at nights. No lights were anywhere. The place looked so dark. To move around the place, all we had to feel where we were going. Just imagine, we were like blinded person. That's how we had to face the darkness.

During the night some one would scream with fright or have a bad dream. She would scream at the top of her voice. All of a sudden you would hear yelling and screaming from all the girls in the dormitory, then, when the noise would die away everybody would be quiet again.

Now it's the boys's turn to scream and yell. Although they don't know what happened . . . the yelling on the other end of the dormitory by girls. They would scream too. Because in those times the Adults told us too many stories of devil or Spirits. That was well in our life, that fear, and that devil can take anyone away. That's why the girls and boys never could have a pleasant sleep at nights in the dormitory.

I can remember at nights I had a sister, who always walked in her sleep. I would look for her then call out. She would get more frightened and run back to her bed. Not because I wanted to do that for any reason, but night mare was not that I knew of. But the same thing happened each nights, so often. I would try my best to help my sister to see she came in the right bed, with me, but as I spoke or touched her in her hand she also would take fright.

But we both grew up in the dormitory, helping each other through her night mare and all, until one day when I was fully grown up, everyone was evacuated because the war was now on. That's in the year 1942, when May William and myself had to stay with my uncle and auntie until my father returned from bush. Well, during the night May William did the same thing. She walked over to the window, from one room to another, then walked out of the house, standing and looking around. When I missed her . . . got up and saw she was missing from the bed. I then called out to her and saw her walking outside. I walked out to go and bring her back to bed, but Auntie Cora quickly and quietly walked up and whispered to me, 'Don't touch her. She has night mare.' Then I asked Auntie why was that. Well, she said, 'If you touch her, she take fright and die.' Then she explained the rest of the things another day. From that on, I understood all about night mares.

Every Wednesday and Saturday, the boys were sent out from dormitory, to learn to hunt, fish and crabbing, also to collect wild fruits, while the girls stayed in the mission and carried on with the work in the garden through the scorching sun, and watering plants, carrying black soil to mix in the hole ready for young plants to be put in, or for vegetables' seeds to be sowed in the ground, while the boys went out walk about in the bush or along the sea beaches to learn to hunt for their own food. Sometimes when the boys were unlucky to find food to kill and eat, anything, the boys always gathered white gum fruits. That was the only easy food they could gather to eat. So sometimes each Wednesday and Saturday we would keep half of our midday meal, rice or some other small food to give our brothers and cousins.

We often felt tired from working but could not make it to stand or sit for a while. We had bosses that saw that we had to go on working . . . our movements didn't satisfy the one in charge of us, we would often get belting, either by a stick or belts from leather strip of a bridle piece. You could hear screams, yells and crying from each children in different places where the work was going on.

We would race across the plants with pain . . . two girls carrying large kerosene tin of water on each end of the stick, while the water . . . splashing out of the tin, before we get to the end of the plant. There isn't enough water in the tin, with all this frights and hiding. I had hard times, it was very tough to live with. Too much work, also too many belting, but it was all dormitory customs. There was no sympathy at all for us by anyone. They, who were in charge of us, were rough and cruel.

I can say no matter what I've done . . . breaking pineapple leaf to eat or banana leafs, potatoes' vine to eat or digging potatoes after the shoots come up from the place

15

they have already cleared before . . . well, you hear shout from other girls calling out . . . I'm stealing or breaking some plants. I am called to be smacked. At the same time, after I am found out, what I've done . . . soon there are the other girls picking, eating green peas, snake beans, tomatoes, breaking cabbages' leaf or any thing that should not be touched. Well, you can imagine Elsie calling out, and telling on them, that they are stealing and breaking leaves. To their surprise they are called, and lay on tables and get much harder strapping with car rubber tube.

When we grew up we never hid another person whenever they did wrong. We also told from each other. It was tit for tat . . . some one told from each other. It was always the same done for the other person. We were brought up not to destroy any thing.

I can remember when I was young, I saw lots of girls, older ones, also boys being flogged with flagellan piece of motor car tyre, saw blood streaming from their bottoms and legs where they'd been cut as they were flogged. They were cruelly treated and for days they would have these wounds with red sores. The missionaries did not care to cure or deal with the bruises and cuts. It healed by itself. I hadn't got hit with one of them because they could not use them on we younger ones. It must have been very awful to use such dreadful thing on a person's body like that. It looked cruel. I suppose a thing like that happening was not nice, but anyway, it was the life away from parents and relatives.

The only time I was happy was when my mother and father would come in to the mission and see me, and at morning worship in Church, especially Sunday evenings. They were lovely moments, because we could see and hold their hands and were able to talk to our parents and other relatives. It was good to see everybody come as one large family to Sunday Service. Old and young, blind and deaf, everybody arrived. The Church Service was held morning and evening. On Sundays . . . no work, no fishing, washing, riding horses, working mustering cattle. Everything was kept as a sabbath day.

You people have no idea of such awful happenings in those days. I'll never forget the hard times I had to face in life. Sometimes things went right, but other times it was too bad for a girl to live with. They were good times as well as bad times. Although, through those awful days, I became to know a lot of the situation of the mission life.

I went around making friends and helping the missionaries' wifes, made good friend with them, and offered myself to line up the damper on the table as she would cut up the dampers in small pieces for the children's meals. I would tell them some funny little stories about other children, and we would laugh about it.

Effie Lane was our cook. She made huge dampers in six large tin trays, put them in ant bed oven made by Mr Wilson and Mr Sydney and some native men. This oven was so large, and that's how our food was cooked, also bullock's rib bones and small piece of meat were cooked. Other best part of the beast meat was salted to go with our every day meal, rice and meat. Dugong also was caught and speared and was cooked in the oven. I used to hang around and help Effie Lane with the trays of damper.

I tried to do some small things . . . how to help. Sometimes if I am in the way, they chase me away, and say, 'Get out of the way. We don't need your help.' I still hang around until they call me back to help. I really like helping anyone, although sometimes it's a bit difficult . . . not needed.

Mrs Dougherty was my best friend, also Mr and Mrs Cain, Mr and Mrs Palmer, Mr Wilson, Mr and Mrs Sydney. I liked them, because I came to be free with them and had good fun with them. Mr and Mrs Scott were another wonderful couples. They played so often with we small children. They showed us many tricks with hand games and gave us share of their food when we went over to their house.

At Christmas time, it was one of the time we longed for so much. For months and weeks we looked forward and often counted the weeks and months. How much days and weeks for Christmas? It was one of the thing we knew that would be far more better to come, where happiness comes

17

to all. Besides, Christmas meant so much to us. We knew the day when Jesus Christ came to earth to be born of a woman, and how exciting it was when all the stories of Christmas was meant real to us at the time. Not only for giving presents, but everything was so wonderful here.

Everybody looks await when Christmas boxes are unloaded from the lugger *Morning Star* . . . now is to be opened by the Superintendents' wives. All kinds of toys are put on the table ready to be separated for presents for boys and girls, men and woman. Within a month's time, everything is put in a bag, ready to be hung on the Christmas tree. There were many toys of all kinds, lots of presents.

The boys and girls sang Christmas carols at night and that too made us feel that Christmas was so near. It refreshed our hearts and minds that we had the real feeling of Christmas.

When Christmas Eve was, we were all given fire arms, crackers. We came out from dormitories and enjoyed the night together. Then Magic Lantern, the old way with powder works, was shown just in front of the office of the mission house. One time it was in our earth floor Church and school at the same time, by the East side of the mission house, by the tank and the bell. The screen was put up. We saw all kinds of pictures. The first picture was of the first missionary Mr Hall. Everyone kept quiet for a while. No one spoke a word. There was a reverence of silence to all. Then there was others like 'Ten Little Nigger Boys' and 'Grace Darling' and 'Mother the Fisher's Wife' who was anxiously waiting to see her husband come home, by the twilight on the verandah, while rocking her baby to sleep. There was a signal from the light house. The fisherman's ship was on fire . . . and many others . . . also the early tribes of our own people, whom we saw in pictures, but never saw most of them in person, only few of them.

As the pictures was over, the Adults received potatoes, tomatoes, mangoes, pineapple, custard apples, melons, sugar canes, paw paws, oranges, pumpkins, all kinds of different vegetables. Besides boiled tea, they carried away in billy cans, damper mixed with raisins and sugar. Well, you can imagine how many people lived in those times . . . were great crowd of people, but there was enough for all. Before our parents went back home to their camps, they would give we, their children, half of the good they got. Boys and girls would stand and watch how things by serving went on, until all had received. That was the custom of Christmas Eve. Everybody was happy because it was only once a year it happened, and that's how the missionaries kept up Christmas, to treat them all in this way, make them happy.

During the night it was hard for us to get into bed. We sneaked by the window of the dormitory to see what time the Father Christmas would come. Hardly would we sleep, hoping to see the real Santa Claus come all the way from Lap Land. We really believed he travelled all that way to see us, with four Reindeer on a white sledge. We knew that he was bringing us toys.

About four o'clock in the morning we are waken up by the Senior Girls to sing Christmas carols until daylight. At the moment, we have the Spirit of Christmas. The wife of Mr Wilson would come and open the door in the morning and tell us that Father Christmas arrived last night and hid toys. There's a rush from the each dormitories . . . girls and boys racing all over the place to find the toys that Santa Claus had hidden.

Then on 25 December, what a surprise. After breakfast, the older men went out and brought in a Christmas tree. Often they sneaked in the tree and placed it in the building of our Church. Trees were decorated with many pretty papers. On the tree hung present for all the people of the island. No one ever missed out on Christmas day.

The smaller girls and boys sang 'Jingle Bells' and other songs round the Christmas tree, while the other people sat on the seats and watched on. We sang and danced as Father Christmas entered the door of the building and he too joined us with the dance and sing around the Christmas tree. Then Father Christmas told us of his journey from Lap Land and how cold it was to pass the snow flakes, just to come along and see all the children on Mornington Island. We really thought it was Father Christmas himself, and soon we found out it was my uncle Gully Peters. But that

19

never minded us at all. Each year was always the same. We always took him for the real Father Christmas who came from far off country to visit us.

Everyone receives a present from Father Christmas. Then there are lot more presents in the bags. Then there are extra presents on the table. You could choose from there, as you pass the door to walk out.

So Christmas day was one of the exciting time, when everybody receives presents from Father Christmas. Besides, friends gave presents to each other. Adults come in from camps into the mission to give their present to their friend, and friends gave them too, their gifts. Times were so wonderful. Everyone was happy, sharing our presents to each other, seeing what we had received in our bags. At the same time when we smaller girls had no present to give to each other, we parcelled up a small gift to our brother or sister and friends which we received from Father Christmas.

About two o'clock on that same day everybody met at the sporting ground for sports. There were first, second, third, fourth prizes to be given to all. Everyone did well on all sports, so no one missed out on prizes. I was a good runner, always came first on straight race, also my sister May, Eva and Molly. There were other girls and boys who came third, second and fourth. Everyone got presents. We were real sports children. Then the Adults were all good for running. Old and young won prizes. I can remember when my mother and Auntie Maggie won prizes. I ran to my mother to see what she got. She was in her middle age but was active. We spent many happy moments together during the sports. I can remember when Uncle Gully Peters was the best runner, also Kenny Roughsey. They were ties. Also one of Mr Wilson's youngest boy, Hugh Wilson. He often ran with them but he also came second. Then Barney Charles was good man for pole high jump. No matter how high the pole may be, that never stopped Barney Charles to lose his high jump sport. He always won first prize. But everyone who took part in all the sports, they all had prizes given to them.

I still think of those wonderful days. Everybody was happy and contented. Best of all was when parents and children met, to see and have joyable time together, after being so many days just living in the bush and not seeing their children too often.

On Boxing day, the boys went bush for holiday with their parents. The Mainland boys who had no parents here, they were taken by other Lardil people to care for them, and looked after them during the holidays. The girls were kept in the dormitory, while our brothers on holiday. We missed them very much, and often longed that February month could come so soon, when we would be able to see them again.

Boys are gone out of the dormitory for one month and two week. So we miss them all. Oh, it was hard to live to understand that life. I hated to think of that life. Perhaps it meant to do with the law of being in the dormitory.

We girls have no holidays but still work in the garden. The girls are free to take a walk on Sunday evenings around the place, gathering fruits and gums. Wednesday evening we go down the beach to bathe in the salt water. We often enjoy our swim, and have such fun on the beaches making sand castles and drawing and writing on the beach. We pick many pretty shells as we walk along the beach and give them to white friends that come our way, because they always want sea shells. So we would walk along the shores, and collect as many shells as we could for these visitors.

In my times, when I was small, we never were afraid of a white person. Our early missionaries always wanted us to come to know them, speak to them and get used to know them as well. Often I would be the first girl to go and hold their hands and chat with any one who came to our island or mission. Of course I was in the hands of the missionary and was in dormitory. So we were able to do what we knew was right to be happy to meet up with other strangers, or people, I should say.

We had, once a year, Government parties come to visit people of Mornington Island. It was another happy times, when the people had to come in from bush to welcome the parties. When Mr Bleakley and his party came off the lugger *Melbidir*, landed ashore on the beach, the old men of the tribes made a straight arch way from the beach to the front line of the fence that led to the gate into the mission. The arch way was formed with spears and boomerangs. It looked so beautiful . . . how the old people made a straight line, and the decoration of their weapons were painted red and white.

All lead their way in front of the mission house. Boxes are opened by the Councillors and the parties. All presents are given out . . . tomahawks, men's belts, pocket knifes, handkerchiefs, hats, shirts, trousers, blankets, mirrors and combs for the men. To women . . . dresses, hats, necklaces, bangles, needles and cottons, tomahawks, hankies, blankets. The girls and boys get their presents of lollies, biscuits, belts for girls and boys, hankies, pocket knifes.

Well, we all had a good time. The Government parties really cared for us in those times. Their visits came with love. Presents were always gifted. When leaving, everybody sang Farewell hymn . . . 'God be with You' or 'Blest be the Tie'. It was always a nice Welcome and a sad Farewell.

Those days, we had real good people who cared to come along and see all the black people. We often looked forward once a year for our dear friends. They were real Aboriginal Government who even cared to look after us all and spent their time even to leave their homes and families, just to come along and make us feel we had friendly people like them to come to our island. Well, I can truthfully say they were the best people in that time.

I was about thirteen or fourteen years then, when all these things happened. Their going away from us . . . we were so unhappy. Often we wished their stay was much longer with us, but just could not stay. They had many other black people still to visit too. But the day they were on the island was so enjoyable time we spent.

As I grew older I liked being in the dormitory. I enjoyed the life, played so many games. I became a good runner, won many prizes on sports day, got lots of presents. My big sister, Julie, looked after all my presents. I now became to know I had a big sister and brother but it took a fair good years before I knew I had a brother and sisters . . . Ginger, May, Julie and myself. Well, those days were good times. We had many funs, jokes together. My family were quiet children at first, but when we became to really settle down in this new life in the dormitory without longing for our parents, we were happy children.

My brother Ginger and myself were full of mischief. We did what boys and girls did. I would do mischievous things with all my girl friends, as my brother would do with his boy friends. Actually, I don't mean bad things, but cracking jokes and fun, touching things, breaking fruits, rooting up plants and many other small things. We did them, and not being found out. My brother would ride calfs and quiet horses, when he was not supposed to. But when he was found out, each Saturday or Wednesday, instead of going out for day's outing my brother, Uncle Henry, Cousin Bambra, Alick Hills, they would stay in the mission on the mission house porch and ride all day in the hot sun on these wooden horses, and that was their punishment.

Things were so tough, but to me it was the custom to all who went to the dormitory in my time. Now children are free, but I was treated differently. I could not speak and play with my brother, uncle or cousins. The only time we could play and have fun was when the missionaries were not watching. Girls and boys were brought up not to be near each other. That's why most of us were in families and relation circle. We never knew that, and that's how we never respected each other as relatives to each other. We just grew up as boys and girls being under the hands of a European. We grew up to do everything what the European's laws, rules and life was like. Although it looked good, the life, but to feel it was very tough, sad, lonesome, friendless of families' circle . . . hardly any happiness to make us feel were contented of everything nice being in the dormitory.

We were not free, even not have fun with our brothers or other relation amongst the boys. We girls had to stay in own side of the place, also the boys. Although, that couldn't stop us at all. We used to sneak to play and fight each other and have funs. Then if we were caught playing with our brothers, cousins or uncles, we were called and got a spanking from all our missionaries who came to work amongst us. Gee they were tough.

But as we grew up, things were not too hard. We began to have more fun as new lot of missionaries and Staff came. Things were getting much better for us to look and understand. But the toughness of my time made me to be what I am today . . . nice, kind, helpfulness, forgiving, to be honest and not to be dishonest with anyone, to be happy. Well, all what I learnt made much different in life I'm living now. So those hard life I once had was to help me to understand so much . . . how to get prepared for when I was able to stand for myself, when I was old enough to keep control of myself. What I never knew in my girlhood days, is those awful days I thought was not nice for me to live with tough missionaries, but I was wrong to announce it. But that was so. I must speak true of that life, or perhaps I was not really wrong. It was the way I looked back upon it, was my way of looking at things. But that made me now free to really understand it all.

I'm thankful I was firstly put in dormitory. Now, when I see it all, it made me how to do everything right. Never mind sometimes we make mistakes, but we fix things up together again, with apologies and friendship.

I am thankful I had old parents, because in the year 1942, I learnt extra more from them. They thought me all above the top line I mentioned before. I did not learn most good things at all much. It was more how to work, keep rules given to me that I should do, and not to disobey, and remember them and other rules and laws of the land, and what belonged to the christian Church. But anyway that was all okay. You can bring forth so much from the past . . . how it was all worked out, to what it is now . . . everyone does what their wishes, so free and not so happy. I mean this twentieth Century is far more different than my time of life as a girl. I was well guarded by my early helpers who were able to teach me the real true life . . . how to grow up, with all I had and was done to me, and how I was able to get along with other boys and girls . . . were so helpful. Then the children of today can compare my time of learning and understanding. When I grew up many good things passed my way in life.

Having school in front of the mission house after the first cyclone that hit Mornington Island when I was ten or eleven year old.

A time for exercise during school hour.

Some where about 1934 to 38, I was much older. I was much happier, I knew the life was much difficult. Now hoping how to be free from the life of dormitory, I often thought how would I grow up to do something bit different. Now I'm old enough, could I do things like the older girls? I started learning to hem stitch edgings on handkerchiefs, then crochet edgings on table cloths, and other crochet work, helping to mind children that had been taken from mothers, for extra care and treatment. I was chosen to nurse and care for them.

As times went by, I became great helper to children who were to be given further mother's care treatment. These children had to be brought into the mission for extra care and feed, because the mothers of whom these children were, were on their way to become pregnant again for another child. So I was chosen to help to take care of them while their mothers or another bigger girl in charge of them was busy. But I was only there to see they were alright, nurse and play with them, also to give them their feed and milk. In those days missionaries were very careful about weaning children so soon. They rather the child grew up strongly, instead of being neglected. But I was always ready to help. I looked after many children while I was young, for their mothers were busy, and some altogether were taken away and brought to the mission to be cared, because also the child's parents often went bush and it was wise for the child to be left in care of the mission.

Those were hard times to get along. Often people travelled for miles and miles in the hottest day, to go bush and hunt for food. White man's food was scarce . . . not enough to feed everybody, except for the boys and girls who were in the dormitory, also some Adults who worked as Stockmen, carpenters, yardmen. That's why it was tough for any parents to go bush with these small children.

I took charges in the work to be a boss or leader to boys and girls as they worked in the gardens, carrying soil for new beds, for the soil to be mixed to plant vegetables' seeds and other small plants. Now I worked much harder. Tired I was, but the job must be done. About five o'clock work is over. We have tea, only damper most time dry . . . no other food to go with it. But it was all the life to go through.

As I write I wonder why it all happened like that. Things were good and bad . . . have been mixed together. Sad and happiness came together at certain times. Everything seemed too tough, really to understand the way I grew up with. Sometimes goodness came out of that new life being in the dormitory. Then again, so much different feelings of people not really dealing with kindness, love, comfort, friendliness. It was a rough, cruel times, I lived to realise.

I often sat around some quiet places. Cool Westerly breezes seem to make me feel a bit different person, whether something tells me there is a nice thing shall happen to me or perhaps I am lonely. I feel so sad and lonely. Something has gone away from me. Could it be love or need love of my families? Where my parents are? When will I see them again, to visit me? Or, why I haven't got playmates? So I shake that feelings off me, I get around to my sisters and friends and have few talks and fun with them. But I think that sort of feeling came around with the breeze, that could make you feel to think you are growing up. You see things happening to you. You feel at times the feeling of sadness and happiness, and where woman hood age creeps on you and gives you feelings of that stage, you are growing up and you feel and think as grown ups do. At nights while lying in bed, we sing hymns, choruses and songs.

I remember when I was a young girl, a young man named Spider, he came from Mainland. He was very sick with wet consumption. He was one of our great leaders as a christian. After his baptism he was named Allan. As he lay in his bed, May and myself would go and see him. He would tell us how he fought with spears amongst his tribes. He was good for spear throwing. When throwing the spear, it bent across the sky like a snake movements. He often had a practice of spear throwing. He showed some men how they used their spears when a real fight took place . . . skipped and jumped when another fellow threw at him, dodged every throw.

He told us many stories of his life. He read bible to us, told us stories from the bible. When he was not sick he was a great ploughman getting grounds ready for the rest of the work that had to be done. He worked as a ploughman with an old draught horse, ploughed the ground for all our garden plants, for potatoes to be planted, vegetables' beds, bananas, pineapples, oranges, mangoes or any other thing you can think of. That's how he was a ploughman getting grounds ready for the rest of the work to be done by girls and boys.

May and myself visited him often, because in our custom he was our father or uncle. Lying on his back in his bed, he would read some verses from the bible to we girls. Spider's best girl friend . . . always at his side after a day's work, or at Smoko time and gave him his water and lunch. We used to cuddle around him and his girl friend to hear the stories he told us. Oh, he was a very nice fellow, loved boys and girls and we often hung around him for his stories . . . until one day, he died. We missed him very much, for his kind, gently loving ways to we small children.

At the same time there was a young man who was a woodchopper. He cut the wood to small pieces, about oven size, to be put in the stove. This man just started going mad. So one day we had jokes with him, as we carried the pile of wood, which he already made a great stack of it. Then he said, 'Now you girls, this is the way Burketown people eat snake.' He pretended to hold up a snake, high up above his head and opened his mouth as wide as he could and . . . 'This is how they eat the snake.' So we stood around him, and just watched everything he told us about and laughed at him.

Then he said, 'Now this is the way they cut wood.' So he picked up an axe and swang the axe about our legs and we all jumped away, not thinking he was turning mad in the head.

So we went with a load of wood and placed it where the cut up wood was stacked and we told the bigger girls all about it.

The bigger girls said to we small girls, 'Go again and tell him to do it again.' So we did and he did it all over again.

He showed us how he was given a hiding when he was small, by his boss. He hit madly all the wood to say that was him, then swang the axe towards us and missed us on the leg. It was told to Mrs Wilson. She then found out that Jupiter was mad. They watched him for a quite a long time, carry wood from the bush after school. Each day the boys went to gather wood for cooking. Jupiter was there too with the others. He belted into every tree pretending it was one of the boys. So they sent him away to Goodna for treatment . . . never heard since, but probably he got over it I suppose.

Later years, my brother, young William, he went bush during Christmas holiday with our father and mother. He was about fifteen years old. How he started . . . he got so frightened of seeing two brolgas not far away from him. I suppose that was the first sight of a brolga he saw. He turned mad.

Dad and Mum brought him back to the mission from Birri. They cared for him. Often he took those turns. My sister, May Daisy and myself always met him to speak to him and have fun with him, like all brothers and sisters do. Once he walked past us both. Then all of a sudden we heard screams and yells from him, chasing to hit one of the Wilson's girls. This girl was our teacher in those early days. She went and hid herself. Then Mr Wilson, her father, came and got my brother and said, 'This girl is not here.' So my brother came down those stairs from the house and played marbles with me and my sister.

Although we girls did not know he was mad, but he was always in good sense when he was by our side. We talked, played and had fun with each other, until one day, he was sent on a small sailing boat to Burketown then to Norman-ton . . . over land to Townsville hospital. He soon got well and was sent back to Mornington Island and was able to be like we other girls and boys with better human sense again.

He then grew up to go Mainland, worked all around Cloncurry and Nonda Siding and became one of the best rodeo buck jumper. He won couple of Melbourne Cups on his show. He worked so long at Granada Station for Mr and Mrs Frazier.

My brother had three children . . . Stephen W., who's now a hard working man on our mission with the tractor, clearing all our roads and getting places cleared or levelling grounds for all our new buildings to be built on. Alex William was another boy. I took care of this one. He was always a very sick child, so Dick and I took him off my brother and his wife and took over him as my own son. But he is a man now . . . already built some small boats for anyone who wanted a boat. He built a boat that could cross the sea to another place, called Bentinck Island, and travelled across that wide sea back to Mornington Island mission. At the moment he stands aside, waiting for more materials to build more boats. A girl . . . Aileen, who is now married to a man from Aurukun Mission and lives there. Her husband is a head Stockman there.

These children's father was a great man. He also was a head Stockman on our own mission . . . worked so hard amongst cattle, breaking in young colts that became good working horses. He did not live so long with us on our own island. He went on a sailing boat, or a whale boat, so small going towards the sea towards Burketown for cargo. But there was a tragedy on the way . . . don't know what happened still today. There was no trace of the missing boat and all other five men who were on the same boat with him . . . still never know until today.

In my time in dormitory, Gully Peters and Paddy Marmies were young men. They were Councillors. They controlled many people, but they were really tribal people, roamed and spent to hunt all their lifes in the bush, but they were great people. But that time only two Councillors really looked after them. They were great men of our laws, European and tribal law they handled. They did both the work on their own. They joined in tribal fights, trying to protect each sides, but people turned on them and fought them, so the fights got worser. So the two Councillors would go home and dress into their Government suit, and march towards the fighting crowd . . . then only to look at the suit, the people would stop at once and return to their camps. My dad helped to work with them.

It was so many wonderful days when I had my brother and sisters all together in the mission. I really now knew that I had them at the time in the dormitory . . . grew up all together. We were happy children. My father, William, had three girls and two boys. Now in the dormitory, my father helped in the mission work, and was a crew on one of our lugger, *Morning Star*. He sailed the sea from Mornington Island, round the North side of the island across the wide, blue sea towards Thursday Island for a cargo . . . then along the Gulf of Carpentaria, along the coast from Mapoon, Weipa, Aurukun, Mitchell River, Normanton, to Burke-town and back again to Mornington Island.

How happy we children of my daddy's when he arrived home again. He gave us all presents each. We shared lollies, biscuits, coconuts, damper, meat with our playmates. Also Daddy brought us hankies, necklaces, bangles, combs . . . then for boys, or at least one brother, red cowboy hankie, belt, pocket knife and sweets. But the boy had more chance to see him. About five o'clock brother would go down the camp to see him, while we girls had not always to see him, except when he called in the mission.

My dad, William, was an elderly man, but he was good for using a gun . . . never came back without twelve to twenty ducks to support the missionaries, Mr and Mrs Wilson, when they ran out of fresh meat. Dad was crack shot and came home with many dead ducks tied on to a piece of rope around his waist, and others at the back of the gun hung on by a string. I don't know what he got for them. I suppose tobacco. I can't remember any other thing in his hand. To me, it must have been part of the mission time job. Then Dad went home, back to his grass and twig humpy. My dad often helped to take messages to people who were out bush, when they were needed back in the mission, either to celebrate King George 5 birthday, or to meet Mr Bleakley and his members of the Queensland Government.

Also, when there are no voyages, Dad lives in the bush and spends most of his time out there. Often he'll come back to see his children. He's able to bring back bush food for us all. We feel good once more to see him again. Then another time, my mother and her parents will come in and see us, and they too will bring us what they have collected and killed for us. I mean they are cooked. It was one of those things . . . was the happiest time for we to see our loved ones, like our parents and other relations.

But then when it's time for us to see them part for the next day journey for go bush, our parents are sad to leave us and we feel the same. I often cry to see them go away, and my mother and my grandparents often cry too, as they leave to go back out bush again. I often very much missed my parents and grandparents. I always wanted them to stay near so I could be able to see them always, but it was not so. They rather choose the wild bush life where there was freedom to roam the bush with all it had to keep them alive. They had many corroborees, feast and meetings and other things to do.

Children came from Mainland for school here. They were taken from different camps on the Mainland, sent by the police. They came by boat, the boat that carried all our cargo from Thursday Island to our mission here. They found the mission life a bit strange, and then gradually got used to the place. Most of them cried everyday and night at first, then found friends amongst we girls and boys. They were so lonely. Burketown to Mornington was long way for them. They watched longingly when their parents would arrive.

I felt sorry for these children. It was so many miles away for the children to understand how far away they were from the Mainland. Everything seems and feels so bad at first, when you no more beside your parents. The children . . . really unhappy and looked for that real protection and love, where only parents can give them. Times went by, they came to know the life of the dormitory and all the laws and rules, work and play. My people began to bring up these children, and cared for them. They were joined into our family groups and for that reason they were happy, as these children knew they had someone to claim them as their own children. So everything went on since then.

Our big holiday was in the year 1939 on Namie Island. It was a lovely place, many large oysters and fish were there. When at low tide you could walk for miles out on the reef as far as the sea is low.

Vera Barney and myself were great pals. We would go walk about among the reefs and small lagoons. We went out, too far out, one day. In some parts out in the reefs, the tide comes in faster. So to our surprise we saw the water was filling in near the beach, where the sea water came in rushing. So we looked back to the beach. In some small lagoons . . . were already high with water. We both jumped faster on rocks, rocks after rocks until we almost gave up with fright to see the salt water rushing with great force in and out of the lagoons . . . were being filled.

At last we were nearing the last few rocks, and it was very difficult for us to get to the shore. So we both had to swim to reach the shore. We sat on the beach to have a break, and were glad we managed to get on the beach. Well, in this part of the country the sea is so big. When the reefs are covered there are many sharks around and you have no other way to get back to land, only to swim back to the beach. So we were happy to go back to our camp, where the rest of the girls were. By the time we got back, the other girls were having supper. But that was the day I thought me and my mate would never see land again. We could have been eaten by sharks.

On that same day, both of us also saw something like huge ship on the sea travelling towards the same island we had our holiday. We both stood and watched. Then two of the boat drifted away from the others. Then it wasn't a ship. There were about six canoes with boys and men in them.

They came ashore on the South East side of the island for dugong and turtle hunting. Some girls had already gone from the girls' camp, to go over to the boys' camp. Mrs

Dougherty was in charge of us. There were some old folks, Don and Rosie Robertson, Namie and his two wives, Mabel and Molly, and other two couples. It was nice moonlight night. Mrs Dougherty and some bigger girls and Namie had to go in search of the bigger girls that ran away. Mrs Dougherty soon reached the place, and found men and boys rushing behind bushes, so not to be seen. She soon drove all the men on the beach, into their canoes . . . and paddled back to Mornington Island again.

Still, we had a good time there. As we spent our holiday we saw the stone at low tide where the two boys were turned into a stone. Only the mark of boys' feet were there, because we believed it was cut and taken few years before we got there. Couple of days after, we left the island and went back to Mornington Island.

For the first time, Mr and Mrs Richard, Kippie and Molly and some boys left the island, to start a new life, to go out and work on a Cattle Station. They went to Abingden Station and soon got used to the place, and loved their work. Since then men and boys were able to go out on Stations. Girls in my time were not able to go out to any Stations, except the ones I wrote about. These girls, their big sister Ellen Richard could not leave her sisters. She rather take the girls with her. As each girls were able to get married then they left the dormitory. That was the only way. But it took so long for a girl to desire to get married, because they were not anxious to get married, unless there were many sweet talks to be done for that case.

I remember when the new building was built, the Church hall. A big storm came with mighty strong winds. It was a cyclone. Being so young I thought it was just a wind and rain. Soon from the Westerly wind and rain, there was a movements of our dormitory being off the timber foundation. That really gave we girls a such terror. We wondered why this thing did happen. We looked at each other with fear. Suddenly the bigger girls grabbed we smaller ones by the hand and rushed out of the dormitory to the nearest house for shelter. Irons were flying off the rooms of houses. Some fell beside us, some over our heads, some iron sheets

35

just behind us as we ran. But no one got hurt or cuts.

The only place was under the mission house, where we had to shelter. We slept among clothes and stores. That was the only food and clothes shop. But Mr and Mrs Wilson took great care of us all. Village people came running in to the mission for shelter. So everybody slept in that one big building.

The next morning we came out to see what had happened during the night. Everything was in mess. Buildings were torn to pieces, irons were lying everywhere, trees were torn to pieces, plants and vegetables were ruined and everywhere the place was turned in awful mess. So we started clearing up the places. But that was the first terrible storm we ever saw and had on the island.

Cattle on the island were hundred and hundred head of herd at those time. It was nice to see the bullocks in the yard. There were many cows and calfs, mickies and heifers and so many stud bulls. At the time we had our own Aboriginals to work and take over the job. Many work had been done by the boys . . . earmarking, bang tailing, branding, innoculating young mickies. Milking cows were sorted out for milking for to keep up the children with fresh milk. Girls did the milking of cows. Boys bailed the beast into the bail, and tied the right leg backwards on a pole, to stop the beast from kicking. We would stand in the garden and see all the work that had to be done by the Stockmen.

Gee, the Stockmen were busy, hard working chaps. They would stay out in the bush mustering for a month and two weeks. Then come home. Coming home on the day from bush, you can hear the bellowing of cattle, striking of stock whips, boys singing and yellowing as they drive the cattle into the mission paddocks. I never saw so many cattle so much as that in my time. When the work is finished by the Stockmen, they let the bullocks out of the paddock out in the bush again, while the best milkers and calf are put in another paddock, and those are the cows they milk to keep the fresh milk going for we children. Now the Stockmen help to work in the garden, digging and planting young plants, working on house building, chopping wood for cooking food, and other jobs they had to do. Stock job was not the only work they had to do . . . but many other jobs to do in the place.

Adults had football and cricket match every evenings, high jump over a tall pole, hop step and jump . . . were the only games they liked and played each day. Mr Wilson showed them all those games, and enjoyed himself very much playing with the men. Mr Wilson and his children Andrew, Hugh, Bessie and Joan played many games with the boys and girls. They shared many games and play with the children. The two girls helped to teach us at school, while the two boys worked with the boys and men. They worked hard, like any other girls and boys did. Work and play were treated alike in those years. Missionaries and other Staffs were really one people enjoying everything together. Some of them were very tough, some were kind hearted, but we still had many jokes and funs.

As years passed I became much grown up. I understand the real true life of the mission and the dormitory . . . I can feel myself in a huge paddock where the place is fenced in. You cannot go too far. If you do, there is trouble. All kinds of foolish punishment you have to pay for getting bit too away where the marks have been measured . . . that's enough, and no more further.

Then there was that time when some children now had to leave school. Instead of working for wages, boys were sent out from dormitory into bush again and learnt to live the same life of the tribes. The boys were taught to hunt, make and use spears and woomera, were taught to paddle in a huge dugouts, even to spear turtle and dugong, also fish, how to use nets for carrying fish or crab in them, also to hunt in the bush, to search for land bush food, and were made to find the right food to kill and the right fruits and roots to collect. They were shown what was no good to eat. They, the young lads, were entering a new life amongst their people . . . were now going into another life, a bush school by the tribes.

Father and mother did so much for their sons. Often for the rest of the life a child is passed on to the mother's brother to take over the child. So now the young lad is really cared for by the uncle and auntie. All uncles are the protection, and responsible people for all children . . . belong to their sisters' children.

While the girls, when they leave school, they work about the mission and are still kept in the dormitory until, unless they get married . . . then live like the rest of the bush people and learn the same as the young men have learnt, and live by their laws, customs, culture and legends. Now they are entering another new life with the tribes.

These little children are carrying sandbags to use in the garden.

Gathering tomatoes from the mission garden.

Gathering around the antbed oven for lunch.

Ladies waiting to exchange bush food for white man tucker e.g. flour, tea, sugar, tobacco (these bush food were given to the children in dormitory for their meals)

Parallel danger

In the year 1940 a battle ship came in to our harbour and it was the first ship that came. I was now a young maiden. My big sister Julie Roughsey had a son born to her at that time, Brian Roughsey. It was Sunday after Service, the girls went on board of this ship and had a look through the boat. It was nice, with some pictures of actress . . . girls, I mean. But that really made me think, why these pictures were stuck on their bed rooms. So they really missed their wife, and girlfriends and perhaps mothers. But that really kept their minds happy while absent from home. That would be navy's idea of being lonely. Still, it was nice to be on the ship, because that was the first navy ship we saw that ever came to our island.

1942 . . . the war was now at hand. *Wambat*, a huge boat, two storey high, well built, came to Mornington Island. On the Western side of the shores of our land, they had to choose a nice deep anchoring spot to unload all they had besides the army's soldiers. How happy we were to know the soldiers came to guide, and guard our island, also we people. We did not worry much now about war, we now had men who could fight with guns for us all. We had many happy days with the boys, made good friends with them. We had many concerts by them that were held in our school room. Sometimes we girls joined them in concerts.

Where they lived was very scrubby and green. The scrub just matched their army tents. Tents were everywhere. They were the first boys that came and started clearing bush and trees to make an air strip with the help of our people. It did not take long before the clearing was done and over. Then we had planes come to land on Mornington, and also many seaplanes landed on the sea. It was so exciting to see planes come and go. Very large seaplanes came . . .

Catalina, well, she carried about 99 crews, sometimes 231 or 140 crews . . . just to come to Mornington Island.

Mr and Mrs McCarthy were here by that time. Before they came, all the missionaries and Staffs left us by ourselves to face the enemies on our own. But we had a nice christian friend. He was the only person . . . said he will never leave us people. He was a German, but he was a nice guy. He was the only white man that was with us then until the war was over. Mr Brownholz was a very good fellow . . . on the island while the war was fierce and frightful, but he knew God was with him. That's why he could not leave us, but stay to the last with people of Mornington Island.

One Officer was going to teach we few girls how to shoot with Tommy gun. Well, we were so excited to learn, so we could help to look after our own people and country. But you know, when a person who is a Superintendent on the island amongst black people, they think and say you never can do that, or it won't be done. So our training lesson with Tommy gun was closed. That's why we still in the same way since and before the war.

We are still in the same place, never really move forward. We are still wondering what will be another forward step that will take place, to learn and train, to be what we want to do. If we try, we'll have to put our feet on a stumbling block by the way, and that will stop us from looking ahead. My country, Goonana, is a nice place. We lived here too long, ever since we were born. But did we ever try all those years to step forward and learn to do things that can take us somewhere? I know many dark people are level with a white person, because they had for the start, good people to show them what to do, and how to live to make things worthwhile. We have so many talent people here, but whether we can go forward and see what we can do for ourselves? I see too much can be done for our future. How to work things out? Then could my people do it? Will they if they get that chance? It's too jolly hard for us to leave the island now of course. So where the help we can get? If we have the money can we be allowed to go for training? I suppose you can go. Then you wonder why my people

cannot always want to do what she or he thinks of doing
. . . because there isn't a chance anyway, at anytime. Only
very few can, not all. The biggest problem here we got up
against us, is pure jealousy. I cannot explain anymore about
it.

But you can see from way back to now (when the year of
1973 closed), that those years did not bring us much to go
through in life, to do something in work, learn, trained to
be what each one of us can do, to face the world ahead of us.
So we start all over again, as how they first found us here. I
know there's not much help here at all from the early start.
If there was, we should have now a level with a white
person, with all its duties, its works, its way of life, all
working together as one. So years have changed. Days,
times, months and weeks have gone and we still have plenty
to know and learn, yet so far . . . There are times when you
get older, you understand well and you're able to pick up so
many things you can see to do. I know as I write . . . was
spent so many precious life in not doing what we ought to
do in the first place. We missed out on many good things of
life.

I went to Sydney Island once . . . only saw the wreck of
the plane that hit the oak tree and swang itself into the sea.
We saw old machine gun on the rocks that some one picked
up, and left it there. Dick Roughsey showed me the place
where they made arrow showing where the wreckage was.
And how sad it was to find the men in the plane. Many
fishes were about the wreckage, also few large sharks were
there too. It was sad to see the planes coming in with the
coffins . . . and were taken over to Sydney Island by a boat.
They picked up the bodies and put in the coffins, and
brought them home. The planes were here already to take
the coffins away.

During that time we had a heavy falls of rain. The place or
the sky was dark and cloudy. Few old people were out bush
at the time. One old man could see pieces of the plane had
been washed up the shore during the bad weather and
stormy sea. To the old man, he thought they were irons
from a fallen house had been washed up. But when they saw

it was some parts of the plane, the old men got so frightened. So they came in to the mission and reported to the Superintendent, McCarthy. So immediately Dick Roughsey and Lindsay Roughsey, who were policemen in those days, went on search with Mr McCarthy to Sydney Island. During the day, as they arrived on the spot, the tide was very high already, and no work could be done. So early next morning they arrived on the scene and worked with the bodies before the tide came in.

After everything was over there were several white policemen came to question the poor tribal men who found the pieces of the wreckage on the beach while living in the bush at the time. The two old men were from the early tribes . . . knew what was right to give report of what they saw and found on the beach. The white policeman went hard in questioning the tribes in harsh english and tried to force the tribe if they knew something of the wreck and the people who fell in the sea with the plane. Besides that, they had guns to show the old tribes. If they had done a murder they would have been treated with the pistols and taken to jail. They had couple of our men there to explain what they understood from the tribe. But no, the things really went hard on the tribes, after the poor men rushed from the bush to the mission for the rescue and help, to let everyone know that somebody was in danger out sea somewhere. Only the pieces of wreckage told the tribes something had been destroyed not far away from the coast of their country.

It was sad to see . . . the tribes were in an awful case of courting, as if they were the cause of the plane coming down. No one in the whites thanked the two old men, for all they had done to find and discover the wreck . . . found the bodies and sent them back to their love ones. They had been ungrateful to the blacks. They rather handcuffed them with thanks, the innocent, helpful tribes.

Our tribes were afraid to strike on a white man. They themselves believed not to kill anybody, but to take care of anyone. The tribes understood all this hurtful, meanful nastiness with their own laws, not from the European's life, but their own laws and customs . . . the way the tribes grew up with everything good, and free life, the way they lived and found good health and a happy, rich life of their own race. I never knew of my people . . . wild and reckless, or a destroyer. They were tame people. I don't know why they were like that. I suppose they came from some good people many years ago, from a good tribe.

I remember hearing stories of the early settlers who came from Mainland, on the coast of the Western areas, who came by walpas to Mornington Island to war against my people, and killed them and ran off with their women and girls back to Mainland . . . and never heard of the Lardil women again. Killings came by these strangers to our island, where as our people had a very small idea about killing . . . but rather lived together as one real people, real countryman and real relation.

I have known and heard, read books of other native people who lived in other parts of Australia and places overseas, that they were savages and did lots of killing, and some still have remained fierce with savageness. I suppose in these parts of countries they had no good leaders, but bad fighting leader who made their people not to be friendly to anyone.

But then the ones who became savages and killers, these people must have met with strangers into their country . . . could have threatened the natives in some way, that the natives could not trust the other bloke. Well, each one did not welcome strangers walking about into their country or their ground. The most fearing act would be the other bloke would steal his woman and kill the others, then one would run away with women of that tribe. Then never another native person would trust any strangers again. No matter if there is a good person to go to the country to help them, a native person will never trust the strange bloke again. That's why if you ever walk into a country of a black fellow, he'll never meet you with smiles of regret, but hard looks to say, 'I don't like you here. Leave me alone. I'll live to keep my laws and customs in my country, the way my father and grandfather have lived.'

So then there was the killing of Rev. Robert Hall. Peter

was born on Mornington Island. As a young lad, he went on the Mainland with walpa . . . with other people to the Mainland for a walk about. As a young man he worked on a Cattle Station. He knew english and was treated nicely and knew the ways of an European life . . . learnt to smoke tobacco. Then in his manhood he came back to our island . . . asked for tobacco. Peter was told, 'No one have tobacco here, no body smokes.'

So he was upset and said, 'Well I want tobacco because I've been smoking on the Cattle Station.'

This is why and how Mr Hall was killed by Peter. So there you see, when you enter the life of civilization, well you know right from wrong. Then why killing went on from a man who already understood the right way to live and should have helped others to live that same way? So he did not live the tribal life that he should. If he'd stayed with his people all the time, he would have not known to kill a white man. Instead he was taken away to the Mainland as a boy, grew up to see some killings and death, and probably that way he had heart to do so. When Mr Hall was killed by Peter, the tribes were so frightened and could not do anything . . . never moved from their camps. They kept to themselves. My people knew it was wrong, so they kept away from the killer. And what would come after that?

These are the men who were responsible for the murder of Rev. Hall.

These men went hunting dugong to feed the children in dormitory.

Some old folks on Mornington Island from long before I was born.
I don't know who they are or where this picture was taken.

During the war time 1942 . . . 43 . . . 44 . . . things were hard for us. We had to leave dormitories and were again back with our parents. White man's food was almost scarce, and it was hard to start all over again, to get around and start learning to hunt for land and sea food.

It took me hard to trace up on some wild vine creepers that had different roots to be dug and found. These roots were good to eat. Well, all kinds of wild plants had these roots. We went miles into the bush.

I was taught how to find wild bee honey, by searching for the honey. This is how. On the tree there are some nice hollow place where you can see a fly [wild bee] go in and out of the tree. These flies are yellow looking with black head. To find a tree that has the sugar bag . . . well, you must make sure they are the right flies going in and out of the hollow. Most times you see a very small hole with wax at the entrance of the home of the bees. You carefully look closely, until you are sure the flies are there. Then the tree is cut down, falls to the ground. From the main entrance where the wax is you chop piece of wood until you come to the last where it ends. Then the honey is collected in place in a tin, or I should say, baskets made from ti-tree bark. You separate the honey from the eggs. Honey goes to one container, the eggs, with some honey, goes in another basket. This one, that is all the eggs of the honey . . . taken home and given and shared amongst all the older folks, because they rather the eggs and not the main honey. The honey of the sugar bag is eaten by children and younger people.

I like very much going out bush for sugar bag hunting. I began to get excited when I first found a sugar bag. Well the flies that I saw . . . it was the right fly. I'll call out to my father, and say, 'Daddy, I found sugar bag.' So Dad walks over, looks at the tree, and then he pulls out the tomahawk from his belt that's round his waist. And when he does that, I feel so happy. That is a sugar bag . . . although Dad does not say . . . oh, yet it's the one. But when it comes to chop the tree, we know it's a right tree with sugar bag.

We went bush many, many times with my father. My younger brother Colin, he was on the South side of the island with my mother and her relation, but May and myself were with our father and a foster mother. We spent many happy days with our father, cracked lots of fun with him. Sometimes Dad didn't take jokes on trips like these.

He wants us to go through the bush very quietly. He walks ahead of us, looking up at trees to find sugar bag, while my sister and myself walk along behind, giggling along as we go, having fun of our own from different things. Dad will look back and yell out, 'Shut up you two girls and walk quietly.' Then all we can hear . . . chop, chop. We stand and look around to hear for another chop. The moment we hear the chopping of the tree, we run to the direction and stand in front of the fallen tree, while he chops off the chips. Dad says, 'Stand away. You won't get any if you come near.' So we step back. But as he chops away, we girls creep back again towards the tree. Chips come from every angle hitting us on the face and body, because we always liked to see how the sugar bag honey lay on the hollow tree.

We had two dogs with us too, but these dogs did not like us at all. Everytime we go to get our share of the honey these dogs snarl at us and frighten us both, but Dad hits the dogs away until we get our share. Then we leave the rest for the dogs to eat, and we go on hunting for more sugar bag, even for goanna, and other food roots that were good to eat on that season.

Dad was also good for spearing wallaby. Everytime he went on wallaby hunting, a wallaby sprang out of the bush to get away. Dad's spear fell right on the creature's back, and it fell to the ground dead. Wallaby meat was good to eat.

How to cook a wallaby . . . we dig a long deep covermarie hole. When the fire dies out we put the wallaby in, then put bark over the wallaby, then put little bit of coal over the bark, then bury it up with sand. When the old tribes think it's cooked enough they undo the covermarie, with another bark for a table, and place the wallaby on the bark. No matter how much campers are there, the wallaby meat is divided into each family.

The same as if there is lot of people moving in the swamp. The swamp is just about drying up and it's easy to track a swamp turtle. If the whole hunters be there and get a lot of swamp turtle, that too is divided into family groups.

When it's dry season they go hunting. It's hard to track a swamp turtle. But the tribes just faintly trace the track of the swamp turtle. Where they think it's lying they start digging and it's not long before the swamp turtle is there lying flat on its belly. You wonder how they survive all through the summer, lying hidden away. And no water to drink. They say he only holds enough water for the other seasons under ground in him, until the lagoons are all full again with water. As the earth is dry, these turtle lie there. The place they are buried . . . is cool, although it's so dry. But that's how they live.

Often when the lagoons are full of water, the old tribes get in the lagoon, and swim in a long line and dive in search of swamp turtle. When they have caught enough, they go home and show what they have caught. The ones who have caught more share with the others. That was one of the customs lived inside of man. If you go hunting together, those who have caught what they've hunted, must give the other bloke that saw him hunt for the food they all went for. So they share, alike.

There is a short story, our legend, that says . . . the wee turtle that lives on the land in the lagoon is known as swamp turtle because of its size. So one day the wee turtle said, 'I feel so tired of living on the land, in the lagoon. I'll go and find a better way living somewhere.' So wee turtle crawled out of the fresh water lagoon, travelled miles and miles away until finally he found himself on the coast, looking toward the sea. Wee turtle said, 'This looks beautiful, but I have very small shells on my feet and hands. I very much like to live in the sea, but how can I get rid of the wee shells?' So the wee turtle scraped the shells from him and left them on the beach . . . got to the edge of the sea, had a dive in the salt water. He was so delighted to feel that the big sea had more room to get around, and more to see of the new life. So wee turtle said, 'Now I'll forget to live on the land. I'll take place of the big sea turtle.' So he found himself that he had already begun to grow much . . . a larger turtle. So he said, 'I will live in the sea, so everywhere I move around and pop my head out of the water, I can see everything, such as sea, sky and land, also birds at the same time.'

Then the sea turtle came out of the sea and took place of the wee turtle. The other turtle got on the bank, looked around and found the empty nail shells of the wee turtle. The large turtle picked up the shells, put them on, and in a moment the shells fitted him. Well, he shrank so small. He found his way to the bush, and soon found his new home in the lagoon and felt happy and said, 'I'll always live in the lagoon now.'

While the other one found a much better life in the sea, so he said, 'This is where I should have been before. Now I can swim everywhere and see the beautiful world.'

If you are walking along the beach by the sea, you see the shells that the land turtle left on the beach. Today the sea turtle now lives on the land, and the land turtle lives in the sea.

It was not easy thing for the life of my people to find a swamp turtle. It was hard to hunt for what you had to find to feed yourself . . . but it was just how you had to be taught, how to hunt when you live on the land. There are many ways how you can live on when you tired of hunting in the sea. You must even know how to hunt on the land. So there are many different food that you can live on. That's if you want to be a good bushman. There are many things I had to pass through . . . how to hunt, by my father and mother.

I saw many things that my father could do. He was very good for spearing fish, also for spearing sea turtle, dugong, wallabies, also goannas and snakes. I had many happy times walking about in the bush amongst my old folks . . . lots of laughs and funs. Dad often told us many stories of the past, especially of his young man life time . . . how he got into trouble over women, and how he fought the tribe and came out with no mark on his body . . . except one fight he was in. While so interested in his fight with one man, he was struck on the leg by another man . . . speared him while he wasn't watching. Dad said that was the only fight ever cheated him. He was speared by another bloke. It was a kind of the same fellow enemy he had a fight with before.

Dad told so many stories, good and bad ones. I don't mean bad stories that you might think of other things, how and what was done, but I mean stories you won't like to hear about . . . Devil Devil . . . how it happened long time. It really scared us to hear stories at night time, when darkness was on. We would cuddle ourselves beside Dad or our grandparents that would be there, while the story went on. We would sit round camp fires and listen to the stories that were told to us. I have always liked stories to be told to me. I really liked to hear what happened and how it happened and how things went on from where I've heard. Everything sounded so good . . . how the old tribes lived with life of great interest and happiness.

Times and days, nights have come and gone past, and the same things happened each time . . . had to get up in the morning and set out for hunting, sometimes along the shores, and sit on big rocks and do fishing. The best sport, I've always chosen . . . to fish on the rocks, because there were nice small lagoons that you know that look good to catch a fish. Not long, when you throw your line in the sea, there is a fish being dragged up to land. I've always felt happy to catch a fish. The whole family of Dad's would be on the reefs or along the beaches. At the same time there's plenty of time to eat oysters as you sit on the rock and feel tired of fishing . . . also gathering some eating shells that have some live fish in them. Oh there are all kinds that you can learn to hunt for, that are good for eating. Another time we would go inland to hunt for other various roots, wild honey and other bush food, well, anything that is good to collect to eat.

My people never knew to call all our weathers by their seasons. I mean of course Winter, Spring, Autumn, Summer and wet seasons. It was by certain food . . . was collected or eaten or plentiful at those times, and that's how they knew that's the time . . . 'My child was born,' or 'We kill plenty of dugong and turtle,' or 'Water lily time, we dig for and eat them,' or 'Palm nut time is on,' . . . that's pandanus palm tree.

When the pandanus palm trees have all their nuts ready to eat, the food that's red is the meal of my people. We call them cumbered because it turns red, but the nut is inside of the curelle. We bash this against two stones, or one stone and a nice, heavy hard wood with a handle, called thubun. This is always a food pounder for everything that is used for eating or mashing food soft to be eaten. These thubun are very handy. They used them in so many different way.

I can remember when I went bush for holiday, I often sat by my grandparents, that's my mother's parents. That was in the year 1942. They always used a stone, lay it level on the ground or dug a small hole to sit the stone in. They got a small, heavy piece of wood with a handle, then lifted it in the air and pounded whatever they had to eat. Often these thubun wood were also used for steel knife, but it was called thubun . . . something that could be known as meat mincer. They used it for many things, pounding dugong or turtle meat, panja or nail food.

We call nail food banner. It's a hairy food that grows in the swamp by the creek that the salt water flows into. These nail roots are gathered when the salt and fresh water dries up. That was the main food to gather in baskets, and in their large net bags they collected big mob of these food or roots.

Bush roots of all kind, and bush fruits were collected in huge bag nets made by grass fibre, also in large baskets made by ti-tree barks. They were called coolamun. Coolamun was the only food and water supply carrier, also for carrying whatever they had to carry. It was used for everything. As for those days, they knew nothing of suitcases and bags. Coolamun was one of the thing they treasured very much. It was used with some strong strings made by women for their use, that they put on their shoulder. The coolamun, with many heavy goods, were hung on their side. It made everything much easier to be carried. They travelled for miles and miles with all their load. Even these coolamun were made for children carrying. Children grew up strong and healthy. They hardly carried children in their arms, always in a coolamun, but that was the custom, to do that. Then, when the baby grew out of it, the mother got another large bark and made a firmer one, which she carried her baby in. Another large coolamun she carried on her head, that's with all her food and other things in it.

Also the mother has her walking stick on her right hand to help her walk, to keep her balances and help her step over lying fallen trees, and logs, and stones . . . crossing rivers and creeks to keep her firm. When a mother wants to have a rest and feels tired, the stick is used to help her go slowly down on to the ground with all her load without falling. When she begins her travel again, the walking stick is used to help to pick her self up and go on. She manages to stand the stick on the ground tightly, and slowly raises herself and away she'll go.

The walking stick was more of a guidance too . . . to clear away grass on the road in case there were snakes, and brushing away bushes from their eyes while travelling. It was meant for other purpose too . . . for striking anyone or fighting with, even for turning over things they may come across on their way. Instead of using their hands to bend to touch a thing, they used their walking sticks.

My people have the life of bush because it brought contentment to live away from the mission. I've seen how hard it was to travel in the bush. I never liked going bush, but I had to. That was the only way I could learn from my old folks how to hunt, how to live on my own when they were not around. I learnt many things from my parents and other relations . . . how fish run in hundreds in small groups, fish run over sand bars where they spear much bigger fish . . . stingray season, when large and small ones were speared and cooked and given to each campers.

When oysters were big and fat, they collected in large coolamun. The people of the past made a big fire in a hole and put oysters in ti-tree paper bark, tied it with creepers' vines and then placed it in the fire or open earth fire oven. Hot ashes were thrown over the wrapped up oysters, then cold sand was thrown over the heat to keep the heat down. We called it a covermarie.

When it's all ready cooked, they uncover the covermarie fire place. The food is then placed in another clean ti-tree paper bark, and the sharing time is on. Everyone is given covermarie oysters to eat. Oh, when I write about the covermarie oysters . . . makes my mouth run water. I only wish I had my mother and grandmother still alive to cook that way for me. The time I saw them do and eat them, how nice it tasted.

Water lilies were grown in large swamps. When the green leaf turn yellow, it's time to be rooted up. The person who was born there, owns that part of the place and the swamp too. So when the boss is there, he gives order to his people. They can go down the lily swamp and dig them out. Women gather their coolamun and walking stick and down the swamp they go. Men are not missed out. They go and dig their lilies too. When they come home, in their camps, they give half of the big share to the person who owns or claims the water lily swamp. Then they all share with each other. No matter they all were there to gather their own, they still had to share with each other.

That was one of their greatest customs, sharing. Most time the one who was born near the place, he claims everything that is round about the country side. No one is allowed to do anything wrong on that part of the area that is owned by that one. If he disobeys the customs and law of the tribe, about the time when all eating thing of that season are on, with the owner of the land not there, they have a big fight and most time he is killed by the relation or the person who owns the place. Through fights he is killed . . . that's when he steals . . . but most time they just have a terrible fight, just to punish him not to do it again, with spears, nulla-nulla and boomerangs. That's why in those time people lived together as one people. They all shared with each other and each one did not take away what was not his or hers. That's how to keep all customs right. Even in the pandanus palm trees, you cannot pluck any nuts off the tree or even from the ground when they fall. That too can cause all that kind of trouble. The one who touches anything that isn't hers or his also ends with trouble or punishment.

Those days, people were never told or spoken to many times, not to do this or that. They just obeyed. Once when the harvest time was on, everybody was allowed to help themselves. Orders were always given by the man who owned the place, where he was born. Today at this present time, everyone doesn't live by the customs. They root and tear and rip trees and swamps today. That's why there is not much of a good season for anything to be plentiful. You cannot hardly see anything when you move in the bush. They are berryless and fruitless. Nothing grows well enough to support us at the fruit season. The customs and laws and cultures are gone with the greatest people of the past.

In those days when Dad had to take we girls out bush, really I hated to go bush. The travel in the hot sun was too hot to carry on travelling. We used to sit under a shady tree and have a break on the beach. It was nice to take a nap for a while under those shady oak trees with all their stories . . . as the wind from the sea . . . blowing the trees, swaying its branches, with many memories, lying under those trees. You can lie there, as if the oak trees are telling you tales of the sea. But then it's time to go on, to get to the next place, where we shall camp. At last the journey has ended. We are happy. Next to gather grass and branches of trees, to make our camp for the night, collect enough wood for the night.

I've found out it was good to sleep by the fire at night. The old people believed that the fire was a health heat for the whole of the body. When the fire died out at night, they would stack more wood on to keep warm, also to give light in the camp. That fire is to go all through the night until daybreak, because out of the same fire wood that is burning

. . . is also for the day cooking. Even when you go out for hunting, you must carry fire stick. Sometimes if you have gone too far for hunting and the evening comes too quick, to be dark, well the fire stick guides you on your way home, back to the camp. I went through all this.

I can remember, in the heart of the bush, the boundary between North and South countries of the people, that cuts off the two sides of our people's land, the limit . . . tells where the end of the line is. Well I saw the place, and Dad showed me . . . this is the place that belongs to his side of the people, and the other side on the South belongs to my grandfather Barney and my mother's side of people. My grandfather is the one who is my mother's youngest uncle (Big Barney). My mother is the daughter of his eldest brother. Well, now I've seen all that part of the bush, and it's long way from the mission side, where we all live.

Well, at the time, we camped there in the centre of the bush. Me and my sister pestered Dad to take us back to the mission. We did not like being out in the bush too long. We rather be home with the other girls, but Dad said, 'No, we'll go home, when I think of going home.' He disappointed us very much.

So one of the other girls from the same camp asked her father, 'When are we going home, Father?'

He said, 'Not yet. We all go home together when we elders decide.'

Then all of a sudden there was a great disturbment, by screaming and fighting by the girl and the father and mother. So we girls of Dad's sat very quiet and said not a word. We thought our father would bounce on us at any time now, for seeing what happened with the other families. But Dad was a nice fellow . . . never hard on us at most times.

Then on a Sunday we all left bush for home. All the way home we hunted for wild honey and goannas and other bush stuff. All the way through the bush, as we girls walked, we were excited that we were on our way home to the mission. As we walked, we had all sorts of idea . . . when we will enter the village? . . . and who will find us first? . . .

and how wonderful it will mean to us to be back with the other girls and boys and relatives. We wandered along the bush, silently, in case we happened to find a large goanna lying on the ground, that was for our supper, or other things that were good for eat. As we walked along our parents would give a 'shoo' to walk very quiet, also in case we find small pups that were asleep or left behind by a mother dingo.

The day was so hot to continue most of the way, so we sat under a nice shady tree for a blow. As we sat we talked and had fun, and shared whatever we had to eat on the way. The old people would put their bundle of bags and nets of articles on the ground, and fall off to sleep, until their rest was enough to travel on. As we passed some creeks and swamps, we knew the places well, we were excited. We knew we were not too far away from the camp on the mission.

The evening came, and it was getting towards for the day to close. Then darkness was over our heads as we continued our journey. Now the old people had already collected some ti-tree paper barks, softened the end of it, got a fire stick, blew it and lit up the bark. That gave us much brighter light to see our way through. Finally we all had a firestick and maga torch. Everyone had something to hold and carry, to show us the way through the dark night. As I walked I looked back and saw a long line of people of all sizes carrying lights in their hands and it was so beautiful. So we were able to find our way through the long grasses, stones and bushes.

Then not far away from the mission camp there were yells and screams from everywhere, telling and letting another person know that the Lewit people were coming home. Then we reached our camps and settled down. All our friends and relations came round us to hear the news of how we travelled, how we spent our holiday or walkabout, and all kinds, etc. The food that we hunted for, and carried home, we now started sharing to anyone, whatever we had. Firstly we would wait and see how dads and mums would go, as the old folks gave what they'd got. Then we girls

59

would give what we'd got. Although most time we didn't hunt as good as the old folks, but it was good enough. What we had to share with anyone made us feel happy. Whatever we hunted for, our old folks and grandparents would be very proud of us, to know how well we could hunt.

If there were children . . . came home with whatever they hunted for, either sea or land food, the old folks would say, 'She or he is good hunter and will able to look after himself and feed his brothers and sisters.' But if a boy goes out and hunts for himself without his parents or grandparents knowing and appears with a crab or a fish and stingray, he is noticed by an older tribe. 'Look that small boy, why he went and got his own food? Why didn't somebody big go with him, and partner him? He goes on his own without father and mother.' As the boy sits down with whatever he may have caught he feels so proud of himself and passes the raw food to his grandmother.

Then the old grandmother would take the fish or crab, make a fire and at the same time she burst out crying for the small boy's catch. All of a sudden you see rushing and jumping, grabbing boomerangs and nulla-nulla, cursing, squabbling amongst each other. Then a terrible tribal fight takes place. But the boy, he is there. He takes no notice, because he is just a lad, without any understanding of the tribal customs. He is busy playing with other children, or sitting down in the camp eating, while the fight is going on. Many people get hurt.

But that was one of the custom . . . never let a small child go and hunt for himself. He must have his father, mother, big brother, sister, uncle, auntie and grandparents to do the hunting for the child. Children weren't allowed to go on their own to hunt, in case something could happen to them without any one near. But the most important of all is, a child must not go on his own, and bring back to the camp what he caught. That always means a fight must take place. A boy is allowed to go hunt when he is a young man, when he can look after himself, but he still must go with father, uncle and grandfather, until he is able to manage hunting himself . . . that's when he can really take care of himself without getting hurt. An Aboriginal man and woman, when children grew up, it was one of the things they must teach their children, also how to hunt, how to find the right tree to make spears ...

These spear trees grow along the beach, where they grow very thick. The ones chosen have nice long, straight limbs. They break these ones off, make a fire, take the barks off, and warm it over the blazing fire. Then the man straightens by pressing the weight of his feet on the hot stick or handle, or straightens it with his teeth, until finally the handle is very straight. At one end . . . is much bigger than the other side (the side that the point piece of the woomera will be put in, by holding it with his hand to hold the spear up with.) First of all the larger side is where he digs a long narrow hole in the centre. He ties that with a piece of the fibre . . . he already skinned it from the same handle. That's to save the handle from splitting any further downwards. The centre hole is now ready for two to three thin shaped gigjie prongs made from gigjie wood. These were one time cut with shells, lowalen. Then out of the fibre bark, they plait this into twine, and being now tied all up together, it then is a spear, ready to be used for hunting for land and sea food or what happened to come by the hunter's way.

But on the other side, the small side of the spear, at the end there also is a small centre hole, for the woomera eye to be placed, for the woomera. It helps to send the spear as far as the man wants it to go, also to direct the straight shot to strike any object that he aims for. Without the hole there, and no woomeras to go with the spear, you never can feed yourself. A woomera was made, and meant for other purpose too . . . for digging soaks, digging hole to stand a broken branch tree for a shade, catching or hooking up crabs and breaking off claws, and other things.

I can recall when every man had his own spears and woomera and never was careless about it, but was well kept. You just could not ask another fellow, can you have a loan of his spear or woomera. That old fellow will tell you, 'Make your own. I won't give you mine to take. You'll break it or I shall never see it again.' They also showed another fellow what to do and how to do and make them, so they may have their own to feed their wife and families.

The early tribes lived hard life, because they had to find the best way how to live, how to hunt for everything, how to look after their wife and families, to make camps, to tear ti-tree paper barks to shelter from rain and many other things. I've seen most of those hard life. It was so hard, if you were unlucky on that day of hunting. I say you would be so tired and hungry. But another fellow would feel so sorry for you. He would send food over to you so you could have something to eat. My people were very kind hearted people, never been selfish. They also had to share whatever they had, even the last bit of food they'd got. They never kept it for themselves, but were always willing to share and give away.

I have never heard that my people were one of those kind you would say lived on an island as being a savages. There is not a talk about it. But how they lived . . . they were people of their own, knew each other, saw each other often, but did not like to see the sights of ships passing. They would run away in the bush. Only three men, and two women would hide behind scrubs, and watch to see them pass or land on the shores, but never go near them. Some times the men from the boats would leave food and other things that the people might like to have, but as they left and sailed away, the old ones went down the beach to see what they left. My people did not touch any of the stuff, but left it on the beach and went back again in the bush. My people had no idea of any value belongs to a white man, but just lived on the land, where they were much contented of the food they lived on.

Times went by when some of the hard life was passing away, when we were gradually getting supplies from the Mainland. More and more good things came to our island. People were looking for something belongs to a white man now, so they were forgetting about our customs, laws and legends. They were looking beyond for the white man's everything, its laws, rules and all its powers of Governments. But what was the use of forsaking their own tribal laws and customs? Where the tribes were so strict, everything was perfect. The tribes of my people knew just how to live, how to punish a bad person from harming the other person. My people did not know of the white man ways, but they lived in their own way of life, understanding each other, never hurting each other badly, but were so loving and friendly, and always kept the laws of the tribe wisely, and obeyed all its customs. They lived a strong healthy people before the white man came here. After the white man came and made a poor black fellow look and listen to them, and showed them now what to do, they were sad people and soon forgot how to live properly in their own tribal life. That too also has vanished and was altogether left far behind.

When new things came in too fast, with new kind of people, all kinds of race . . . well, you could say they ruined every precious life of the Lardil people and all it had on the land with so much happiness. Friendly humbleness of mankind was now gone or taken away from them. The new settlers thought these kind of things were no good. So what they had, the new settlers, they rather their own idea which can be much better than the ones I saw and grew up with. I grew up not knowing what selfishness was like, even greediness, thoughtless, unfriendly, cruelty, meanness . . . well, everything I can see today. I only knew the opposite side of these things in life, the goodness for all mankind, because I was taught to share and be friendly with everyone that passed my way, in life.

More old women waiting for the picture to be taken.

I can remember when I was small, there were too many people lived on Mornington Island. They were tall, well built men and women. Most of them I did not know by names, but by just looking at them. But some years later there were not much of them seen. Most of them died at different times of the year out in the bush.

In those days, when a man knows he will shortly die, he goes to the place where he was born. That's where they would bury him, after he died, and always the customs . . . bailer shell with water is left on the grave. He must not wander away too far to torment the campers that's camping not too far away from where they left him in peace. In early days they believed a dead man's Spirit goes everywhere and gives bad luck and sometimes good luck to anyone.

If a dead man tells you there's a dugong or turtle in a certain place, you go there and you will find the food there. That's your good luck for being good to him while he was alive. So you get up in the morning and think about the dream you had. So you say, 'Well I'll go', and for sure you do find the fish, dugong, turtle, stingray or whatever it may be, also flying foxes, wild honey and other such food. But of course, some times they speak to you in dreams, to go by yourself to catch for a good feed. But when you get there, instead of the right food . . . the right food is either turtle or dugong or fish . . . it turns into shark or some other bad signs if you never showed love and friendship to anyone who passed away, or even did not visit him at anytime when he was alive. He will surely punish you in Spirit after you have seen him go. But if you were good to him or her while they were alive, then when they die they speak to you in your dream and explain where to go and where to find this food. To your surprise you will find the food that was told to you to find, then you soon find out the Spirit is true in giving a fortune.

Even if a man is suffering in agony from sickness, he would say certain thing will happen for certain food will appear on that day or time while he is still alive. Perhaps turtle is floating in the channel. He tells anyone, the only one who is to go for the turtle. No matter some one else saw the first sight of the turtle, he is not allowed to go. Because if he goes, and was not told by the suffering man, he then spears the turtle, and when he jumps in after it, it turns into shark and will rip him up. Then again, the real person who was told to go, he is the right one to go, so when he spears the turtle, it just floats on the surface . . . is sometimes just caught by the right man in his hand. Sometimes he just gives a small poke and drags it into the canoe or walpa. And when it's cut up, it is so fatty, and when they see the fat, well, the old tribes say, 'That's his tucker, or his food, from the sick fellow or dead man.'

When these things happen, other people on the shore must be silent, not one talking, yelling, screaming or moving, running about the place, because we were taught the Spirit of the man that's within the turtle or dugong, fish, stingray, mob of crabs or schools of fish, will vanish and nothing more will be there to see. So that's a bad luck.

Many years ago, when I learnt to understand all these things, I knew these things did happen. I also heard things told by a sick man, then I waited to see how it would happen, what day or time of the day, and gradually, to my surprise it did happen to these people who were told to receive these gifts of wonders of sea food . . . was real true.

I've seen it happen, and understood everything that was done in those days. Some people got lucky stones in dreams to look after themselves from evil things, so that the man and his family would not be sick. It's a power to keep evil Spirits away from the families . . . not to get sick or any harm done to them. It's a power to cure a sick person from evil Spirits of the sea, animals or land Spirits that could cause illness to suffering and death.

The only way to cure is a smell from the under arms. Give

a blow of wind to the hands that already were held at the (healer's) under arm. Then he had touch . . . slightly rub over the painful part of the body. Then that good Spirit touch already has helped to cure the sick one. By that time of cure touching, he is well and not sick again.

I've seen all these good things happen. That can show you that in their tribal ways they were Doctors among their own people, who can cure anybody. These stone magic were given to some of the people, who were lucky to grab at nights during their sleep. That's why we can say these are from dream land . . . gift to a man to have power.

I can remember when I was newly married in the year 1946. One night a man was very sick, Edward Namie . . . stayed late that night cooking up some food. He fried scones. Everyone of his family were asleep. Also, the rest of the people nearby in small cottages were sound sleep. I and my husband Dick had a home by the other end of the ridge, by the water front. I was half asleep when I was awakened by painful crying and suffering. The sound was too bad to hear. So I woke Dick up, and shook him to get out of bed. 'There is someone crying painfully.' Everyone was asleep everywhere. No one was awake, everybody slept soundly. I could not bear to hear the bloke suffering. So Dick and myself walked down to where the sound came from. We walked everywhere to see different homes . . . whether someone was awake. Then we went to the spot where the groaning was. There, all by himself, was Edward Namie with people not far away from him. He lay there paining and suffering, rolling around with great pain. I asked, 'Where are your families?'

Edward answered, 'My girl, they all asleep.' So I went to the door of the house and woke the families up. They were that sound asleep and had not even heard any noise.

It was past twelve o'clock. No one was allowed to disturb no Nurses or Superintendent in those times. So what next to do about the sick man? How can we help him? Our fear was at anytime he would die. So I said to Dick, 'You wait here, and I will go and find and wake Alick Hills.' Then I walked a few yards away to Alick Hills' house. The home of

Alick Hills was only ten foot away from where I lived. So I knocked at the door.

From the inside they asked, 'Who are you?'

I said, 'I am Elsie Roughsey.'

'What do you want?'

I said, 'Uncle Alick. Come quickly. There is a man down there, in one of the cottages, suffering and rolling about on the ground.' So we walked down together to get to the spot of the sick man. I had confidence in him to make that man well. So I watched what Alick did next.

He said, 'Get me bushes and a dripping.' So we gave him bushes and the dripping. He rubbed himself with the bullock's dripping then rubbed some on to the suffering man, still crying and still suffering painfully.

The only words being said were, 'Oh the pain is too great, it's cutting me like knife. I'll die. Oh, it's too great.'

I looked as Alick Hills worked on the man. He rubbed himself with dripping, warmed himself on the fire and touched Edward. Edward lay in pain there. Alick rubbed his hands on his under arm, then on his tummy, then warmed himself on the fire and touched and rubbed Edward on his chest, side and tummy. He still yelled and screamed with pain. Just after the hand of Alick held him, he gave the last great big yell, 'It's gone.' I thought he was now dead because he lay there without another word. Alick gave three hard brushes of the bushes, with a blow over the body of Edward . . . and then all of a sudden, the sick man was quite well again.

Edward told us how he was sitting by the fire and fried some scones. Then he was struck by something that went in his body. Alick soon found out it was a small knife, like Sheerblade, that ran across the sky and hit him. While we sat there talking to Edward, Alick Hills told me and Dick to wait till he went after the light that came out of the man's body from the last brush of the bushes. Next, Alick raced along by himself following the light of a stone. He caught up with it . . . grabbed it in his hand, but it hopped out of his hand and fell into the river. So he missed it. He came back to us where we stood waiting for him. So Edward was quite well again and we put him in bed and left him.

There were by now many people awake and saw what Alick Hills had done. I could not get over all that I saw, especially with a man in terrible pain, almost suffering to death. Then with the last yell, it was gone. In few minutes he was sitting up good as before, before he was struck with a pain. I then knew this man Alick Hills had healing touch. All he did on the night of that terrible moment. Next morning Edward went to do his job same as usual, as nothing really happened the night before. So that's one of the things I really can say. This was my eye witness of how a man can do good work, with another person when they in need of help, without European Nurses or Doctors.

I have great belief of my people that they receive great talent of curing and saving life of young and old, whether it's a baby or anybody . . . all is the case. I have a brother-in-law, Kenny Roughsey, who is a very talent man . . . also Lindsay Roughsey. These men have wonderful talent of healing sick person. Most of the healing touch and chant songs of the past they receive during the night when they are asleep. These are part of the gift from people who have died . . . are for ones like them who care to do good to others. Especially it's really only to care for their own families, and keep them in good health. But with all they have, they help others too, who go to them rather than going up to hospital.

The tribes had songs to revive very sick person to life. They chant songs over their head and chest to keep them strong. While the heart throbs with pain, they sing the heart and belly to be running in order so he may live. And for sure the songs do heal. They known to be medicine chant alright, and it does work . . . other songs again for Mulgree when a person gets sick.

The Sea Serpent is one of our greatest legend who can harm any one who goes to the sea with a smell of greasy or oily stuff on their hair or body. Even if they eat some food, that is not supposed to be taken out and eaten on the sea, and Sea Serpent smells that and causes that person to get sick. They start feeling pain in their tummy, and roll about with pain. Also it makes them to vomit. Most times it stops them from doing their motion as well. But most times they are lucky from death. They go to these men who have power to drive the evil Spirit away from their body. This is not a fable to write and talk about. It's real thing. I've seen it happen to too many people, even to small children and infants. I've seen many of these people get sick and be cured by my two brother-in-laws . . . not only by them, but by old folks who have lived and are now dead.

The only way to get them better . . . they have songs that are for the Rainbow Serpent, to chant over some one just on their tummy. Also they chant a song to drive the pain away from the forehead, then put under arm smell on the suffering one, rub their hand two to three times on the person's body until he feels better, and then give three blows of wind from the mouth to say the boy or girl is quite well again. That mouth blow is also some how part of the cure. Then at that time, the sick person is no more a sick person. He is up on his feet and runs off to his camp, or the child is once more running around again and enjoying fun and laughs with his friends.

There are many children in the four brothers of the Roughseys. These children really trust and know they have fathers and uncles who are their great healer to any kinds of sickness, pains and illness . . . their troubles, they take it to them. These children have great belief of these men. They got sick and went through all this. They were treated for being sick with tummy ache, head ache and other different ways. They've seen things happen to them, and how they felt after they were touched by these magical and wonderful hands. Inside of them, there is that wonderful possession of healing.

You might wonder how these things do happen. You might then think how can these happenings be done. But it works. They have been seen by the people of the land. So as we live amongst ourselves, these wonderful things are happening. We see it all, and we do believe, because when we were sick the same was done to us. So amongst our people there are people who work different from our European

Doctors and Nurses. As I write, I've seen so many miracles have been done by our native Doctors. But truth to say these miracles only come given to few people in dreams. Luckily what is given or told to them, how these things must be done or treated, they must be smart to remember them all, and then test and see if it can work. Then if it works the way they saw it in their dream, then they have already received such a blessing of healing.

I can remember when my daughter Eleanor was a very small girl. She often took many turns. So many weeks and months, I almost lost her. But I've looked after her well. Also, Sister Yappa did so much wonderful things to help my little girl too, to live on. Every time I brought her home her uncles would grab her and give her their blessings to give her a nice good rest for the nights. She never gave us trouble at nights. She was always well. All my children were treated in the same way by their uncles. That's why my children and their children never were a patient at hospital. Until now, they are all grown up men and women and have children of their own, who are now happy families.

Why I write this . . . there is a true touch of healing, how they work with their hands and by chanting words of songs to cure or heal anyone who is at the point of sickness and death. People who will read this book may wonder how this may be done, how such men as them can do all this. Well, we too wonder about such wondrous things, what a man can do to help others. I often wonder why that healing touch comes by these men. Where is the magical origin stands within them? Well, we do not know, but it is there.

We see a work of a white Doctor, and how they treat people and how they do their skill and help to revive a sick person to life and health. Some of us know when we pass operation in hospital by Doctor, we cannot see their skill. All we know is when we are put back in bed and awaken by ourselves, we then know that something was wrong inside of our body that was cut and taken out. This is another way to cure a body to life from death. But these Doctors had to pass a test whether they can do it, and these sort of Doctors were interested in what they would like to do to help people to live without suffering. But now look at this Aboriginal healing . . . is far more different to the kind of a European healing. This one is another thing that the European and other different people in other parts of the world I suppose, do not have or do not know.

Fancy, just a smell from under arm, then a blow of wind to the hand, then on to the body of the sick person. Also dripping or fat of a bullock may be used to rub fat on to the hand, warm the hand on the heat of the fire, give a puff of wind from the mouth on to the warm hand of the Doctor, and rub into the sick person. Then all of a sudden, or in two to five minutes, the sick person is well again. But then, can you imagine how wonderful such a wondrous healing can be done? You might say it's superstitions, but it's not. It truly has been done and still is done today. I've seen many people who have survived from sickness and death, and are now strong and well. I tell you of many men of the past who I saw once . . . were these type of men who did different goodness to save life.

There is another one that comes to my mind. It was in the year 1947 that I saw happen on this day . . . man named Jimmy Dugong. He was a tall, thin fellow and very quiet. He was from the old tribe. Although he was born and reared in the bush before the white man came to Mornington Island, but he could not speak his own language in the end. Before that he spoke his own tongue among his people, then all of a sudden his sense of mind, to speak not his language but only english. Well, this fellow was one of the smart men too.

One day my youngest uncle, Henry Peters, was very sick for days and days, was almost at his death bed, when I watched Jimmy at work. He got a human hair belt that the men use when they put around their waist for corroborees. Well, he had a ball of this hair belt, got a long steel wire, pushed it into the ground, then tied the hair belt in a long string on to his feet and ran his hand up and down with his finger and worked that way until some blood flowed from the sick man on to the hair belt, and fell on the bark that he placed on the ground. Then Jimmy Dugong picked up a large sewing needle, the largest one he had. He showed we who were around him, to see. We did and to our biggest surprise he thrust it into Henry Peters' lower part of the waist line below his tummy. The needle he had, he gave a poke into the skin. The needle went further and further into his body until it disappeared into the inside of the man's body. There was nothing to be seen. The sick man lay down very still without moving. Then again the needle was once more seen in Jimmy Dugong's hand. Then he put the needle back into his pocket, wrapped in a small cloth. He told his brother he soon would be alright again. Today he is now dead, but Henry Peters still lives on and is now in charge of a turtle farm here on the island, and also he is a good hunter and hand craft man.

So that will give you an idea how clever these men have been in the past. One thing that really surprised me . . . how on earth he did not bleed the other person where the needle went in. There was also no mark left to be seen of the needle. Also even where the needle came out from, there really was nothing to see on the body of the sick man . . . where the needle went in, and how it came out. The skin or the body of the man was just as it was before it was handed by this 'nother bloke. Also you could not see the blood flowing in the hair belt. All your eyes could see, the blood falling on the bark. It was miraculous sight.

We just cannot really explain how these things were done and how clever these people were. It was something belongs to them. The talent was theirs, and all we can see, the only thing of a man, is his skill. How you call this? Is it then Aboriginal dramatists to a physician man for his healing? It's something that you see but you really cannot explain. So it's a skill of healing from dream land, given to them while they are asleep. So many things to man are given in dreams. While he sleeps he receives dances, songs, bad things in dreams that mean something awful will happen to him or his loved ones. Then again, good luck will be given to him. All that is told to him from someone who has died, so he can help others to save others, warn others of some evilness of

73

mankind life that will or can hurt you. So most of these things are for good health and to beware of the things that will take you for trouble, for sickness and death. A native man had too many good things come to him. Not all receive these gifts, only very few of them.

How I learnt about these . . . I saw some of the people of the tribe in early stage. Once my little brother, Colin William, went hunting in the bush not too far away from our camp. We were both with our mother at that time. Little brother went gathering some bush fruits amongst the bushes, when all of a sudden he was stung by a hornet. The hornet stung him on the side of his ear, and there was a terrible swollen. He ran crying and rubbing his ear. I asked what happened. All he did was keep crying with pain. I got him and carried him to the camp to Mum, but he jumped off my arms and ran to another camp, where an old man was. The old man was James Bush. He grabbed him and all he saw was this awful swell on his ear. So the old man put his under arm smell and rubbed his ear. Then old James put his mouth to his ear and sucked his ear until he had mouth full of blood from where the hornet had stung him. Then old James spat the blood on his hand to show Colin William what he had done. The swell went down. Colin was alright again and able to play with the rest of the children. I wondered how Colin knew about old James could do something for him. Though we were hundreds miles away from the mission, but the old fellow did the job.

Since then I have closely watched all the life of my people, even to little things that had power of healing. I can also remember the old folks attended to children and took great care of them. Even if they had head ache they would chant over the child's head to keep him cool, from getting hot and sick. Also if the child ate too much and the child's tummy got tight, the old men would get the smell from under his arm and rub the child's tummy. That helped the child to get better. Why children [know these things], like I saw Colin William consider James then. I was taking him to Mother, to comfort him, but to me, I suppose he knew something about old James that he could do something for him, that I would not understand to know.

I asked my little brother Colin why he went to that old man. Colin said, 'Well, he Doctor too. That's why I went to him, because he is my jumba.' That means . . . he is my grandfather. So he really believed that old man could help him out of his pain. So since then I took notice of many things, things I have never known and seen.

In the year of 1942, when we all went bush . . . this was the day when four Spit fighters came over Mornington Island. They formed V for Victory. Firstly we ran and hid ourselves when we saw the planes, and put all our fires out and ran in the scrubs and trees. But when we saw the V shape we were alright because then we knew they were our men in those planes. I saw children eating damper with butter, syrup and jam, then go down to the sea for a swim. All this happened out bush, away from hospital. The children had wonderful time swimming, but this child forget what he ate. Also the parents did not take much notice of that child.

All of a sudden he feels something wrong with him, so he comes to the bank and rolls on the beach with pain. Then a cry breaks out from the children. Something is wrong with the kid. You see a rush of parents running down to the beach to see what has happened. Amongst the old men, they would take the child to the one who chants the evil Spirit of the Rainbow Serpent, to drive pain away from the child's belly. So the old man sings and rubs the child with his body smell, and rubs it on to the child to where the pain is. Then the child is now well again.

There is a custom to all . . . never go to the sea with a smell of a fat or meat smell. You must firstly always wash your hands before you want to make your way down to the sea or rivers and creeks. But if anyone, like Adults, wants to have a go they may do so. If you are unlucky to be caught by the Rainbow Spirit, if there is one of the tribe there to cure you, you will be Okay. But if no one is there, you get swollen and you'll have terrible pain. Then the next thing you die, because you did not have anyone near you, to drive away the sea evilness of the Serpent. It's same if you eat land food like sugar bag or wild honey, goanna, swamp turtle from the lagoon or pandanus nut seed, also cumbered of the same tree . . . you go to the sea or fresh lagoon water, you will get sick. Just the same bullock meat, a wallaby meat, tin meat, butter, milk or mother's breast flow when it's full, also cause death and sickness. We believe all this. That's why we are careful not to disobey the customs of our law. It's there to keep us away from being sick. These great beliefs . . . still we have, and will always depend on them for cure and safetyness. So there you can see our people are very talent people. They knew just how to live, and find different ideas . . . what they may or can do to help one another. Being a healing man is one of the things that we shall never understand really, and how they became one of these special people.

I suppose it is the Lord's way, to give and help them, as most of us grew up with the tribes of the land, and if they did not receive such blessing, most of us would have died in hundreds without a Medical treatment from a European Doctor or Nurses around us at those times. So we are lucky too . . . still have some of these people, still with us today. So the Lord looks down in mercy and pity, also to a tribal man, because He placed us on earth to take care of ourselves. He gave power to whiteman, too, to become famous healers with all their skills and talent today.

So you may wonder how we can live also, with all our unknown powers. But there you see, white and black are equal to gain all that belongs to them and what was meant for either of the race, to help all men of the world who are sick and those who look forward to be healed. It is a miracle when you can understand how many people have gone under operation, and the European knows what he is doing because he learnt about the inward part of the body of all human . . . so people live.

Also, this other healing is far more different because it's in a man's feeling that he too has a power to heal just with the touch of his hand. You think that's the same way of our Lord Jesus Christ? When He was on earth, all His works were just by speech and touch, and everyone was healed. So it was given in like manner to all who were anxious to heal. They all had the gift of blessing, to raise the dying and sick and helpless people of the world. They all have some one to care for them. So we are all lucky to have people like these in all islands, cities, towns, missions . . . for people who live where ever they live. I suppose we all should feel happy about one of these people who can heal, and take care of us.

So as I lived amongst my people I have carefully watched many things that I never knew when I was young. I have learnt many of my people's ways, of all they had and how they lived in those early life. So this will give you all some idea of each person, what they can do, and how we live in different parts of the countries. Everyone has something belongs to himself that was given by training or from dreamtime. They all have something to be proud of.

In later years many of the tribes were being wiped away very fast, from sickness of a whiteman as missionaries settled on the island. They died of fever pneumonia, heart trouble and other sickness they did not know of. Some of them died by snake bites, but those who knew salt water was good to cure snake bites, bathed themselves in the salt water. The time they got bitten, they would race down towards the beach and sit all that time until the salt water had killed and washed the poison away from the body. Sometimes some of them died because they were too far away from sea. That means they were too inland in the bush.

Many had idea . . . get medicine grass and leaves off the trees. They warm this grass and leaves on the fire and place it on the parts where he was bitten. That also kills the pain and the swollen goes down. They keep acting on this way each time the pain comes on, until he is able to walk again.

These medicine grass are used for any illnesses . . . colds, headache, for sores. The grass has a perfume of eucalyptus. They are curly leaves when they are dry. It's good to collect them about that time when it's dry. It looks brown. Well, all you do is pluck the leaves or grass shrub, burn or warm it over the fire and rub it over the body. Also now we boil the grass in a drum, or smaller tins, until it turns tea colour. The grass is separated from the water. Then you bathe with just the water. Strange thing, the water is so soft. It smoothes the skin, and that helps to give strength to the body. Also it cleans the sores on the body and dries them up. Also, whenever you have bad colds, on your nose and chest, that same grass water is used as cough medicine. You drink it and that also clears the cold. As I write I've tested them myself and I found out the bush medicine is good. I've bathed in the water after I've boiled it and drank cup full of the water to help to cure my aching legs. I felt it did a bit good for me. That shows how we treat ourselves with these bush medicine.

Also, creepers that grow by the sea beach, they are good for burning in the fire, pressed on your tummy to cure your tummy ache. That always cures you. Also, there are trees that grow by the edge of creeks, rivers, swamps, in lagoons, in fresh water. These trees are white gum trees. The leaves are picked in bunches, boiled until the colour in the water has changed its colour to dark tea like. This is also to bath with when you are sick and weak. Also, it's for sores, rash, and other skin diseases. Dog balls are grown in small bush fir. You eat the food or the seed. Mix it in baskets made by ti-tree bark, and squeeze with hands until all that sticky sweetness is all gone out of the seed. Then you drink the water, also its leaves can be chewed when you have belly ache.

Another native medicine is white pipe clay. This is dug in the ground beside water stream, by the side of the rocks. It is collected, put in a ti-tree paper bark, and then it is moulded with clean water and put in another clean paper barks and left to dry out in the sun, to dry it hard. The white pipe clay is used for medicine also. If you have tummy ache and head ache, you eat some of these clay or mix it with water, and soon you find it does you good. The white clay cools the whole body. Also, when a tribal mother has not enough milk for her baby, she drinks this white pipe clay, and that gives her more milk for her baby to suck out of her breast. If a child is old enough, and is not strong in body, the mother gives her baby to eat the clay to make him grow stronger.

When a person's body gets hot and the tribe doesn't feel well, they eat, or smash the clay into powder and mix it in water and drink. This gives them much better feelings, cools the body and also strengthens them. Most of the time the white pipe clay can just be eaten as a meal.

I can remember how the present time children were made to eat clay to stop from eating sand. Most of them were soon knocked off from eating sand and were made to eat clay. I know. I had a son. When he was three year old, he often played with sand. He used to dig well into the ground until he comes to a cool sand away from the top surface. When no one is around to see him, he eats the sand, and when found out or seen by some one of the families, he runs away with a spoon in his hand, and hides.

We smacked his hand to try and stop him from doing it. There was no way. So the little boy, with two other boys and one girl, had to be sent over to Cloncurry for treatment to stop them from eating sand. But while they were there, that feeling of eating sand, made them to wander out of the hospital and find a good gravel place, and there they would sit and eat. So the day they came home back to the island, I found out the little boy of mine never stopped from eating sand and mud. The treatment did him not much good at all.

So I still had my mother and father, a foster father . . . were still alive. So they went out for awhile, going to search on the salt water plains for clay. They both brought back as much as they collected. They worked up a small ball of the clay out about the fresh water course, to take most of the saltness out of it, and soaked and washed it in the water and made a small ball of it, then put it on the rock to dry. The others, they kept it in their baskets or coolamun. Each day the little boy forgot to eat sand, but ate the white pipe clay, everyday when he felt like eating. Mum and Dad beat him to knock him off from the sand and mud. He ate clay until he was much bigger and soon forgot all about the clay any more. Now he is a fine healthy lad, also a strong man. I had few of my children eating clay. They found it tasty and then they gave up from it.

So as I came to move around the bush, clay was a thing to

be used for many purpose. Guyil was the name from the tribes. White pipe clay is a European way of saying. Guyil was also used for painting on a body for corroborees and also for tribal fights.

Now when they have to make wars between the tribes, they appear to the camp with painted bodies to say they are going to fight with their enemies. All that the enemy sees . . . the man who just came in from the bush. His enemy gets ready too by collecting his weapons. So each side of people are now ready. So they play salt water. The man whose totem is salt water he plays and dances pelican and brolga dance. The other side is also a salt water. They dance and play, imitating the rising of the salt water, and the rest of his brothers and sisters play the redbill dance. Also the pelican and brolga totem people imitate these birds. Then the play stops from both side and a fierce fight takes place. They use guyil for painting spears and boomerangs.

The red ochre is also used for the body. The ochre is first found on the salt pan. It's a yellow mud dug out of the ground, then taken up on a piece of ti-tree bark. Fire is made, then the wet yellow mud is put on the fire until it turns red. It's then called red ochre. Ochre is rubbed on a child's body, also Adults'. Many years ago when I was with my mother, she rubbed turtle or dugong fat on her body all over to head and foot, then slightly over with red ochre. Then my mother would get hold of my little boy and do the same . . . wipe the boy with dripping or fat, then red ochre. This means the ochre is a health. It also smoothes the skin. So whatever we had, it was for some good purpose, for Medical treatment and other use.

I can picture back in those days, how the old tribes used to sit under oak trees along the beaches, and sit all day long with red ochre on their bodies, while others, who weren't well, had white pipe clay or guyil on their body to make themselves better. On the humpies were lumps and heaps of these guyil, all there to dry and to be used.

When a person, whether a man or woman, wants to hunt on the sea for fish, crabs, stingrays or turtle and dugong, they must first wash the red ochre off their body with water. It's against the law, because the Sea Serpent will smell you because that's also another thing that disagrees to the sea. That's why you must wash before going down to the sea, also in rivers, creeks and swamps. No matter where you are, the Sea Serpent smells you anywhere, because he lives on land and sea. There are many legends from the early stage of our tribal life, so we must obey them still or our penalty is sickness and death.

As I grew up I learnt many things of my tribal people, got many stories as I possibly could get off my father and other relatives. I was so interested in them all. That's why I became one of the women who took parts in the tribal ways . . . hunting, dancing, also learnt to fight and defend myself with nulla nulla, took part in the initiation ceremony . . . how to nurse and care for children, how to treat my children with many of my tribal ways.

Before I had my own children I cared for many other children. I mothered them as they were my own children because I like to help to take part in love and caring for children. As times went by, as these children grew, they soon forgot about me and fled back to their parents, with no thanks as they left me. They were strong and healthy, and were now ready for school, to join the other school children in the dormitory.

But does any one else care to look at these things? It means nothing to the parents of these children, or the children themselves. It means plain nothing in caring. They give no thanks or regards back, it's just a big fun. Everyone thinks that you did it for nothing, to help to rear somebody's children. I just cannot understand it all. Why in the first place did I do that? It was that these children really wanted to stay with me when they were small because their parents had another smaller child to care for. Also, it was just like being a part of life, as being a God mother to these children.

These children were brought up in a tribal way. They slept and stayed in my home, ate every meal with me. Their parents had nothing to do with them. But it's strange, when it comes to that time when they are big. That respect is not shown from the child back to the one who cared for them. They then rather their own parents. All they think . . . 'Blow you. I would rather my own parents. I wouldn't look back to you, as long as I am strong and grown up man and woman.'

These children I've cared for, they were sick, and needed more further motherly care and better treatment. But that's Okay now with me. I have all my children of my very own, who grew up so strong and healthy.

One thing I am proud of, my children never had to be a sick patient in the hospital. The only one was a girl I had. She was a child that always had turns from when she was infant until almost four years old. But then on, she has never been a sick girl, but is a strong, healthy girl, growing up a fine young lady. Now I have a good working healthy girl out of her, who is so quiet and timid . . . only laughs and plays a lot among her own families. She too is so fond of children and nurses and loves small babies. She often gives chance to some mothers, to do their home work in the kitchen and bottle feeds the babies and makes them go off to sleep. She also has five brothers. Three grown up men and two small brothers that go to school with her.

Also in my young woman's life, I've been nurse to many mothers and nursed for their children. I myself cut their cords and cared for their navels. To your surprise you would be amazed . . . the scissors or razor I used on the mothers and the child were rusty and blunt, also dirty. But I quickly made fire out in the open camp fires and put boiling hot water on, quickly sterilized the only thing I could see around me.

When it was just right there for the right time to use, then I use it, as the baby lies yelling with cry. All I have done to the mother . . . put her in bed. I then see about the baby, and tuck the baby in a comfortable bed in the room. I always have to go and see that mother and baby are quite well and safe.

These were the days when we had no Sisters in our mission. Some of the trouble I had while Sisters were here, but it was too late to get the mothers to the hospital in time.

The delivery was in my care. I always felt so happy when I had to help with mothers and a child. How I came to do all this . . . I very much wanted to learn more about mothers and the birth of children because I was so interested in learning and caring for babies. Since then I've learnt more from Sister Creagh. She was the first Sister who came to Mornington Island.

All our babies were born down the camp in our own huts and humpies. Some people had small iron house built by Mr Wilson when he was here, for newly wed people. They were the only houses, five of them, with two rooms in one. It was just for ten married couples to live in them. When they had more children they moved out of these cottages, and made larger houses made of bush messmate barks and ti-tree paper barks and bush timbers. They built larger houses where the big families could live in.

When these huts were built, it was a very hard work to be done. We people went so many miles out bush to get all our barks, spent all day just collecting barks, making large fire to burn the barks to keep them firm and strong . . . flattened them on the ground and put weight of logs and stones on them, until the evening came. We all came home with great loads of barks on our heads and on our sides, hung down from the shoulder by a string or a belt. That's how we carried extra load more, was that way. The men had much heavier load on their heads. That's how we had to work hard to build a hut for ourselves. We had no other way to carry all the load. Some were lucky because they had dug outs to go out to bring back all their barks. So you see, it was very hard to start to build a house of bush barks. Everything was done by walking.

Then people who were able to go out on different Stations, worked hard to get better money. Others went on ships as deck hand and crews to make money for much better homes. They spent money for new iron houses and bought timbers that came by Cargo ships, and were able to build better houses.

Yes, talking about the white pipe clay which we native people called guyil, I once sat beside an old woman. I had noticed she was one of the early aged person. She had a large mass of white clay which she used for eating. Also she put some of these clay on her head and face. The most of the white clay was so thick on her head. I sat beside her, watched every movement. We both sat there in the sun, beside her broken humpy. I asked her if she had a head ache. The old woman replied, 'Yes, I am sick, got head ache. I need to cool all part of my body to make me feel better.'

As I sat there, most of the white clay was already dry and hard. To my surprise she started picking out the dry clay from her head and started eating it. The ones that were on her face were much too wet for her to pick on, but she waited till they were dry, and she ate some of it. She let me mould the other rest of the clay with water.

As I did that, she, the old granny . . . packing the rest of the clay, piling it all on her head to have them dry. As the sun beats on the clay, it dries fast the clay. The old granny picks each time and eats them all until the white is left on the hairs of her head.

That was the only way she could get herself better of all the pain she had. Also, the old woman was not in a good sense of humour. She was on her way to become mad, but her madness was in silence . . . felt just like eating clay all the time. Each day was the same, and finally she died in her old age.

I was able to get around the mission doing all sorts of daily jobs. Being one of the Senior Girls, my job was to take in charge of the girls for jobs and see they did their jobs well. Also I helped to cook meals for the boys and girls . . . get them in line before their meals to say their grace. I was chosen for other jobs round the mission. I· liked it all, especially minding the children at work, and working with them. We had many funs and play as we worked, cracked funs and jokes with each other . . . more fun we had, we got on faster with our jobs.

Many people say, I've heard, we cannot work and play at the same time. What's the use of working quietly? You never get on well together. But I realized more fun at work, you come to know each other well and you do more work fast, with all your jokes and fun. I cannot understand . . . if you had to work all the time, the same way in silence, you find yourself unhappy and you probably find out you have no friends. You will never learn to understand somebody else's happiness by remaining silent. Someone will think, 'What's wrong with you?' or 'Are you sick?'. Then they ask all kinds of question . . . 'Why are you sad?' 'What's the matter with you?' 'Have you got troubles?' 'Did anyone say something to hurt you?' Well, the only answer to all this . . . be happy, best to laugh and play. You find yourself go a long way with so many friends. You'll love all your jobs. Even at playtime . . . is good to enjoy yourself. You will find happiness all around, no matter what you are doing.

I know when I was young, I got into many holts of trouble. I got spank for some things I did, and some spanks I got for somebody else's fault, but that didn't worry me at all. It was all the kind of life that a child gets, and it matters you not much to take it deeply in yourself. I was still happy. I still liked the person who gave me a spank with strap or board, or a piece of fire stick or a swish . . . well, you could say with all kinds of things, just enough to hurt me, to make me cry. After it was done, everything seemed quite Okay again . . . just got along and joined my other mates.

My young day's life was a fairly good life. I can think of the times when some times were so tough for me, and other times were good times, but I found life rather pleasant.

Then as I grew up, I much understood many things. I began to find things much harder. How can I do now, without a real boss to guard me, to show me how to do the things I've learnt to do when I was much younger? So the time came when I had to practise which is the right way, how to get on, how to behave like a young woman. This was the life I had now to face, to be careful of the wrong life that could lead me into trouble. But I knew how to come a good behaving woman. I did my best to do all things in right way. But you still live with people who blame you for things you haven't done or you knew nothing about. The best way I always fought it out . . . to speak up for my self.

So as times went by, the things I've written about were at the time when world war II was on. I've mentioned one. There was the night I saw happen when I was married, but that was just to give you some idea. The rest is all about when I had to go in and out of the dormitory.

During the time if a Superintendent had a trouble or a fight with we girls, we used to run away from dormitory and go out to our parents. Well, we just wished to do any thing we wished because in that case we just left our parents for shelter from rain. But when we needed to leave, it was then our own wish to stay in dormitory or leave to go back to our parents, where we found love, kindness and freedom being with them, instead of starting once again all over in some one else's care in the dormitory.

Dormitory life was hardships of all different way to make you feel sick, tired, friendless . . . hopeless if there is hope for you to get along with something new, for you to try and give it a go. You'll never get anywhere to understand to learn any other good things, no matter how talented you are. To do a thing . . . they never let you have a try to give it a go, but expect you to go along the way of life without helping you. They rather we black fellows stay where we are. Don't make a move, or you will go above a white man, or I should say equal with them. That's why now, at our present time, when we should be able to do something by ourselves, it's no use, because the past years have gone past and all our training should have been by that time of years, if we had had some one to give us that help. But the advance of our time could not possibly have given to us. Our time of doing or learning was just enough and no more than to that, just half way. Then you walk out of school and live in the bush as the boys did. We girls had bit more better chance until there was a time when marriages took place.

Well you go out, you start all over again the hardship of learning to hunt again, and learning all the laws, customs, legends and all the tribal ways of life. But by that time you are really walking the proud land, free as the Summer's bird, back again with mums and dads and able to move around wherever you want to go . . . no one to worry you with all that white man laws, no one to tell you, 'Do this, do that, don't do that', but happily roaming the bush, living and travelling together from camp to camp, dancing, laughing, hunting, having all funs and jokes. No one was too sad to worry about anything, but lived that peaceful life amongst our old tribal people.

Something rich they really had, that really and truly the white man can never understand and will never learn of our tribal ways . . . how things we had to live by the law of our people. If you start explaining some of the tribal ways to a European, she or he will never understand how it is, how it goes, why it happens. I often heard from some cities and towns when you tell them of our customs, they just cannot understand. Although they say, 'Of course, it sounds all right. They have wonderful customs and laws' . . . but truth to say, they really haven't got the dimmest idea of such and such a life we had to depend on, to keep us out of the white man laws.

It was too perfect. Hardly there were troubles of the tribal race, because they helped each other by doing most good by all they had from the past. So many wonderful times they had, too good . . .

The present time is with too much troubles, small and big, too much laws that make you sick to hear it being repeated time and time and again. Nothing is done . . . how to help, which our people cannot understand today. It's too much of these new rules and laws of present time. You just can't really know who is your boss or leading person. You just don't know who is the law keeper at these times. Everybody everywhere says this and that, and when the law should act. You see plainly the law deal with a harmless people, and then the laws are so strict with some one like that. The law should really punish those who really should be dealt with for the wrong they do, but then others bear their punishment.

But if it was on my tribal way of life, the laws say . . . punish the only one who tells tales and causes disturbments. So they, the elders, bring forward that person. They give him nulla nulla. He has to stand there all alone and fight, himself, against five or eight men until he cannot stand to hold any longer. That only shows or teaches him not to do it again by causing troubles with anyone any more. That's how the old people taught all their children how they should live in peace and friendship towards each other. That's why the real tribal man's child is good.

Also, you find people who live by tribal laws know right from wrong. If they go against wrongness of other person, then they say, 'Why don't you punish him? He did something that was not right and was unfair. He must be punished.'

But no, there is the other way. One does wrong. All parents and families get involved in fight, then they all get hurt, because they haven't taught the child the way they grew up with the tribal laws and customs. They rather take the trouble their way or the European way . . . take it easy, just jail him for certain time, months or years.

That can plainly be seen by a tribal man. He should suffer

by fighting alone, or also by being speared during the tribal fights which take place in a different form, which the tribes meant real for actions, bloodshed and death. Although it happened like this, but they also got rid of the troublesome person who could never live without trouble. The best way was put him or her away and no more troubles they could give. That also taught others to live friendly.

The tribes never allowed anyone to spoil their laws or customs. Everyone had to live alike, as they were really in full blood relation line. Those who were born not too far away, also were treated as full blood to each other. That's how you just could not really believe that everybody was some one real to you. The old tribe really meant relationship, and loved each other as their own families.

I noticed many things during the last war II where my people had so many good laws and customs. Firstly one of these customs was, a daughter-in-law could not speak to her tribal in-laws, who were right skin to her father and mother-in-laws. Although the girl never marries their sons, but that was against the tribal custom. You must not speak to them but the father or mother-in-laws may speak to their daughter-in-laws. You can take it either ways, whether you marry their sons or not. You cannot speak to your in-laws. Then the other thing.

As for the case of my big sister, Julie Roughsey, when she married to Lindsay Roughsey I took notice that my sister could not speak to her husband's mother. Although she visited old Minnie, her mother-in-law, so often and never spoke to her, but she would speak to my sister by her children. My sister would listen and do what the old woman said to her by her children. Most time she would talk to her son, Lindsay, about different things, but all that yarns seemed even for my sister as well. Minnie would just speak in whisper to her husband, then her son would do all the speaking having all the good yarns to themselves. I was out of the mission's care by that time. I too was not able to speak to that same old woman. I now had to respect her as well. Although I was still single or unmarried at that time, but the laws and customs were there for me to see, and do the same as my big sister was able to do.

Secondly, there was the other thing. A brother would not speak to his sister or even go anywhere near her. Although a sister and brother had many funs and play during the time when they were both brought up in the dormitory under European eyes and care, but as I lived amongst my people, there were different laws and customs to be taken over for me to understand, and become as one of my old people. For instance, when I was told by my folks, 'Now, Girl, you must not go near your brothers,' or 'Don't go near them. Even you must not speak to them, you must keep away' . . .

Well, when I heard that, I laughed and said, 'Daddy you cannot stop me from speaking to my brothers. We were meant to speak and play with each other. That's why God gave us brothers and sisters, so we can enjoy life with our parents, to make everyone feel happy.' That's all I said. Dad was so angry with me. Why I did that . . . because it sounded so awful for me to be not able to speak and play with my brothers.

Then Dad and Mum, uncles and aunties and other relatives spoke to me, 'Now you are a young woman. You must keep away from your brothers.' For quite a long while it was upsetting to we sisters. Everytime we had to get together for meals with our parents we would all sit down and crack some jokes around the camp fires. Then May, my youngest sister, and myself would forget the customs we must face against, so we start laughing and joking with our brothers again.

Then the whole thing is explained to us all . . . 'Now you boys,' Dad would say, 'don't go near your sisters or speak to them.' Dad would say to the girls, 'Keep away from your brothers. You are all big enough to understand the customs and laws of my tribes. This is the way you must respect each other.'

The respect was mainly meant on the side for the men and boys, to teach the men or brothers of the sisters not to touch anything that belongs to their sisters, even not to fight and growl at their sisters . . . the only way they taught all brothers to take care of their sisters. No one must hurt their sisters in any ways. So later on, we began to learn to keep away from our brothers. We respected them, and the brothers kept away from us.

Truth to say, in an Aboriginal way of life, our parents and other tribes' people knew the age of a young girl by the bust. That time is the case that everybody in the families and relations of the girl must really regard her with respect as being a young woman. The young woman must closely be loved by all . . . see that no trouble comes upon her. She must be treated with love and care, and above all is that respect. Anyone who breaks the law of this matter is punished by tribal fights. Sometimes death takes its place. That's why in that case you break any important customs of the tribal man you be punished. They won't show you any love, how to forgive you, if you show no respect for the other person.

Say for instance, I walk past by my brother and sister-in-law at their camp, I must not get too close. I must walk ten foot yard away from their camp. I'm even not allowed to speak to my sister-in-law. That too is how we show our love and respect to her, because she got married to him. And I am not allowed to go or even speak to her because that woman is now one with my brother. Therefore it is the way I cannot speak to my brother or his wife.

It also concerns about the other sisters of my brother's wife. They also, I must keep away from them. It is also against the law, because my main sister-in-law and her sisters can have a chat and crack jokes with each other and they are meant to be together always, joining each other's companies. Besides that, my sister-in-law won't speak to me. She must show me that respect more seriously because she married my brother.

These laws and customs, I soon found out, were worth to be carried out. It was something that was valuable to be kept, and that was how our relationship was real in our way of living as one real people. The love for each other was strictly kept and obeyed. If there is no respect for each other and some sneaky stuff enters in a heart of two people to allow themselves to do wrong, when they are found out there is always such a mess of troubles. There's a fight on. These bad people have to stand all by themselves and face all that comes to them. Their uncles and aunties and grand-parents deal with these two couples. No one takes up for them, not even their parents. Most time mainly sisters' brothers are responsible to deal with their nephew or niece.

Also it goes my brother's children are under their aunties and uncles again. The main person to handle all this kind of stuff over children of each parents is their own aunties or uncles, and not their own father and mother. These parents would leave everything in their sister's and brother's care. Then again, if the child is given a smacking by her or his parents . . . is sometimes a bit alright, but the parents can't go too far by hitting the child too hard, too much of a hits. The poor parents, before they know what happens next, there is a boomerang being thrown and then there is a big smash up. But not for long, because there would be other people go to stop the fight.

Now here is the track to this life that I am writing about. I have brothers and sister-in-laws. If I were to hit any of my children beside these people (my families), they will bash me for that, seeing the child is small and cannot hit back. So in looking at this, they do the same back to me, for the child's sake. The child's uncle gets hurt and he must hurt me in the same way. In fact I get much more heavy bad treat-ment on me, than what I gave my child a hit, because the uncle to that child doesn't want to see my child get hurt in any way, not even by words. It all costs troubles and fight, and it lies heavily on me. That's why I must take care of my children and don't hurt them. That was one of the customs. Feelings of children would also hurt his uncle and my sister-in-law. Also my grand parents would belt me too.

Now if I was to fight or just quarrel with anyone, other people would take no notice, who are nearby. They would sit in their camps without moving to stop me and the other person. So some one would call out to any of my relation, 'Hey, there's a fight or quarrel over there. Come quickly!'

My brother would come, but he speaks not a word to me.

I happen to see my brother standing there . . . he's come in peace. Then at that very moment I must stop at once. So I walk away and the whole thing is finished. Also it applies if my brother or my sister-in-laws are fighting with some one else. Well, I must go at once to break it up. My brother or sister-in-law see me there, standing by the person who they having a fight with. Whether there is another blow with the nulla nulla to strike the one they are fighting with . . . well, the moment they see me there, they stop immediately, drop the stick, and walk away without a word, and go back to their camp. Everything is over now, both sides say no more and fight no more.

In the other case there is another feeling also. If I fight and somebody hurts me by bleeding me on my head or some part of my body with a stick, all my brothers and sister-in-law, my uncles and aunties and my grandparents from both sides see me being beaten and blood pouring from where I got hit . . . well, you can say that other poor fellow will be in a very bad way. They will bash him or her with a nulla nulla or even spear him or her. That was how they taught other people not to hurt and fight another person. That also taught us to mind our own business, leave the other person alone or not pick fight with anyone, but be friendly, be happy and share and share alike with everything that we had.

When there is corroboree performed by the tribes, elders of the tribal men use their own blood for painting feathers on their body. Some blood is given to others . . . pierce on the arm and pour the blood on shells or bark. This blood is spread on the body where the feathers are put.

At the time when the men are in the corroboree ground, other men or young men who do not take part in the dance, are to keep away until there is a signal warnings with a shout by one of the men. The corroboree is now ready to begin, so the women, children and young men sit around the main dancing ground . . . wait for the show to be put on. Some women take part, not all. In those days, the tribes only choose the best dancer in men and women. These people are presented with feathers from the tribes as the singing and dancing is going on. They perform an opening dance during the day, sometimes at night. Then the main dance is held on the following night. Only these group of people gives the show. This show goes on for two or three performances, before other people are allowed by the tribes to dance.

When the corroboree is over, the one main man who offered his blood for the men, his sister is not allowed to pass the brother's camp. Although the sister and brother-in-law do not know what happened at the corroboree ground before the show, but all he or the sister knows . . . only by the boomerang that was thrown by the brother who gave his blood away. As sister turns to ask why her brother threw the boomerangs, before she opens her mouth to speak, someone, either cousins or the wife of the man, quietly speaks, 'They have used a blood of your brother for the dancing.' So sister and her husband who is a brother-in-law, walk away without a word. They feel ashamed of passing the camp of the man's sister.

There was no fighting back to the sister's brother, because it was one of the biggest sacred laws of the tribes, part of the life. Sister and her husband show a respect to the brother. They cannot speak, but walk home with their heads down. They know the law of that. But there is the time when you don't know what happened earlier . . . only is nice surprise . . . tells the story, a boomerang is thrown, then the sister realizes she must keep away from her brother's camp or not go anywhere near. That's the only time a brother can turn on his sister. Two or three month pass. Later, everything is alright again, and sister can visit the families. The brother still loves his sister, all the same. He gives her everything a brother has to give in their tribal way. Children are the most important to pass things or food to sister or brother. They speak to each other by children's activities.

I saw one of this customs on action one Sunday, as I was passing to go home after visiting my parents . . . and this I saw. Brother did not speak to let his sister know of the secret of himself. Only he spoke in throwing the boomerang. I really was surprised at that, as I did not know of these things. A sister must be careful.

Our tribes never wanted any thing to move in a wrong portions . . . or even not to ruin the customs of our land. Our tribes were wonderful people. All they had has made us to be what we are today . . . not all the people, only very few of us who live with those customs still, as all people don't carry out the laws of the tribe, though in them it should not be forgotten, but live by it because it is good to live by two world. Only if they really understand the laws of the tribe, is so important . . . where you find there is no pride of loving yourself at all, and forget about the other person.

There were not selfishness, cruelness, hurtfulness or greed, or any sort of illness in any way with the tribes. We were taught to be kind, friendly, generous with whatever we had, to obey, be happy. Well, you can say and think of everything that old tribes did have, but you just cannot understand it all. Where these wonderful way they got? I know as I write, it was not from a white man. It was their own customs, before ever a white European had never found them. It was their own feelings . . . how to live as real people. These dear old folks, who lived those years ago, found everything really satisfying . . . made them really happy people. They had their own schools amongst the tribe, their meetings of their laws, shared fun and happiness, also their own good back ground was perfect.

So that's why the blackman himself is a real unknown people to all people at this time. The Europeans have not the slightest idea of all that the tribes have, or what they have lived with. Though you hear some legends, customs, laws and rules, but you just cannot understand how on earth have these people found to raise themselves as these people. I suppose the black race has something that no one today can look downwards on. Of my people, of asking more questions about all this, only I can say they were man and women of rich wisdoms and knowledge.

Then you would ask how they've forgotten about all their ways of living, as one of these early days people, if the laws, customs, rules, Government of their own people . . . had them, and now they are gone from them. The big reasons . . . the white man's law came in and made the people of the past to wipe it off and look and take the laws of the white man. Then christianity came with much heavier force, at the same time with the laws of today, and soon scarred the background of the black people. Now as you enter the life of the future, with all its troubles of laws and rules, they make you to live by them, with very small feeling how really to punish those who need to be punished when they do wrong. All their new laws today are all being said, and no true action can be laid on anyone . . . just to teach and learn people not to do it again. But the things which really can't be cared and protected by the law today, stand uncared, unprotected and most of it is useless. Then the same things go on for ever . . . go to jail and out to do the same thing or something else.

Then there is a murder done to others who would like to live as the killer would. That poor person is well out of this world by then, where else they would have liked to live on until there was an accident of different other way to get themselves hurt. I have often wondered how innocent people can be killed, like children of other parents, man and women of other families do . . . all the hurtful, harmful, thoughtless, meanness of the one who does these things . . . that the same things do not happen back in place of the loved ones of these ones who were killed. Why should they do these things of selfishness . . . or whether these wrongdoers have no parents or bigger sisters and brothers, uncles and aunties or grandparents from both side of the families, to help and talk to them not to do these sort of a thing. If they had, these people too should be responsible of them. There would not be too much sorrowful, worried, unhappy people in the world today. Everybody would feel unharmed and safe if only they had somebody to help to stop all this sort of bad life. They should have their own families from both side to guide and make sure that their own families should not do all this.

But a tribal person has another step of looking at this

awfulness of killing. They teach all their children . . . don't kill anybody, don't tease, don't hurt anyone, don't fight, don't hit, don't blame anyone else for doing something unless you have eye witness to see the thing was done. So they really protect each of their families as well as the other families. Black people all help each other to live together in peace and friendship. To my people killing is dreadful thing. It is the baddest thing among black people. To punish anyone is to hurt them, just to teach them not to do these things because they would not like the things to be done to them in the same manner, as they do to their fellowmen.

I often wonder, now, at this time . . . you may look for the past to be right at our door of our lives. Could we have them again? But how can we revive the dreamtimes again? Some people think . . . start them off in school and teach them. But how can it be done in school? Our customs and laws do not belong to school . . . but get together in families groups down the village each day at certain times and speak, explain to parents and families. Have a chat perhaps round camp fires at night, or anytime where there is a thought for it.

Then my appointment is take children out bush for a holiday . . . two to three different places on Mornington Island, and make it like school business for three weeks or month until the children can clearly understand all the laws and customs told to them and then force the action on them, whether they can take and hold it with interest. Teach to hunt, make their own hunting weapons, what time of the season certain food to collect and how to find them. Teach the young men and women also to dance, how to sing corroborees, besides the rest of the laws and customs. I'm sure something might take place if only something like that can happen. It really depends on fathers and mothers of these children. If they themselves can step forward and help the children to continue with the old ways, everything will come back to what it was before . . . happy, laughing people full of fun and happiness.

Why I write about the early life and speak of those days . . . people of mine were different to what they are today. If

I express the real true life of my people you would not really understand how wonderful were the days. The people were fantastic. The way they lived, they had everything that was good and perfect that you could have pride the fact of life, if you were interested. If you had to see it all in action, you would stand firm to the laws of an Aboriginal man, and not allow too much of the European laws to come and ruin and spoil all we have.

I can recall how as I worked in the garden in the dormitory reserve, I listened day after day, noises of people . . . laughing, yelling, screaming. I often wondered what was all the noise about. But it was my people enjoying themselves with the fun they had, also teaching some young men and women to take part in the fun. It was the same customs of a European today. You have two to three people acting as funny people in show room and all others just sit and listen and enjoy the fun. Well, my people were just like them, those long years before the white man took hold of them, before the people really could understand of the Government laws. Well, the people had all these ideas of fun. They gathered some of these people and played and joked amongst each other. It was everyday thing with different funny ideas. I'll tell you some of them later on when I can express it to you, how the people learnt themselves to gather all kinds of customs. They had most enjoyable times, when you just could watch, sit and laugh.

If now you try to recall to some old people, if they can remember of the times, how it was spent by them, some of their customs, laws, also ask some of the legends, it would be very hard now to get most of it from them, because their poor brain cannot altogether gather them back from memory and hold them all. They have almost lost all their culture, customs, laws and legends . . . just lucky you have some Europeans who are interested in the black people's way of living from the past. They ask you about the way of life and that, too, can make you think, and look back of the time when it all happened. You can get half but not all. It was one of the best that I shall never forget of all I have seen and done . . . the way of my people, how wonderful it was in those days when the tribes had to live on such customs, laws and cultures which made them a hero to their own people, and how they lived together as one big family, with all its glorious life.

Most people shall never know of all our life time from the past . . . was absolutely important, but now it is all gone. Only memories can remember them all. But to look at it, it so faintly can be seen on actions in a very small way. That makes you feel so sad, to get rid of all that was ours.

When two young people about to have a baby, firstly the baby shows many good signs through its parents and by near close blood relation. Something nice may happen while going out for hunting on land, or sea food. The baby gives plenty of food to the hunters. Although, the other families don't know the woman is going to be pregnant . . . keeps that business to herself. As each day comes, the man and woman who are going to be future father and mother go out to hunt. The man goes to the sea, spears dugong and turtle or big, fat stingray, comes home, while others come home with nothing. Well, the old folks talk about the catch the young man caught. They say, 'Mungada', means . . . baby gives them food. Only the other person have bad luck. Then the whole campers begin to talk about the young woman who will have a baby. They chat all day long with happiness. Then one sign to another of good luck follows the two couples. Everyday they hunt in abounderous and share all they hunted for.

By that time before the baby is one or two month old in his or her mother's womb, the father must tie a piece of twine or a piece of cloth around his left arm. That's to give him good luck for the day's hunt. Sometimes the tribes don't know the man's wife is pregnant. It's a surprise to them, when a man picks up his spear and woomera to hunt in the sea. He sits in his camp, ties the piece of string on his left arm without being seen and walks down to the sea to hunt. The other tribes see him. They get so excited and talk to each other . . . 'Aye, look that man got his arm tied. So his wife going to have a baby.' So they all rejoice with him. The grand parents from both sides are very happy, when they see their son or nephew shows the customs of the tribe. It means good luck, and his hunting will be successful one when he returns back to the camp.

Also the mother, she goes out too for hunting. She finds lots of wild bee honey, goannas or plenty of crabs and fish. No matter what sort of food it is, it must be plenty because the baby gives all that, even to his other relations, as well as father and mother.

When a woman, any woman, before she is pregnant, or any sign of pregnancy . . . most women get sick, have bad head aches and vomits, some get very ill . . . also sometimes death to father or mother and most times the last baby that already is weaned gets very thin, cries a lot, because the baby needs more attendance from the mother. Baby must have plenty to eat, to be satisfied. If the baby is not really cared well, the baby will have a very bad time, crying for food. When it sees some one eating food, the baby wants some. When the food it is given, the baby feels better.

Mother gets crabby most time. She gets cross and angry and begins to pick bones with her husband or other people, then there is a fight on. Besides that, most troubles are over jealousy. They get in holts with old friends from the past, really for no reasons. Sometimes that's all caused because the baby that is on the way in a mother's womb makes the mother so angry. At most time the mother is so friendly, so loving towards other people and her husband. But baby makes so much miserableness, crabby and makes the mother get so cranky that all this happens. Many good things happen, many bad things happen also.

They say it's a boy because father gets thin, and the mother gets bigger or the baby shows bigger in the mother. If it's a girl, father gets fatter and the baby in the mother doesn't show much.

When the child is six to seven month old, the mother feels much better. All her differences disappear and she gradually becomes a proud mother after all.

When a mother is pregnant she is not allowed to eat any deep sea fish such as rock cod fish, dunga, large blue fish and other deep sea fish. Why? Because it dries up mother's breast from flowing. Also, the baby will be born cripple. Something will be wrong either with jelly knee cap, cripple legs, or thin arms and jelly flat back. The baby grows up unhealthy and cannot crawl and learn to walk the right time of its age to a certain month.

To cure all this, all you have to do is sit by the fire, put your hand over the fire and warm and rub the child. You do this each day and night, whenever you feel to do, to help the child to grow strong. You use the kissing act by your mouth and squeech your hand on to the spot where the crippleness shows, and rub the child to straighten the form of the baby. You finally find the bone and flesh get tightened and the baby will be able to move and crawl and walk about like other children. If any mothers disobey the law of our customs, these awful things do happen. That's why, when most of us were pregnant in our time, we had to obey all customs, and not eat when it was against the tribal law. When we obey, our children grow up healthy and strong and have plenty of breast feed.

Tribal lullaby songs for babies were often heard by the tribes . . . sings baby off to bed. Some songs . . . to make baby grow strong and fat, stop baby from crying, so they can play all day without crying. They real stuff. Baby quickly turns on its back, and before long baby crawls, then learns to stand and walk.

Also, when a baby is young and sucking, mothers are not allowed to go down rivers and creek beds for fishing, because if the mother does she gets sick and starts vomiting. Then you know the Sea Serpent smelt the smell of the mother's breast milk, or probably the mother had her periods at the moment. Sometimes mother dies unless she has a song man to chant over her to drive the evil Serpent away from her . . . then she is well again. All this has been experienced in early stage of the early tribes of dreamtime. When things did happen to certain pregnant mothers, tribes carefully watched why things did happen to a child or to a mother. That's why all customs had to pass down through all ages, to be careful of what you eat or you should not touch to eat. No matter how hungry the mother can be, she cannot touch the forbidden food, unless she eats only the smaller fish, or fish that's given to her by her parents and grandparents.

Also mother is not allowed to swim or wash herself and baby in any running water from the land that runs into the sea. That too causes sickness and death, either to the mother or the baby, and sometimes other people who are hunting round about the place . . . that can harm them, all through the carelessness of the mother who has a young child, and doesn't care less about the laws. That mother doesn't think that the law of those early days no more can hurt anyone now, but as I know, these young mothers are still mistaken. Things still do happen yet in our time. Children get sick, mother also gets sick, also it applies with others.

When it goes for other people to get sick, which the mother has done, what she should not have done, we all blame the mother who disobeyed. So in our tribal tongue we call it 'Billmaree'. This is the word means . . . blamed the other person to get sick, or . . . my auntie or sister is to be blamed for that sickness or death, or you could say . . . I caused it or my silly auntie or sister caused it for some one else. That's when you forget to remember the laws and customs of the early days of my people. That means when you don't bother about any tribal ways. You think those days are gone now . . . no more of those stupid ideas can we live with or obey anymore . . . they past, and no more with us. But to all that carelessness of today's people, I say they still with us, and most of us still fear the creeks, swamps and rivers, and all it means to us.

When a brother's sister is pregnant with a baby, the brothers in family of hers, or out of her family line . . . would be her cousin brothers from other relations or countrymen . . . they too must 'shut eye', or not see or go near her. This is a respectable law.

Also, when the baby is ready to be born, mother of the woman and the sister-in-laws, of her brothers, are not allowed to be there on that special time . . . only the aunties, cousins, grandmothers. They are the only person to attend to the birth. Fathers, brothers and grandfather too, cannot see the baby or the mother until the child is a month old or more, until the mother and baby must have a bath.

103

After these times, then they allowed to go and visit the father and grandfathers. They are kissed by the whole families, nursed and loved by them. Gifts are given to mother and baby, also to the father of the child. Bush bark baskets are made and presented to the child. Mother must always carry her baby in it at all times, until the baby grows out of it. Later another bark basket, larger one, is made for the mother to use for her baby.

All the time brothers are not allowed to nurse their sister's baby . . . but his wife can nurse the child and show her husband the baby, but he must not dare to touch the baby. Later years, when the child has grown up and crawls around, then brothers can have a nurse of his niece or nephew, but still he must keep away at all times and don't speak to his sister. That's a tough law, but it must be obeyed by the tribes.

In early days, when the tribes saw two babies born to a mother, twins were not allowed. I just don't know why. To my idea they might wonder how twins could come. Probably they might have thought these were two fathers for each of them and that shame came upon the families, and that's how they meant to get rid of one and keep the other. I suppose the one they would keep would be one who looked like the father. If the other one seemed different they would kill it, and get rid of that one.

I know of a woman, when no white man came to this island. This woman had twins. They killed one and kept the other. The one whom they saved grew up to be a fine young man, and in his youth life, he walked along the cliff, missed his balance and fell down the cliff and died.

This situation would have been . . . they hated to see twins because they only believed one baby was the right thing for a mother to have. When foundation on Mornington was developing in a better civilization, when I was quite young in my teens, to our surprise there was a woman who born to her were twin girls, out bush on the next island, on Denham Island. This woman was accompanied by another lady and her husband. She sent her husband on message to the village cottages on the island, to give report to the

Superintendent on the other island where the mission was, saying two babies were born. During the time, one of the eldest of the tribe was so afraid of the birth of the twins, he desired to kill the other one, which meant to him and the other tribes, it was wrong to have two babies born. But this other woman, who came from Mainland for Education, knew that firstly these twins must be known to the Superintendent and his wife, before anything could be done to one of them.

Well, in those days, two babies was not what they expected, and it was a thing that really scared the life of the tribes. So the children were brought to the village cottages. The missionaries and the Staffs were so excited about the twins . . . the first twins on the mission. But somehow, the people themselves were not too happy about the twins. They were more terrified about the babies because they never liked the kind of twins, as I mentioned before. They only knew one was enough and was right to have one . . . not more than one. They thought it was wrong, because they knew it was against their law and customs. But now we people, we know the love for twins and everybody seems to feel as good as seeing twins in our midst today. So civilization brought much better sense of mind to us all. Now twins are much to look and value for.

As I was thinking on these things, to me they are here for anyone to understand the way of life we had to pass through, if we were interested in our culture, laws and customs.

Our legends have really taught us something. We must be careful about our babies, and also for ourselves. A mother could not go down to the sea for fishing or walking on the reefs, and sit to eat oysters, also along the banks of the creeks, rivers or also crossing a channel when having periods. There were these strict customs . . . do not touch any salt water. Fears were upon the Rainbow Serpent, it smells anything that is no good. So we were taught to keep well out of the sea coast.

You can say or watch out for the night when you'll get sick. How the tribes know someone is sick in the camp . . . there goes a big bright star runs across the sky, and that lets the people know somebody here will be sick. So as the star falls across the dark night, there is a howl of pain from a woman or man, may be a suffering tone of a painful cry from a baby.

So the old tribes get bushes in a bunch. The main tree leaf is a wattle leaf. Here they warm the wattle leaf over the fire and warm the person's tummy, and repeat the warming, also chanting at the same time. Everything is over. Then another big star with blue and red colour drifts across the sky. Fire sticks are grabbed from the camp fire and thrown the same direction as the star went. To our belief, the evil Spirit of the Serpent is gone out of the person, back to the Spirit that lives in the sea.

Our customs, cultures and laws and legends are true activities, one which I am proud of, and hope one day it may come back to real life of interesting people to learn to understand the problem for our future life and happiness . . . how to learn to obey what was told and shown to us, so we may really care for the things of the past. They are real, and true, and what my old folks had was one of the best that I will always keep to hold and guide my children and myself, because I know what was told to me, and all I saw and went myself through. All activities I lived with amongst my tribal parents and relations shall never be forgotten.

I can look back and think of so many happy life of my people. How wonderful their character was, full of happiness. Many laughs were often heard. They lived as one individual race. Although they had two tribes of people,

Winded and Lewit, but they were all as one big family, and the true relationship was real in their whole community as one full blooded people. As I grew up to understand my people, I soon found out that most of the people weren't real full blood relation, but somehow they were countrymen, because they were born, and were not too far away from each other. That relation among them was as you would think they were full blood relation. But it was the way. The customs were taught by their parents and grandparents, how to show and respect those who are around your part of the country, and who are your friends, that so often visit you when passing through to go somewhere.

I know there are many Aboriginals who lost their culture and customs, and are now a very unhappy people because they have no other tribes from the past and cannot pass it to the young people of today. When they hear of the past, and they themselves, wish they had lived in that time, and done and took part in the dreamtime activities.

Sometimes when I have some children sitting round my fire place or any where around my house, I can talk over to them of the life I went through, and what I saw their parents do in my life time, of how they kept the laws, customs and all their good culture, how they acted on them and really respected one another, especially their father and mother-in-laws, brothers and sisters-in-laws, brothers and sisters, grand parents from both side of the families . . . all other good stuff that was worth keeping, with a very strict elders of the tribes. Most of the things I recall, and these children were so interested on hearing. They sat there with heads hanging down with great pleasure, or I should say, with great interest.

These would be children who were about sixteen to thirteen, twelve years old. The rest were younger. To them it seemed as though their small minds were looking back to the past . . . how good it was, for how the way I explained to them and told it, as if I was telling a story to them. They kept on asking, 'Some more, tell us more.' So I did. This kept their minds opened to hear as I told the children the culture and the customs. I could read their thought, as if their thoughts were mine . . . they hoped they were the days they could wish for to live by it, with all their folks had. You tell them something funny of the times, the fun they had . . . kids would laugh, then sit very quietly to hear. To me, their minds or thought were far away, back to those good old days, where people lived in provision of happiness and love.

All our customs has taught me many wonderful and careful things which I know are really real. You even could not go near the sea when eating wild honey, flying foxes, pandanus palm nuts, cumbered flesh from the same nut fruit . . . eating goanna, swamp turtle, wild fruit such as wild figs, wild cucumbers, and many others that I cannot mention . . . also bullock fat, salt meat, tin meat of these present times, and butter, tin fish and other stuff. They are all disagreeable to the sea and fresh water lagoons. We still fear the Sea Serpent, because it enters in the tummy and gives pains for sickness and death. Also you get swollen all over your body . . . and that creates sores.

You may be well aware of all this. If you have to face to eat the food of the land, you must always wash yourself if you think of walking about, along the beaches or in the bush where there is swamps or lagoons. Always wash in the camp circle . . . but if you forget about the custom, you fall into trouble. Just towards the cool of the evening, something makes you feel a bit tired, and you sit around the camp fire quietly while others are having fun and laughter. All of a sudden you have a sharp pain in the tummy. You roll about on the ground with pain. As you suffer there, the others ask, 'Where are you sick?' or 'Where the pain is?' or 'What you ate today that cause you to be sick?'

Then the sick person tells what he ate . . . and then went fishing, or doing something that was not right. Then the song man, he comes along and chants over the body where the pain is, warms the body with heated leaf, then on to the tummy. The evil Spirit is driven away from the body. He is healed and is quite well again.

Many years back when I was young girl I can remember when some of the tribes went out hunting in the sea for turtle. My daddy, William Peters, was on that trip, when he speared a turtle on Birri waters where the Sea Hawk lives. There is a big reef out there, that's the home of the Sea Hawk. Well, my daddy speared the turtle. They were so far out at sea. It was a nice fine day. The water was so clear and still . . . you know how fine days look like when it's a fine day.

Well, one of the men jumped in the water to hold the turtle at the side of the dug out. He held the turtle, while the others in the dug out pulled the turtle in to the boat. Then Adam lifted himself out of the water, but he found out he was held down by the master of the place. So my daddy and others pulled from the canoe, and Sea Hawk held fast on his side with its claws. So the men finally pulled harder and soon got him in the canoe. On his left side of the tummy he had an open scratch from the claws of the Sea Hawk.

All of a sudden there was huge waves come from the sea. It was now rough, the huge waves almost swamped the canoe. Everytime the waves came in a huge roll, the old men paddled faster and faster to get away from the waves. The poor old man was bleeding fast, the canoe was almost swamped in blood. The men kept paddling, and when they turned to see the rolls coming behind the canoe, they saw the head of the Sea Serpent chasing them too, to take the turtle back, because the tribes believe he guides the turtle and dugong around that part of that area.

The old men got very frightened so they chanted to drive the evil Spirit away. One or two of them prayed to God in languages, asking the God to calm the sea, and drive back the Sea Serpent. So the sea came calm. But the rolls were so big, as the huge waves came, it sent the canoe drifting, gliding itself fast on the waves, much further still. The Sea Serpent followed them. They were nearing the beach when one, two last big waves landed the canoe on the beach. The men looked back and there he was, not very far away from them. The men hurried to shore, dragged the boat up to the shore and lifted out the man who was hurt. By now the canoe was just mass of blood.

They took Adam up the camp, chanted over him to give

109

him back the strength that he already lost of blood. They warmed him beside the fire. They chanted the wound on his side and closed it up, without being stitched. As the tribes chanted the cut on his side, it finally closed up. Then Adam felt for a motion. What happened, to the people's surprise . . . his motion was the bird's feathers of the Sea Hawk. Soon after he was well again and was able to come in to the mission, showed and told all what happened to him. He told the Superintendent, Rev. Wilson, how they managed to get away from the Sea Serpent, and how the Sea Hawk attacked him in the water.

Although it sounds foolish to anyone who knows nothing about the dangers of the sea and land customs of our native island, and all we believe, they are not fables to pass to the world. They are true life in our history . . . how things do happen, and how in certain places these creatures do live in these parts just there waiting for that time when strange things happen on those forbidden areas.

If you see a whirling water somewhere in the sea, well that's where the greatest history is seen and tells of where Sea Serpent lives, although at low tide, where he lives you cannot see him. He is in the hole on the sand banks or under great holes under the reefs. He sleeps all day. Then when the tide rises, and now it's high tide, he comes out of his hiding place, and floats on the surface, and travels round to seize his prey.

There are many bad places on our country where you can be very ill or die if you have no one to help you. Though we can be happy and free with all we have, except the laws of our customs must be noticed and obeyed. If we care to look at these things, we will be safe from all that, but when we don't care about these customs and laws, we are punished by illness and death.

Once when having holiday, it was on a time when school children had their school term holiday, a boy about three year old, he ate butter with his damper. Also, this same little chap still suckled from his mother's breast. In those times children still sucked mother's breast when they were so big running about and playing along the beaches. They still had the breast feed as well as other food. Well, after eating and sucking breast milk, he ran off without his parents noticing him, and forgetting to wash the child's body, his hands and mouth, so the deep sea fish or the Sea Hawk wouldn't smell him, also the Rainbow Serpent. This child's parents were so young . . . about twenty-four years ago, not too far off when most of our laws, customs, legends and culture were almost gone from us, and most old folks had died, and more young people had come, and everyone seemed to forget all our tribal ways and life. So as this little fellow played in the sea and had a nice swim in the water, enjoying himself in the water, he was alright. But the moment he came out of the water, he felt sudden pain in his tummy and his eyes were red with blood flowing out of them. Well, the Dunga fish went into his belly and poked him in the eye. That fish has a strong legend too. The two young parents were so worried and upset, they ran with him to the mission hospital for to treat him. On the way up they met one of the tribes . . . asked what happened with the child. The only thing they said, 'He went down the sea with butter smell.'

So the old bloke told them, 'There is a story of the Dunga fish there, that poke anyone in the eye and that's how he goes into our belly.' So the old tribe man put his underarm smell on the child's face and belly and blew a puff of wind on the child's body. That made the child seem to be alright again, but still the parents took him to hospital for further treatment from the Nursing Sisters. The Sister asked what happened. They told her the child was in the salt water swimming and that was how he got sick. So Sister gave him something to take for the pains. During the time he was getting further treatment there, the tribesmen miracle already had killed the sea fish Dunga inside the boy. His motion was so dreadful, full of foul smell. That Dunga fish died in the boy's belly and caused him to pass out a stinking motion. Then the boy came home and played beside his mother.

But there you can see, if the old man did not touch him by that time before he went up to Sister, he would have died on the way up to the hospital. The Nursing Sister also treated him, but I can say if the old man did not touch him, Sister would have not known how to treat him. She would have given him the wrong treatment for customs and culture because she did not know what had happened to the boy.

For what reason how it happened . . . well, it was . . . no one is allowed to go down to the salt water with butter smell, tin meat or bullock meat smell or any such greasy food. For sure, these two couples were afraid to tell the Nursing Sister the boy got Mulgree.

In later years some Nursing Sister did get an idea of some of the facts of our laws, of how things happen to certain people when they are suffering. You must always tell the truth so it can be clear for others to understand, so the right treatment can be done and that others may not do the wrong things to have their children suffering for what was told to them, and the customs they believe on.

On the same area in the sea, my youngest father Gully and his wife Cora took me out one night in a dugout for hunting fish with maga light. Old Gully stood up on the forehead of the dugout. I held up the maga torch. The sea was so bright you could see everything that moved in the water. Old Mum Cora was at the steering part, back of the dugout. So slowly the old woman paddled at the back. I laid the maga at the side of the canoe and held it firm and steady, so that Dad could see and spear the fish. We caught, or Dad speared plenty of fish that night. All of a sudden we heard the Fish Hawk . . . came from somewhere out of the sky or perhaps out of the sea, somewhere near by us. I stood there very quiet, holding the long burning, blazing maga. When the Sea Hawk appeared, Dad said, 'Something wrong here. We better go back. How you feel Cora? You girl, how you?'

Well, we said, 'We are alright.' But that night I had periods. I knew all about it. I should not be anywhere on the salt water. But nothing happened because I wasn't in the water, but inside of dugout. Anyway, still the Sea Hawk did come around. So Dad and Mum and myself, we all went home again, and carried up all the fish that Dad had speared. We made a huge fire outside of the house and began to cook some fish to eat.

No matter how, a young girl or grown up women should not be in the salt water or crossing creeks and rivers. It's no good, because only will appear the harmful creature that lives in the sea.

There is another creature that also attacks anyone, and that is the Sea Frill Lizard. This Frill Lizard is so large, if anyone goes in the water with a smell of a child, infant milk smell, or their breast if flowing, that also could affect the baby to get sick or die, also the mother to get sick and take sudden illness and die. But these two people can be alive, if there is a song man right on the spot to chant or put under arm smell on them.

You might wonder how all this happens. You could also say and think, 'Where lies the power of that all?'. No one knows, but that great belief belongs to an Aboriginal person. It was meant for him to cure anyone in those long centuries where they themselves could handle to cure each other, before the white man ever reached them. That same thing is still being carried on to help one another, today. I've seen all these things happen . . . how a person can be very ill suffering from the things that were caused by these creatures of the sea, rivers and creeks, also running fresh water streams that run from the land, cutting their way to the sea.

Perhaps now, at the present time, Nurses that come to live on the island may have some experience how to find out how certain people became ill who have gone to them for treatment, and have treated anyone from the things that only we understand . . . that's if any of the Nursing Staff did happen to hear something of Mulgree, and was told to them of our customs. I think they have now some stuff that can kill the poison inside of a human body. These creatures of the sea make you very sick. You roll about on beds or on the ground, it causes you much pain. Also you vomit slimy green stuff, that is the deadly stuff that the Sea Serpent has entered your belly and made you sick.

For that case, you have been warned by the tribes . . . don't eat land and sea food and go to the places where it is forbidden. Also a mother when suckling her baby, she must not go eating oysters or fishing when she has a young child because the smell of an infant is not good. Even if a father, sister or brothers or any other relation, touch and nurse the child that still sucks from mother's breast, still the smell of the child and milk is on that person too, and they all must be careful of themselves. They must wash their hands or their body before thinking of making another movement for either of these bad spots. Also young girls, women must take care of themselves when on periods from eating anything like tin meat, salt meat, butter, milk, either sunshine or condensed, tin fish, anything that has grease, also turtle, dugong, flying foxes, wild honey, pandanus palm nuts, wild cucumbers, wild bananas, goanna or swamp turtle. These are all no good for the sea and fresh water. These things happen . . . after eating or handling any of these food, you must always wash yourself. That's the law and customs of our tribes.

They tested and noticed all these things. That's why the Aboriginals must take heed. They are all for safetyness of yourself. If only you can obey these laws of our forefathers, you won't have these things happen. These are all dreadful laws and customs. It doesn't concern only for Aboriginals, it's also for white people too . . . that's if you come to live, and visit our country, and you try it out for yourself. If you don't want to take heed, you'll find out why you feel sick and why you are vomiting or also, you can risk your life by death. That's if you think it is all big fun to you. You may give it a go, and you soon will find out what will become of you. It also applies with wild bush fruits and berries when eating them.

You have all read the book of my husband's *Moon and Rainbow* . . . one of our greatest true legend, I mean the title. Moon also is one of them . . . you eat and touch any of these food and other things I mentioned, the Moon smells that also, and he enters your belly. Your belly rises like a big balloon until it is so tight that you suffer and die. He also lives in the sea. Lucky if near a song man you can live

Some years back, an old man by the name of Robert Burns went out fishing, out from the very cliff that the story once told. He caught something like fish pulling on the line. He hauled it by the side of the dugout. It was a strange fish. He looked closely. It was a bright, glittering diamond like colour, so soft and jelly like, but to the old man's surprise, he saw it was the half quarter Moon. As he held the Moon in his hand to take the hook out of its body, there was a sudden big swell of waves tossing the dugout up and down. Finally the old fellow got his knife and cut the hook and let the Moon slide back down to the sea again. The little dugout was tossing up and down with the old man. He quickly pulled in the anchor and paddled towards the shore. He was so scared, and went home, because he realised what would have become of him if he still stayed to do his fishing. The old fellow, he knew all the story about Moon. That can give you an idea that our legends are not lies but true . . . so you know how the story goes. Moon's spirit is still with us, he lives on earth in the rock also in the sea, and he is in the sky. Are you quite sure of that?

That Moon was once a lonely man living all by himself, until he met trouble with some strange people of the same strange country, called Spring Point. He ran off with the meat, and was tracked by some of his countrymen and they followed him and killed him, then chopped him in small pieces with stone axes and tossed his body everywhere. Some half flesh fell in the water, other half on the rocks, and some fell in spring water holes and other three pieces into the sky. That's why we have three shapes of him in the sky . . . half quarter, half full Moon and full Moon. Sometimes the full Moon turns to the eclipse. Well, that was his sad ending, but his Spirit is still with us today, and that's how he pays the people back who destroyed him. He now punishes us with illness and death, and also causes pain and suffering.

Then again we have another sea creature, and that is a Water Rat. He also is a deadly one too, because if you go to the sea with greasy body in the sea and creeks, and in lagoons where he lives, he comes around at nights to seize his prey, to enter into your belly. Before that happens you are already suffering. For instance one of these things I did not know happened on that part of the island, on White

Cliff, Uncle Sandy's home . . . now it's cousin Maurice's part of the place, seeing the old fellow has passed into another life. Well, this is where I happened to see this thing happen.

One day Dick, myself and others, we all went on a wild honey chase, also for goanna and swamp turtles and wild roots and fruits. As we went along the bush, we came to a very scrubby place where there were swamps and thick trees and long grasses. We came across an old man and his wife cutting a huge tree for a dugout. It surprised me very much to see a huge ti-tree had been cut down by the old man, Popgun, Dick's uncle, and his wife. The tree had been chopped down several months ago, and we had gone back to the mission for some time. By that time we were out as a working team for fencing. A new cattle yard was put up for the bullocks to be kept in.

So, to our surprise we found these two couples all by themselves, living out in the bush to continue to finish their dugout. They were not young people, but in their old age, but they managed to chop that great tree down with two small tomahawk. In that time they had nothing like axes, but with that small tomahawk they managed to get themselves a canoe. It was sad to see them at work, and living alone amongst the thickness of the trees and grass. So we said Hello and Goodbye and continued our search.

On the way Dick found a small tree about five foot tall, with wild honey. So he cut the tree down, but the most of the honey was going downward into the ground. We collected enough of the honey and filled our billy can, and went off again. Soon we met up with the other people on a small island in the bush, beside the plain. We found them gathering hundreds and hundreds of conborras or wild cucumbers. I got excited and started pulling it down from some very tall grass or ferns and they were nice and sweet. So we took some to eat on the way home. We wandered everywhere and saw different wild plants and fruit trees. Then we spotted two other persons. One was my tribal father-in-law, and his wife . . . Sam and Lily Bush. So we joined them and had a good time, chattering and laughing as we walked along, still picking and eating conborras.

Finally I came upon a strange tree. The tree was hollow inside, but on its branches hung green leaves. I stood beside the tree and saw lots of white motions on the ground. I looked up to see if there were birds on the tree top. I called out to Dick, 'Hi. Come over here and see what could be the mess at the foot of the tree.' As Dick came towards me where I stood by the tree, suddenly my father-in-law came running without a noise. His wife Lily, too, she came to the spot to see what the mess was.

Then the old man called out, 'Go away from there, run away quick.' So three of us, Dick, Lily and myself ran off, and he walked up to us and said, 'Inside the tree lives a huge bird, like a man's body and the motions are his.'

So we stood far off and watched him. Soon we heard the noise of as an eagle's wings flapping inside the hollow tree. He heard us talking . . . so woke him up from sleeping.

Then the old man said to Dick, 'That man is our skin, Booralungie. He is our brother, he was a real man once, but he turned into a bird. I'll go over and talk to him before he gets angry and comes out to chase us.' So Sam and Dick talked over things with each other. Then Sam said, 'Dick, you go first with your wife and Auntie Lily. I'll go over and talk with him, and let him know we are all brothers, straight head brothers, we one skin Booralungi.'

So we stood there with fear, and watched what next would happen. The old man hit the tree with his woomera or club. The bird struggled to get out of the great hollow tree, but Sam still stood there. 'Hey, Brother, I am your brother. Don't do anything. We just come for a walk, pass your way,' . . . Still flapping his wings in anger. Then Sam called out much louder, 'Hey Brother, me Booralungie just like you. Sleep now Brother. We go home.'

All of a sudden there was quietness. Sam hit the tree with his woomera, and said Good bye to his brother who lives in the hollow tree. Then four of us quickly walked down the beach and the old fellow explained to us about the creature, as we walked along the beach.

These two couples had a small girl, about three year old,

Mavis Bush. She was eating conborras . . . the ones were sweet and ripe, she ate them. But among them, one she bit was not ripe, but raw and bitter to her taste. This one she threw into the salt water. Her mother saw that and quickly ran in the water, and grabbed the fruit and threw it away, on the beach. The father said, 'Oh it's too late Lily, it already was in the water.' The old man did not worry. If anything should happen he already could chant the Water Rat away from entering into the child's belly.

We reached home, and along the beach stood other people fishing with lines and rods. On the beach lay hundreds of fish that had been caught by them. So it was great fun fishing that day. Most of the fish was just left on the beach to be wasted. I thought it must have been just a sports of hooking the fish for fun, because it was too much to take home and cook them all. The rest of the fish . . . just left where they were lying.

Night came on. After supper the men all went up the ridge to make a corroboree, and left the women alone in the camp. Suddenly there was a great big blue star, ran across the sky towards West. Then a great, big light . . . out of the water, sailed towards the launch . . . had been anchored there. We women stood quiet with fear. On the beach there was another flash of light shone on our camps. We called out for help from the men. There were millions and millions of lights in the water. They told us it was the eyes of the many Water Rats that came for to seek after the one who threw the fruit in the water during the day. The brighter light was of the Mother Rat who controls the sea there.

The men came running down and asked each other for the song to drive the Water Rats away. They stood there trying to think of the words, until one man started chanting. Then all the men joined in chorus, chanting as hard as they could. Finally the eyes of the Rats disappeared. All we now saw was the eyes of the Mother Rat. She swam round and round the launch, or the boat, then disappeared.

Oh, I was very frightened that night. I had a restless time during the night, that I could not sleep because my camp was not too far off the sea mark. Dick lay suffering in the circle wind break, we made the day for the night. He had toothache, and could not sleep. To cease the pain he lay beside the fire and warmed himself. He put a bit of chewed tobacco . . . he bit and chewed, put the tobacco into the hollow teeth, but that could not do him any good. At the same time, I worried him to shift our camp further up the beach near the ridge.

But all the answer he gave to me . . . 'Stay here. I'm too bad to try and shift away now. Don't worry, the Rats are all gone. They won't come back again.' So we stayed there. I put Dick at the mouth of the wind break to sleep beside the fire, while I had a good sleep.

That was the first time I ever saw the like of all that lights in the water. From then on I believed there were creatures like Water Rats who controlled the sea. These various creatures are in different areas of the sea, and where they live we just know where we must be careful of whatever we are eating or doing . . . the things that might happen if we are careless.

In this area, at White Cliff, Dick and myself were walking along the creek bed. The water flowed slowly into the sea. The place looked scrubby with tall brown grasses, and the trees were green. In this certain place where there was quietness and a lovely North East wind was blowing . . . seems to make anyone feel of the past, that tells you certain nice things have happened, or some sad thoughts bring back few sad memories. I felt myself looking with thoughts of few nice thoughts of the past . . . when I was in dormitory or some things happened few years ago. I enjoyed the walk very much in the still quietness of the day, as the wind was blowing freely, silently creeping over the trees, swaying the leaves up and down as if they were, too, enjoying the nice summer breeze.

During all the quietness, all of a sudden, there was a great big white furry creature as tall as a huge tom cat sprang from the bank, walked along the creek, sprang and jumped into the creek water. I stood on the bank to see what happened next, but did not see the creature again. Firstly I thought it was a wallaby, then a white cat, but it was the Mother Rat.

That's where she lives. I was amazed to see a Water Rat so huge as that. I could not believe my eyes looking at that strange creature. Its furs were of a sheep's fur and so white. I never thought a Water Rat could be as big as that, so I was happy to see one for a proof, and that's why I am now able to write about most of the dreadful things of my country . . . because I have heard stories that were told to me and I was able to see for myself.

There is another strange thing also where we have heard from the past. There lives a man, he comes in form of wallaby and then turns into a man. He lives in the mangroves, where there are mud shells. When gathering mud shells, you are not allowed to count them as you find them in the mud. The tribes say you must gather them without counting. If you do count aloud, you must hurry and get out of the mangroves, before the man gets you. He comes with a huge noise of a wind and then grabs anyone who is there.

The tribes say there was once few people, man and women, went for mud shells and somebody started counting shells as they dug them out of the mud. Suddenly there was a loud yell for help. One man of the tribe was caught by this fellow that lives in the mangroves, but he could not release himself. He tried to fight his way out, but he was used back way by the Mudshell man. The tribes tried all sorts of way to get one of their countrymen away from the Mudshell man, but he stuck firmly. So the tribes got fire sticks to burn his penis to loosen him. They cut him with sharp shell, with stone axes, set fire with maga on him. But that was no use at all. They could not kill the Mangrove man. He ran off and loosened himself from the old man. This man got very sick after that, and shortly after some time, he died. So that's how the legend has been passed down from the witness eyes of the tribes . . . not to count any mudshells when searching in the mangroves for these mudshells.

Many strange things are here that could happen. If you will hear these stories and do what the tribes had seen . . . strange things happening, and that's how they prevent anyone being caught by surprise by all these action legends that can scare the wits out of anyone.

It's so frightening, although the mudshells are good to eat. Everybody likes hunting for mudshells, because it's something interests you. We often get to the point . . . who will be the first one to find, and have the most? These shells are buried in the mud. How to find them . . . there are marks of yellow red very slightly on the ground. You follow that mark of the colour, where it sprays its water on the surface where it's lying. Then look closely. You can see a small split of earth and that's where the mud shells are. Sometimes it takes twenty minutes or less a time before you can find them. There is always notice given to everyone before they enter in the mangroves. Someone will say, 'Now remember, don't count any shells. Just find them, pick them up quietly, or crack the shell and put the flesh of the food inside a billycan or a piece of bark from the fallen trees, or put them in your coolamun.'

We spend hours in the mangroves just rooting the shells up from the mud or under the roots of the trees, and gather as much as we can collect to take home for supper. We boil the food, sometimes mix curry into it and eat with damper. Most time it's boiled and just eaten, the soup being drunk. Although gathering the shells really frightens you, you've got to keep your ears open to hear if there is anyone, like children especially, will count. Sometimes the children forget. They get excited and say, 'Mum I got one.' The moment the child counts aloud, the rest of the people say, 'Don't count, or the Gooroodmanda will come.' So there is a silent search carries on until everyone has enough and goes home.

I remember once at Birri, a number of us went on mud-shell hunting.

We spent most of our times in the bush, for shortage of water in the mission and round about the village where we lived. So we desired to go bush and have the children schooling there also. There were plenty of water holes had been dug along the shores just below ten foot away from the camps. We made windbreaks to shelter ourselves with and a huge fire to keep ourselves warm for the rest of the night.

One day we all went out. Some went to the river for fishing and crabbing, others went bush to search for wild honey, goannas, swamp turtles and wild fruits. Again, others went for oysters and fishing on the reefs, also collecting shells and corals. Men went for turtle and dugong and spearing fish, while we others went for mudshell hunting. There were large number of us, men, women and children. The bigger boys had their spears and woomeras too. We all started to search in the mangroves. There were too many mudshells lying so closely together. We just had to sit and stretch out our hands to dig them up with sharp sticks. As we were busy digging and cracking the shells off, my father-in-law Sam, and his wife Lily Bush, came round the other way following up the river to find crabs and spearing fish and stingray.

The old man knew we were in the scrub, so he made up his mind to frighten us and pretend he was Gooroodmanda coming to take one of us. So as we sat there talking and cracking, and gathering the shells into one heap, one of the women heard a strange sound . . . sounds like the Mangrove man made. This woman looked around. She did not tell anyone, but she quietly and quickly picked up her bundle and raced out without giving warning to us all . . . all the warnings were with the movement of the eyes. There was a big rush came from everybody, no shouting, no calling out . . . but just ran out of the bush, out in the salt pan. We stood there without a word, wondering what next would happen. Then the two old people appeared, and came out laughing . . . put on the joke. So we all had to laugh for the way they frightened us. One thing I killed myself laughing, was those bigger boys. Although the mangroves was close and thick, but just imagine not one of the boys' spears or woomeras were caught between the trees and the branches. Their hunting weapons went right through, without the boys getting scratches and cuts in their bodies or even getting their eyes poked. They made themselves very thin to slip through without breaking their spears and woomeras.

Then we made for home, chattering and laughing as we went home. The rest of the mudshells were left in the mangroves. Even to this day, our children also have the belief of the Gooroodmanda is a real man who controls the mudshells in the mangroves. They say he lives there always. Sometimes he wanders away to other places and frightens people in their camps.

Recently, several years ago, it happened at Dugong River . . . three women went in the mangroves for mudshells, took with them their sons, to teach the lads how to find and gather shells. As they were busy collecting mudshells, the boys got excited when first finding the shells. They began to count aloud. The women hushed the boys. They began to find more, then the boys forgot. They called out, 'I've got one, two, three here, Mummy.'

So the women said, 'Come on, let's get out of here.' As they were making up their mind, all of a sudden there was a great wind. Trees were bending and swaying to and fro, the place looked gloomy now. Then a bird flew past one of them. 'He is not too far away to grab us.' So they quickly grabbed what they had already collected and ran out. During the escape, it appeared white as it gave another big circle to come towards the women and children. By that time, these people were out of the mangroves, down the beach, still running, and almost out of breath. They came home and told the story to the other campers, what had happened. The only answer to the happening, by the elders of the tribes, was never take any children in the mangroves again.

So there it is. Once it happened so many years ago. The legends are true, and the action is there all the time, as a life history, to teach, to take heed, obey, and always remember . . . do the right thing and everything will be alright. Many people may say or think it's foolish about these things, but they are very, very important and true life to us. Although it's a nice place, but there are in different areas, bad places where these creatures of the sea and land live, and where different creatures can take their form of another Spirit. All our legends are not false. They are true. They have been noticed by the tribes of their early life . . . how certain thing did happen to someone on a different times, on a certain place, and those things are meant to safe guard any other person, who carelessly does the wrong thing. But there was always a song man or a medicine man to save and to heal from all sickness and death.

Since the last world war two, I began to see many new life amongst the tribes, learnt and noticed so many useful, wonderful, brilliant surroundings happening. It was all of the good, happy, spiritual life of happiness and laughing. Everybody were real people. Strangers were invited amongst them in a very friendly way. Some one would come from any part of Mainland, and he was warmly welcomed by the people. I've noticed that the best of some food was first given to a stranger, then the tribes' families came later on, for a small share, but the families never made a fuss about it because that's the first thing I was taught by my father and mother . . . always share with others. It was always being repeated by the old folks.

These words were pressed to us in languages not in english, but I understood all my parents, what they said to me. I always spoke back in english, and they would understand. So that's how we grew up . . . parents talk in language and the children in english. But it never went wrong, we all understood each other. Year by year as times went by, I could speak a little bit of language but not all. But I am still learning as I go visiting the few of the last tribes.

One thing that really surprised me . . . there were very few men of the tribe. There were about six of them had a very, very strange language called Damen. Three of them spoke it very well, and have always talked it at all times speeches. Probably these men went through second degree, and had to stay on these languages until certain time when they had to pass other laws of the land and were given an order to leave off the speech, and continue with their own Lardil language. I have questioned my father, uncles and grandfathers . . . where or how they picked up this way of talking, but they could not really say where or how they spoke. Others say the people from the top end of the island, round about Elizabeth Creek . . . that's where they heard some old people start talking in this sort of way. It's all mouth hissing, hit with tongue and finger talk, but using the words without the real action by sign. It's good to hear them talk, when talking to some one or telling stories of the past. It's so strange, but marvellous to me.

The first coming of the Bullimbanda people . . . they came from the West country along the coast until they reached Mornington. They were Marnbill and Gin Gin and Dewaliwall . . . to work on the island creating trees and rocks, fish traps and searching and digging wells from little soaks and fresh water streams. They were believed to have given names of different foods, sea and land, and named them all until they reached the top of the island called Elizabeth Creek. The last camp was there. They made one last water hole and that's where Dewaliwall was killed by Marnbill because be broke the law going to his niece Gin Gin, and that was his punishment.

I suppose there must have been some foregone people living there, about the death of Dewaliwall and absence of Marnbill and Gin Gin, because if there were one kind of other people living at that time, this is how the legend of Marnbill, Dewaliwall and Gin Gin had to be passed and continued still passing. So there could be somebody, some-where was at that time to see all the life of the coming of the first people to Goonana. So these people could have lived strangely with each other for so long, and probably died soon later.

But if Marnbill and Gin Gin did not die, then could it be their ascendants who lived with them at the years later. Then Marnbill and Gin Gin could have had troubles with these people . . . would have done something with these people and could have disobeyed some of the laws and probably then turned into a stone. From then, these people they left behind were the ones who passed the legends down to all tribes of our people, because if Marnbill and Gin Gin disappeared at the same day after Dewaliwall got speared, no one could ever know the legend of these three people. So that's why I still say some people were there, but were afraid to show out. Or could they be the families of Marnbill and Gin Gin? They would have seen something happen at that time, and said the stone statue were Marnbill and Gin Gin. There too, up at the top end of the island, stands the rock of these two people and a small baby.

Also, a place called Bulletgear . . . the tribes have found out that there lived people who are known as unseen people. To see them moving around you have to be very quiet and hide yourself behind trees and scrubs, to really see what they look like. As the old people say, they look like real human, but they hide themselves away and live altogether in the bush, where the trees are so thick and where rock shelters are. They call them Bulletgearmanda. Often the tribes in early days saw some of these hidden people as they wandered along the shores to do their hunting. The moment these unseen people see Goonanamanda people, they disappear that very moment . . . but they are real dinky di people, no doubt.

In early stage Goonana people heard the clapping of the boomerangs, shouting, and men singing, women calling out to their children to sit down and watch the dance. Everyone is having a merry time, while our own tribes sit round their camp fires, with great fear, wondering who can be these people, and where they come from and how they live. They hear every sound plainly, so close about thirty foot away, or half a mile. Fires everywhere at the dancing ground, but not sign of a real person. Noises are every where with singing, talking and laughing.

If any person strays away from the crowd of real person, they believe these unseen people can make you to go the wrong direction. You wander away without taking any notice you are going the wrong way, and are already lost in the bush. Most of our people have lived in these parts of places. They've seen people like them, they heard noises they made, and they are quite certain they are real people like us. But you cannot see them face to face. They are very fearing tribes.

So you remember the time during the war, last, fighting

bomber passed the top end of the island and went down to the sea. They came ashore on rubber dinghies. They came up to the shore and walked along the beach, wandering around, seeking out for help. To their surprise they were chased by savages of Mornington Island on the oysters' reef and plunged into the sea on their rubber dinghies, and paddled away with fear. These white men, they thought it was the nice kind of people of that island who went to kill them, the real Lardil people. But no, it was these people who live and claim that part of the place. They are unseen people, or we call them Bulletgearmanda. So that was them.

One or two of them could have told the legends of the coming of the first man and woman to Mornington. Perhaps they, too, got around few of the early tribes of our people and lived with them, and already told them the legends and spoke the Damen tongue. Then out of these two kinds of people, from Marnbill and Gin Gin, and the Bulletgearmanda, could we come from? Because no one on this island ever was told, or heard, of our third grandparents. Even the old folks themselves don't know any more from their two grand parents.

This is how to look at our tribes . . . my father's father and mother are Peter and Ma. This two folks father and mother . . . Father knows his grandparents, they both have bush names. Then from there, everything is not known or hasn't been seen. No one can recall any such history of the third and fourth generation. So you can see, that's the limit to our race of people . . . it goes that far.

So the two others, Marnbill and Gin Gin, and Bulletgearmanda must have raised families to make Mornington Island or Goonanamanda people carry on. Then first people, the three workers, died. The second race could be Bulletgearmanda, married into one or two of their own race. Then as people of that time got scared, they got wild and rushed away into the bush. Probably the unseen man and woman must have wandered too far off the secret country and got lost, and found a better way to live on the land, then brought up children and it grew into a big family called Lardil.

So that's what I think this Damen could be . . . the Bulletgearmanda speech, because in the first place, the old people say, they exactly do every thing like we people. They hunt sea food, also land food, they have their dances and fun, also initiation. Only, you never can see them, but they can see us. Sometimes you think you looking at someone you really know. You call out to that person . . . but you look again, it's gone from your sight. All you do . . . go home, back with fear as fast as you can. That's how we all believe, and keep well away from those places. When the tribes saw all this and knew all about these people, they never camped or hunted around these areas. They kept well away until to this day.

There also too . . . another place called Birri. From Oyster Place to Baldie Head Point to Lammatha there is a legend of Cave people. These Cave people are like us too. They hunt sea and land food, and they are very timid people.

At times when we go for sugar bag hunting, we must move very quietly without noise. When wild honey bees are found flying in and out of the door of the tree, where the bees are busy carrying flower powder to make more honey . . . well, that's how we know that the tree has something for us to chop down, and collect the honey. But it's not for that reason we have to be very quiet in our hunting. Also, it is not a good place, to be there, because about that time the Cave people are hunting too, for whatever they are looking for. You find a sugar bag tree, you go to cut the tree down, where you think the honey is stacked away. Well, to your surprise the tree is without honey, because some body from the group was calling out, singing, whistling, banging trees with sticks or tomahawk. Well any sort of noise, you'll have bad luck. Cave people give you many bad lucks.

Now this part of the place is my father's home land, where the Cave people live. They too live there, but up the bush where the caves are, and where the bush trees stand so tall and spread their branches far and wide, touching from end to end . . . place looks fresh and good scents of perfumes and scented soaps can be smelled, where the creek is. It has lovely, blue running water coming from the top of the bush. To my surprise, I said to my father, 'Where the water coming down from?'

Father said 'You are standing on the ground where the entrance of the cave, and this is the first sight you see. Further up the stream into the bush are so much water in the caves, water never runs dry, and this is their country.'

Well, as I write the story of the Cave people . . . because I have seen things up at that place. Once my father, foster mother Kate and myself, we went bush for walk about for roots, goannas, sugar bags and swamp turtles. We walked so far, then I looked around. The place was so very beautiful. The place looked green. Although it was in the midst of Summer where everything should look dead with brownnesss, but way up the bush, where there is so much stony and rough places and where water seems to be very scarce, seemed to look so lovely and green. The air was so fresh all around. The North East wind was blowing so lightly. There were no songs of the birds or twitting of honey suckers and other such birds. Everything seemed to be very calm and still. We walked along very quietly, in case they, the Cave people, were around, so we could sight them first.

Then we came across another pool. All around were rocks, two sides were flat rocks. The pool looked so blue, but the water smelt scented soap. I said, 'Hi, Daddy. This place smells nice. Perhaps the women were here swimming and washing and ran off.'

Well, Dad said, 'This is where they wash their clothes and bath themselves and babies. Now they gone. They saw us coming so they went away and hid themselves.'

I got close to the edge of the pool, hoping to find pieces of soap. The place on the rock was very clean, but the water mark was left on the flat rocks, as they were using it for their washing. But the striking thing of all, was that of a perfume smell, as if they had Chemist shop there. I looked around. The trees were so tall. It looked dark and gloomy, as if the evening had come so soon. But the sun was up above our heads, it was middle midday. It only looked and felt like that because we were not too far away from the main places of the Cave people's home, where they lived.

Dad tried to find sugar bag. Mother dug roots of different kinds, while I looked around everywhere with my eyes to see if I could see any movements of the Cave people. I felt so frightened because I could not see the sun shining down on us. Although there were no clouds around in the sky, but at that spot everything had changed into a gloomy moment.

Then we returned for home, downwards to the sea, where we had our camps under the oak trees . . . looking out into the sea where it was so calm and still, only turtles spouting their head above the surface, and fish swimming past, also few sharks too.

That night all were in bed. Every camps had fire going all through the night to help us warm. Few yards away on the beach there were Stockmen mustering and camping on Birri, so Dad and Mum and many other old people were there. Margaret and Phyllis, who were adopted by Dad, they were there too, beside May and myself. We were sisters. Then we had another mate, Thelma . . . and Muriel. They were sisters. We had so many excitements together. We had a big camp there.

That night while we were asleep, many people were snoring at the time. I was going off to sleep . . . not really, felt a bit restless, so I lay there with my eyes open. The moon was shining brightly. You could see so far as your eyes can see in the moonlight. So I lay very still, eyes still open, looking up to the stars. I closed my eyes, then opened them again. What you think I saw in the night? A nice young man gazing at me, and stroked his hands on my right cheek. I looked up at him. He was so strange, but handsome . . . the nicest looking fellow. I got up and looked around. There was no one moving. I knew everyone was asleep. So I lay down to sleep again. I really closed my eyes and went off to sleep this time. But again the same person bent over me, and looked at me, and rubbed my cheeks again. This time he said, 'You are my girl friend.' He rubbed my cheeks and disappeared. Well, I lay there. I could not move . . . really stunned to see invisible one. But instantly I went off to sleep, as if he put a magic spell on me not be be afraid of him.

Next morning I woke up and told my father what I saw and heard. So Dad said, 'There are people here all the time. That's why we must be careful not to make too much noise or talk loud when we up the bush. These people get mixed up with people during hunting or visit anyone at day or night, and that's how you are lucky to see them. Then they vanish in your presence.'

On another day, we girls of Dad's went down water lily swamp. The water was almost drying up. Dad took us to show we girls how to find tracks of swamp turtle, and how they bury themselves in the ground and hide away until another year comes round, when the rain comes again. Tracks were everywhere, but we could not contact the right marks to follow to where they buried themselves.

But Dad found about six that day and called out to we girls. He shows us how you must dig into the ground, and there it is lying in a nice round hole just enough for it to rest. On the surface ground, there isn't a mark to tell you where they got it, because the top ground is so smooth that you cannot understand how they work to bury themselves.

That same day, as we were moving around gathering water lilies on the muddy ground, besides we girls, Father, Mother and other old folks, we suddenly spotted a small boy, about five year old. Well, we looked and gave a call to this little boy, taking him for Hector Thomas. He was exactly and real of that boy Hector. So we all looked and said, 'Hector. Come here. How did you come? Who you came with?' Then we took our eyes off him. He was gone. That Cave boy, Hector, was gathering lilies too and tracking swamp turtle. That really frightened us, so we said no more and cleared out of the swamp and went home.

That night Dad told us all the stories of a Cave man, women and children, how he knew them. Many times he saw them and often they saw each other from behind trees while hunting.

There is another experience reveals my watchful eye and listening ear, that I really did not believe could happen. One day we went bush. We camped at Weereejerra, that's Oyster Place, my homeland. I was there with some of the old folks, my fathers, uncles and auntie, cousins and other relatives. I was the only young woman, unmarried, at that time. We first made wind breaks, gathered fire wood, and then walked down the beach to crack and eat oysters. Our only water was between two rocks, with a spring water coming out of the rock. The rock was so narrow, also the basin wasn't very big, just enough for a small mug or bailer shell to fill your billy can with water.

It was dark now. Each people sat round their camp fires, talking of the past . . . others singing corroboree songs. Then they came together in one camp, at the song man camp. Uncle Sandy, he was the main man to lead the songs. The singing went on until they had enough. Then all returned to their own camps.

Next day others went spearing fish, gathering oysters. Again, others went for bush roots . . . Katey, Big Mary, my father's aunt, and Auntie Jessie who was my father's sister. I went with them. We went up the bush for wild honey and roots . . . well, you can say anything that was good to eat we went on search. Up the hill we went, climbing upward searching for wild honey, until finally we were on top of the inland hill. To my surprise, I found out, taking each step at a time, it did not make any difference whether we were walking on low land, but climbing as walk until we were at the top. Auntie Jessie told me and the other two, 'This is the hill where Cave people lives . . . but on the other side of this hill looking towards North East is the caves where they live, but still they roams all over these parts.'

Well, on that hill, looking far down below on trees and creeks, looked beautiful. But the best scene was looking across the sea, to Rocky Island. It was a nice warm day . . . sea was so calm, the distance was so clear, you could see far away to that lonely island. As I write now my mind goes to the time when Water Rat could see the trees on this island, from Rocky Island. So now those legends are really true. If only you could see these places and see the distances from

133

where it happened to where it ended.

Leaving the hill we came down for home. The trees were so thick although they were small trees. So we followed an old native road. Although it was now all bush, and grasses grew large on the main road way, that we could not find the right place, still the same we knew where we were going. We all walked behind the other, talking as we went. All of a sudden we heard the rustle noise of the bullocks rushing past, as if there were some beside us on the same run as we were returning home. I looked around. There were no cattle anywhere near us. From the rushing mob of cattle, I could almost reach my hand to touch them, because it was too close. So the rushing of the cattle kept being near our hearing. The old people heard it too. I looked at the three old women, they too looked at me. I said to them, 'You heard the noise of bullock ran pass us.'

The old women said, 'Don't take any notice. Stockmen mustering their own bullocks here.'

We went on, still in the thickness of the hills. There for God's truth, so clear and plainly, the Cave men were rounding up cattle. I heard the sounds of stock whips cracking, the yodellings of three men. The other fellow shooed away a dog which they named Bella. So I said, 'Listen Mummy, they got dog there too, Bella'

She said, 'That's their dog.'

Others were whistling. Gee, I will never forget that. It was too true to hear all that. The rounding up time in the afternoon was one of the happiness time in their life. To me it was so exciting, because I never knew they got their own cattle and working men . . . also a cattle dog.

So of course they are real people. But how we really can contact them . . . really to see them as we are? From that time on I knew Cave people were real, human race but they are much clever people than we are. No wonder the tribes say they are like us, they work, they dress in good clothes like us. So they got everything.

After that, another day I was out bush and we were on a way to Birri. We had a break for lunch. The old people sat under the oak trees and rested. All of sudden one of the old men called out, 'Look, plenty horses on Birri beach, galloping with man on them.' We had other girls there also, so we all jumped up to see them ride up on the ridge. But we watched there in vain. They all disappeared among the oak trees. The horses were all colours. Some were white, most were red brown, others white and black dots. The men who were riding were dressed in black trousers, white shirts . . . all had hats of a real cow boys' suits . . . and well dressed.

As we stood there, we stood there shivering. All our hairs stood up from our body. We were really frightened, because they had disappeared in front of our eyes. Then the old folks told us, 'That's all the Stockmen going out to do their mustering.' There were about thirty to fifty of them galloping madly along the beach, hurrying to get into the bush. So the old people told us, 'It always happens like this . . . you see them at riding, hunting, spearing fish along the beaches or sitting under trees. They live daily each day the same as we are, doing the things as we do. But they are unseen people, which we call Cave people because they live in caves, or Youngul is the place. As you know, we call them Youngulmanda.' So they are my father's people because they all belong to that place.

I had an uncle, Jimmy Dugong, my father's cousin brother. Jimmy Dugong was adopted son of my grandfather Peter, my father's father . . . that's how it all came about. Well, this fellow Jimmy, he often was carried away by these people, the Youngulmanda. They knew he was one of them so they would take him to see the Cave people, then bring him back inside a huge net bag, bring him back to his people. Everytime he was taken away, his relation would miss him from among them. The people searched everywhere and called out to him . . . but no trace of him. So all they did was chant and chant. They chanted to soften the stomach of these ones who carried him away. Although, we began to know they were known as devil people, who carried him away to take him to the Cave people, or elsewhere. Old Jimmy several times was taken by these devil in the net, who were also called Cave people, because in early days, devils did carry other people too, to kill and eat them.

135

But the old tribes had songs which can return the devils with their relations.

Now old Jimmy, I believe, spoke his own Lardil tongue. Then, from since he was taken away to the Deep country area, and was told by the Deep people . . . that's how they suggested the tribes of these people to us, the Deep people or Cave people . . . said, 'Now we twist your tongue speech from language to english.' From then on he was able to speak only english to the tribes, but could not speak in Lardil.

I often wondered when sitting with the old folks. They chatted away, talking of the past. Besides, Jimmy Dugong would be there too, speaking in english back to his people. Although he was of an old age like the others, but they understood each other just the same, because when I mixed up with the tribes, they never spoke english, but language. That's how it beats me to the point why Jimmy Dugong could only speak english. Then one day my uncle Jimmy told me, 'Long time I been talk language, but devil been take me away from my father's camp, and now I can only talk english . . . but I can talk language belongs to Deep people but I can't use them, unless I am with the Deep people.' Then he continued, 'That's all my people . . . also belong to my brothers who own Birri country. That's why they never hurt me when they take me. They bring me back to my camp.'

One night in 1942, we all sat around our camp fires with our parents. There were not much noises on the place. The old people had a very funny, different feelings that made them very quiet. To our people the solemn quietness within the feeling made them feel something not good would happen, but awful thing would turn out. Soon, while we sat warming ourselves by the fire, the old people said, 'Poo, something smells like fish and shark vomit.'

The others said, 'Mulgan or devil is around to carry some one away.' To their surprise, without a thought Jimmy Dugong was standing by a blood wood tree waiting to be picked up by the devils in a huge net, and was carried away. Soon, later, the tribes found out that Jimmy was carried away. Then the old men started chanting. They got in a large group by fireside, and sang, hoping the devils would bring back their love one. As they chanted, all camp fires were put out.

The camps were all dark by now. Then the same smell came out of the sky . . . fish and shark vomit. They knew that the devils came back with the man they waited for. The devils threw him down from the net on a high tree and he climbed down from the tree. The moon was shining brightly. He walked up to his camp, and sat down without a word. The old men went around him, and chanted on him and drove the evil Spirit out of him. They sang over his head to take his mind off the Cave people. They washed the slimyness from his body, and the smell of vomit, and warmed his body with leaves to get his strength back. Then he was well enough to tell the story of how he travelled. The women and men sat around him to hear how he flew. He said, 'I went with the devils from mission area, over Birri, then across to Rocky Island. That's where they suppose to leave me.'

But, he said the devils were sorry for him and said, 'We'll take you back.'

'So they lifted me again inside the net, and flew back with me, and had another landing with me at Oyster Place, near Baldie Head Point. I thought they might kill me and eat me,' he said, 'but again they took the net . . . four of them, up in their hands, and flew back home with me. I called out when I knew I was over the village near my camp. Then they let the net open. I fell out and landed on a tree, climbed down and walked home to my camp.'

From then on, he was taken away and came back to his families, until one day he was standing up the sandy hill, looking around the country. His eyes and minds were looking far beyond, to the Deep people at Birri. I suppose they were his last thought of moments. He walked over the river . . . the tide was low, the creek was dry. He came home to his camp . . . stood there with loss of memory.

I was at the time with his wife Topsy and his children Nicholas, Lawrence, Rosemond . . . James was a baby then. So we all were there. Then old fellow lay on the blanket where we spread it out for him to die on, not thinking he would die so soon. He lay there, and to our surprise he started talking to himself, the rough languages of the Deep or Youngulmanda language. Old Gully Peters was there, and asked him, 'What are you talking about?'

But he only said, 'Now I talking to all my people, here they all come. Look, everybody come to look me.' And I looked around to see if the people were really coming, but no, there was no one. He was the only one could see the people who came to say Farewell to him. All the time he spoke of their tongue. It was a long yarn he had with the Deep people of the cave. It was a tremendous and a wonderful method of languages. I never heard in my life, and never heard it again spoken by no man. Jimmy was the only person ever used them . . . he only spoke the languages of those Cave people.

So we sat there until he finished speaking, then he turned to his big brother Gully Peters, and all his families and relatives, said, 'I'll go soon and leave you all. All my people came to see me, but they all gone back now. You know Deep people, Brother.' Later on, before bed time, the old man died. But one thing, he wasn't sick at anytime before all this had happened. He was quite well, and strong. Once he had black outs, on the very day, before he returned back to his own camp. It was so strange. Fancy walking around, speaking to anyone . . . then the flesh and limbs of his began to give away to be weary and then to death, to the eternal Glory.

As I write about my uncle Jimmy at the moment, I wish in those days, I had cassette recorder. I would have taped the languages. Anyone could then trace up to find out if ever in the world, any race of people near by, can speak this strange language. I bet there would be no one but the unseen people of the Deep country or Youngulmanda. I've heard so many different languages of other people of other countries. They are short words although they're rough, to grab quickly, but this one the old man Jimmy spoke, it's the roughest, toughest of all languages, longest words. I say as those when you spelling words like Ornithorhynchus. Well, the words would be as long as that, when he was using one word, to make a sentences, as he was talking to these strange people. Although, the old man did not explain any of the words to us to tell the meaning or what he was talking about. All we did was just sit there, and listen. So never will we hear that talk again, no more, and never will. It was the first and the last.

So what are these people? Who can they be, and how do they live and from what generation they belong to? Because all these unseen people have everything as if they living in city life, like other people living today with everything that we see with bare eyes. So if any of you don't believe of what I'm writing about, you could live in these areas for a month or more to learn and hear and see things for yourselves, just for proof. If you get lost or taken away, it's your own fault, to become one of them, but it's always safe if you have a tribe man who knows those places and tells you, 'Don't go near the place.' I had to live by the laws of the land . . . keep away, don't wander too far, don't disobey the tribes, because they have discovered all this for us, wherever they went, camped and roamed about in our country. What is here, is true life of everything.

On Sydney Island they also have people living in the same manner, over on that part of the country. The first thing happens is at night, while you are asleep. You dream of the people of that land. They talk to you, but all the time, they are really with you at your bed side. Next morning you think so much about the vision of a man or woman you saw in your dreams. Now your thoughts are really with them, you wish you could now see the person you dreamt of. It's sort of haunting you, but these people they live a different life. They are nice and they are good looking. They are gifted people on corroborees.

On Sydney Island they have some rocks that tell of the life they had and did. It's a well known history to the people of that land. These markings on the rocks really represent woman legends, and they are very, very sacred life of the early days' people. You cannot muck around that area. You

139

get yourself into all sorts of trouble, that you cannot understand how the things happened to you. You become crazy and chase after any man, or men run around with any young girl or woman, and it keeps that way of life all the time. That's why no one is allowed to go anywhere near the place, and start hanging around there or even pointing your fingers or pointing sticks on these stones. It's all against the tribal laws . . . people or the unseen people of that island see you, well you in for a bad time.

You know they are around when these people set the place on bushfires, but they don't hurt you by bashing or killing you or burning, but appear all romance life, in dreams. They say you belong to them . . . either woman picks a man, or a man chooses a woman. You already feel you belong to each other. Although it was a dream, but the feeling you have . . . they already chose you for a sweetheart, or wish to marry you. All you have, it's that feeling of love. It makes you not like to leave the place. But some people who are older and know what will become of you, well, they quickly move out of the place . . . or some very big changes will take place, and you become to live like one of the unseen people.

Besides all that, they give a man songs in dreams at nights. These songs mean love songs and have nice actions. With these corroborees amongst your own people it forms a love just sitting there seeing the dance. These dances affect you very much, and it's all the life of romance when it affects you. You cry any time of the day or night because you cannot see each other in person. But it's only a dream. Behind it all, it's a story that never cannot really be understood, but it affects your real human life.

I know of a young woman who went with her husband once to that island. These were her own words . . . told me, 'Well, Sister, I went alone on the beach. To my surprise I came across a beautiful rock. Everywhere I looked were all kinds of colours of the rainbow. It looked so pretty. I started breaking the stone to bring some home' . . . not knowing that was the area she should not supposed to be there.

This woman goes on, 'Well, Sister, I did not want to

leave the spot. It was so beautiful to be just there.' All the time this woman did not know the secret or the sacred place lies just where she stood. There was no one else around where she wandered along, to tell her to keep right away from the place. The wind was blowing from the North. The sea was calm, but to this woman even the cool light breeze had already hit her feelings, that she would not leave the colourful rocks.

Late in the evening she went home the way she came, sat down by the fireside with the others. She told her husband and the two women how she saw some pretty stones. At once her husband spoke to her and said, 'You the first woman went there. You should not go there.'

But she replied, 'I did not know, I just went for a walk and happen to come that way without any thought of the legend.' Anyway that night, she went off to sleep. She dreamt of a handsome man, came to her and asked her to marry him . . . but all she said, 'I cannot marry you, my husband is here with me. I cannot do that.'

The dream boy said, 'I don't care you have your husband here. I can take you away. I saw you today amongst the rocks.'

She woke up the next morning and told her dream of the man she saw. Although it was just a dream, but it really affected the woman very much. She could not help but thinking of the man she saw in her dream. She told me she did not want to leave the island. She was upset and her minds just went for this man. So next day her husband and the three women were returning for home. She told me she cried to leave Sydney Island, but she had to come home. For some time, all her thoughts, heart and minds were calling her to go back to Sydney Island. She often thought of his vision, of this young man, and cried to herself.

Few months later she forgot about everything, but that can show you it's a real life because you can feel it. What I call it . . . a place of romance. You not allowed to go near the rocks. Young men and women must obey the laws. Old tribes close their eyes, when passing that way. They put bushes over their faces as to go by, without looking that way.

Bushfires were the most important thing. When a man or woman is there on the island, or after they leave the island, all they can see is the bushfire burning with love . . . those have been affected by visions at night, or day are also affected with love. So the only thing is cry about the feeling that entered in their hearts.

I often wondered how the people became to have all this good things among all their laws, customs and culture, to be there with the way they have sought out the life to live with. Although many people would say or think the white man has taught them all this good things, but no it's not at all. They had all this ever before a whiteman, ever they say or ever reached the island to where these people lived. It was something they worked out . . . how to live, by the tribes themselves. So among the tribes they had good leaders. They had their own Governments to keep these laws.

Within the tribes were good hunters, good fighters. Also these men were safe guarders to the weak and the needy ones. They shielded and protected those who needed help. These were their own laws, and that's why we had brave men and good leaders . . . also to protect dingoes, which they hunted for to grow them up, and tamed them to be their friend and help to hunt for them.

Also trees were not destroyed, only for purpose like cutting down large trees to make dugouts. In later years, light wood were torn down to make walpa for travelling, hunting and fishing. Trees like the wild honey were chopped down. In those days, they had to find a heavy hook wood to use to cut down a tree for wild honey. You may not believe that, but that really happened in those days before the white man came and brought tomahawks.

In 1953 . . . a man was not right in his mind. He was of an old age. At the time we were all out bush. The mission was short of water for drinking. So we went bush . . . everybody to their birth place, or where ever the place of their father and mother. So while we were out bush, this old man, Archie, he came to where we were camping. He was mad most times, and other times he was well.

Teaching girls to cut and peel bark for coolamun.

Then one day, he came across the bush and found our camp. My mother, Raymond who was only four year old and myself were down the swamp, tracking swamp turtle. Mother found one, and the boy carried it home to our camp. As we climbed the side of the hill to get up to the top, we glanced at the old man.

How frightened we were. My Mother was a cousin to this old man, but she was so afraid of him. As we went towards our camp, I called out, 'Hey, Mervyn. Look what we found.' That was the only way to let all the children to see the old man before anything was stirred up. Then there was no noise or calling out. Everybody just had a glance at the old man, and the children, men and women creeped slowly to their camps, and never made a sound. All sat in their camps with fear. The old man sat down out in the sun all by himself. Many of the old tribes were there but did not make a move to say Hello to him. All were so frightened. Archie carried a wooden tomahawk and a billycan of sugar-bag, and a woomera. As there was not a move from no one, the old man sat there for half an hour all by himself. I said, 'Mummy, I'll go over and talk to him.'

Mum said, 'No. He might hit you.' But I did not hear my mother. I got up and walked up to the mad, old man with cup of tea and damper . . . everybody still hidden in their camp, not a move.

I said Hello to him and sat down in front of him, and passed the tea and damper to him. The other tribes, also my mother and foster father, were watching from behind their windbreaks, to see what he'd do to me.

Then the old man told me how he went for hunting, and lost his way, and ran into our camp. Archie said, 'You look girl, I found sugar bag tree. I had no tomahawk to get the tree down, so I used this wooden axe.' The wooden axe was from a broken tree. So he used it and managed to get the honey. He gave me the billy can of wild honey, and he went on eating damper and drank tea. I sat there talking with the old man.

When the other people saw old Archie was alright, the rest of the old people and my parents came to visit him and

145

sat with him. Now children from their hidden camps were running around and playing as before, but my feelings were . . . how sorry I felt to see how people kept away from him, and how he came to our camp without anyone to go over to see and talk to him. Although sometimes you must be careful of mad person, but this fellow really upset me very much, because of his own people were afraid of him. But to me, I wasn't afraid. I just had to go over to him, to make know that some one had time to see him . . . and not afraid of him. If I did not go over and talk to him, I knew he would have got upset and started his mad fits. But it was good to see that the old people were now having a good yarning and laughing.

We made a windbreak for him to sleep for the night, and carried wood. Next day he left us, and went back to where the other people camped, where he stayed. So there I learnt from Archie, and saw one of the old stuff they once used . . . a wooden axe.

Also, dunarga was a shell that was picked from the beach and made for cutting meat, like turtle or dugong, when no white man knife was not known to the tribe yet.

Coolamun was out from trees that had strong barks. This was taken out with sharp sticks . . . stripped the bark off the tree, warmed the bark over a fire, and then treated on both side, tied together, and made a nice deep basin like to carry their water or carrying babies, also their own tribal things or whatever they were used for.

This coolamun made babies to have strong backs, legs and arms, and they grew up quickly. Also it was made for sleeping, to keep the child's sleep warm and cosy. Mothers never had to carry children in arms. They knew the safety way was to put them in these baskets. Small baskets were made for carry food and belongings. Nets or mejeals were made for carry food and other things. They also were used for carry fish, stingrays, crabs and other land food. Where ever they went, these were the only possessions which they claimed.

Weeare was their cooking stick for all their use. Weeare also was for digging roots, digging crab hole, goanna killing and other such things. Yamma stick was made for woman fighting stick, for digging at times, for guiding them clearing grass and trees as they walked through the bush where it was scrubby and grass grew so thick. When using these sticks in fights, they poked large deep holes at one other's body.

Bailer shell were much larger shells that too were used for carrying or lasting water for day and night, also for clearing water hole. They used cooking stick to dig down and bailer shell for scooping up the earth. Bailer shell and small shell we call dunarga, we both used for drinking, and to draw water with. Cooking stick and digging stick were used for all kinds. So everything the tribes had were all useful stuff . . . and used it for different purpose at all times.

Many things seem strange to us now, when we think how the days of life were with the people of the past, how they lived without the things of today. It seems hard at these present time, but to the people of old, they were contented behind it all. God was with them and he gave the things they could find . . . how to use everything that belonged to them, for their purpose. Now let's try to hold and use some of those things for chopping trees, and for using to rip large dugong and turtle meat, and digging water holes with sticks. It will take three or four hours to end the job, or perhaps never will continue, unless you start now looking for knife or tomahawk or shovel. So you see they had all theirs, and now we have all what we have today. Fire stick, too, was hard to make one time, and that's how they kept up making fire. Today everything is easy. You go to any shops and buy matches to start your fire.

They even made fish traps with tree leaves and rocks, to keep the fish in when high tides came in. At low tide, they go down to all the fish traps and are able to collect a large number of fish, crabs, stingrays, also dugong and turtle. They find all kinds of sea food.

They only thought to shelter from rain and stormy weather . . . was just to lie in the windbreaks with ti-tree paper barks, and then grass was thrown over the top. They lie very still until the storm and rain clear away. Sometimes when the rain is pouring down, day and night, they shelter under cave rocks, and make great fire to keep themselves warm and dry. The men and women also don't give up hunting during the rain to feed themselves.

It was so dreadful the way they lived especially when rain was falling. I've been through all this. I can truthfully say the life was terrible and so hard. Living out in the bush, everything got so wet . . . children lying in the poor, sheltered windbreaks with a small bough shed over head, with raining leaking through every thing, water trickling down on the head and faces of little Mervyn and Raymond as they sat together in the corner of the roughly made shelter.

The little boys made me sorry, to see them both cuddle together to get themselves warm and dry. I am doing my best to break and root up grasses to put on the top of the bough shed to save the boys from getting wet, while faithful father, Goobalathaldin, is racing up the bush to bark some barks off the trees to shelter the two boys, at the same time collecting huge logs and other small twigs to start up a fire to the entrance of the windbreak to keep the boys warm and dry. Dick and myself stand out in the rain with one each barks over us, enjoying the warmness of the fire. As the rain is pouring the two little boys have fun and giggle. Although the blanket is wet, it means nothing to them. They have the barks over them and sit by the fire.

After the rain has gone away we hang out everything on the ground to get dry. Sometimes there is not enough sunshine and wind to dry the blankets and clothes. Darkness comes so soon, and we have to use the damp blankets for the night. But Goobalathaldin is a careful father to his families. He always makes a huge fire to get the blankets and clothes dry for the boys, before they can use them. When everything is dry from the heat of the fire, the children sleep in warm and comfort.

Other people found it hard too, during the storm and rain, and most of the people and children sleep with damp blankets. Food gets wet. Everything you have really goes through the soak from the rain. I can remember when there was not enough fire at the other camps. Some people would come over to our place, to get themselves warm and dry, also their children's blanket or clothes.

Some people are very useless when storm or rain is approaching, especially men and boys. They just sit there without moving to get ready for the rain. Poor women must do everything . . . on her own. Before everything has been done, already the rain is falling, then everything gets wet. To my way of looking, I think these people must have got so used to the old ways . . . just sit or stand in the rain, only with barks or grass over them, no matter the other things get wet because it's not worth while trying to protect everything while the rain is falling. I've seen men during the rain walking along the beaches at low tide spearing fish and stingray, also women gathering oysters for a meal before bed time, while other families are drying out the camps and other things and making fires.

There were times when I did not like getting wet in the rain, after being in the dormitory, whiles being out in the bush. But I had to live to learn the hard ships of my people's life . . . get wet, stay wet, hunt in the rain, until finally I and my husband had to do the best we could to make proper shelters out of small huts made with messmate barks, to keep our children from getting wet. Dick bought nails and carried in a shut up tin to build a small house, which we have always done when out bush.

Although those times were hard and awful, but it was a good life to us and our children. They really liked bush, it was a free life, and we all really understood the happiness of the old folks. During heavy falls of rain, the old people had something to crack jokes about, and have funs with each other. The rain mattered them not. They still had fun and play.

In our midst we had some funny people in men and women . . . Guthan-guthan they were called. Well, it's a teasing thing, but not the real Spirit to tease, what we all know today. This is another way of looking at it, with fun and plenty of laughter. Uncles and nieces play their part. Cousin brothers and sisters take their part. A woman would sit and talk with others in the camp. Her brother or brother-in-law would poke his finger at her nose or eye, or snatch her food and give it to the other person. They would stand and eat it all together until the woman chased them with a stick. Then they all hit her. Others would come and turn on the ones who teased her, then all sorts are happening. After the play, they all sit together and have a great feast, with others joining in the eating. Then a big corroboree takes place.

Well, all that way of fun has continued from early days, with all kinds of fun to laugh about . . . but it meant happiness to the tribes. It kept on day after day also at nights. It never stopped. They were people of great happiness. As I noticed the people, they had all different ideas how to be happy. There was something to be done. I saw the people never liked to be idle doing nothing. So these funs were to get them moving, having something to do to amuse themselves. They never liked to sit around their camps, doing nothing. All their fun meant something to do with the hands and minds, and often had these terms part of the life . . . was happiness. I hardly knew of sad times amongst the tribes, hardly quarrels and fights. Most were these small funs. Then the crowds gradually became large numbers with many people joined in the fun.

Why I write this . . . whoever wants to find out about my people. Well, there were all this sort of tribes at work.

They made boomerangs, but it meant for preparation for war. Small size were the deadly ones. If a man wanted to use the small size of boomerangs, it never missed to hit the right person. Also, the small boomerangs were mainly for singing corroborees. They also made a fighting stick called nulla nulla. That was used for fight, to hit and protect yourself.

Nulla nulla was a weapon to guard the boomerang . . . from being hit. To use a nulla nulla you have to be very smart, to protect yourself or you get hits on your both legs or head, arms and ribs. The way the other fellow who swings the waddy . . . means to do the best job of the other bloke. But if you are active in handling and watching all the swings, you come out without being hurt. If you are not a good person on the nulla nulla you can say you have broken leg, arm, or even your fingers are cut in half, or are cut on the head. Boomerangs are likewise. They do the job . . . that your eyes must be perfect to watch the other bloke that is using, to throw towards you. If you are not careful in watching the man on action, you are seriously hurt.

Then when the fight has ended, I watch how they make friends with each other. You see people come from two sides and present the two people . . . and give each sides a gift of other things, like spears, woomeras, fish nets, hair belt, tassels, and other such things. Also, they sit in family groups, all eat and share alike with food to eat, and that's how the whole trouble ends in friendship.

Then all plan for corroboree. Away the men all march to the dancing ground, and paint up for a night corroboree. About five o'clock the men are just about ready. The women are at the play ground, burning fires for the dancers. Every women have their own fires lit up. The women sing and dance other dance. The other group sings and helps the men, while others again clap their lap legs, to make the sound better for the dancing and the singing to go on.

They also make nets for trapping fish in the rocks, large and small. Men and women do all this together. They hunt bush for the grass, that are called galgar. The green fibre is bent over the second finger and the thumb. On your right you take the fibre with the thumb and the second finger. To do this you bend it over on your left. Place it on your leg then pull the green fibre right off and leave the white strand, give it a roll on your leg again to twist it and it becomes firm. You repeat it over and over again until you have a big stack of the grass. It's left there to dry for two days. Then you work on the strands, and roll that now to make a twine. When you have finished the string, it's then rolled into a huge ball. From that you cut a small stick, make two opening in the centre of the stick, tie one end with the string, then work it up and down, to and fro, until you have enough string in the stick, break it off.

Then stick another stick in the ground to hold the twine. Make a small loop with the stick that holds the ball of string and turn it backwards and inside until you have enough loops. When there is about five or six rows of round loops you carry on circling repeating as before, until it grows bigger and bigger.

When you've done enough, it is turned into a net, either net for carry belongings, or fish and crab. The large size is for catching dulnu. This net is held by two long sticks and comes in V shape and the net is sewed on to the two sticks . . . and that's how they make them. The two side of the net stick are then used for two men on both side to draw the fish into the net and that's how they meant for to use.

With the same grass and twine . . . to make a jaet or dancing skirt for the women. It's only used for hip to hip. A long twine is tied end to end, and tied on to the half waistline on the woman's body. That was only how it was for women, to use for corroborees or at anytime. That was only meant for front piece only, nothing at the back.

So the grass is called galgar. From it the green fibre is plucked off. After drying, it's then rolled into a twine with red ochre . . . winding into a ball, it's called mooru . . . from mooru into mejeal or net.

At these present time, to my biggest surprise I saw fish-men in white men. They sewed their nets exactly as a tribal man did in their early life. So they both worked the same, but a tribal man and woman had a tough time, in finding their stuff to work things out like this.

Man's hair belt was made from a human hair. Tassels were made from wallaby fur. Now with this wallaby . . . is killed and eaten, fur is left to dry before it is used. Then a hot ashes are put into the inner of the skin . . . then pluck the fur off while the skin is soft, repeating all the time until there is no more fur on the skin. Then the fur is worked up with ashes, until the stiffness is gone. The ashes help to soften the fur. Then the fur is weaved with a hook stick, and made into a long strand and then twisted with hands from under the person's feet, picked up by the hook stick . . . twist the fur until it's strong enough. That is rolled and twisted on the same stick on which it is worked to do all the jobs.

Later on, the ball of the wool is separated into two parts of the strands, put in a tin of water to soften, then it is held in the right hand, and rolled on the lap leg. Another big ball is made up of this. When the wool is big and strong it is then measured for a front piece, held by two sticks that are firmly put to the ground. Then it is rolled, twisted on to the leg again, and sewed on to the main string, until they have done enough of the front piece. This is tightened on the top end with several knots to end the job. It is then called thunda-malmal . . . front piece.

Human hair is cut and used for to make a hair belt or waist line. It works only in an easy way from the thundamalmal. It's only worked, twisted on two sticks fastened down on the ground . . . only you do it like this. ⟨image⟩ When it's done, it is tested on the waist of a man. It is then called burrumbad or waist line. Forehead piece is made from the same string that we get out of galgar, that has been made from the same twine. The piece of that twine is worked the same as the waist line, by two sticks with a long, single string to end off the job. White paint is put on to keep it firm. Hung on the end of that, hangs a wallaby's teeth. This is used for beautyness when there is a corroboree on.

I often watched my mother at work, when she got ready for a dance. She saw that everything she had to use, it was carefully handed and straighted out, before she could put them on. I liked my mother when she dressed herself with jaet. It really suited her. And the head band she always had on made her look so beautiful . . . painted her body with red ochre, and clay on her face with two small dots. My mother was a good dancer. No matter in her old age, she still danced. That's how I came to dance. My mother always got me to join her at the dance.

Since then I always took part in any dance. Then as times went by, I was always chosen by the tribes to open up new dances with the older ones. I did not offer myself to join in any tribal dances. The tribes always pick out the best dancers. You are given a feather, and that feather shows you are invited to dance for the opening show, that's only opened up by few people, the older tribes.

When a man or woman dreams a dance at night, they see some one who is dancing. In their dreams they see all the

153

action, the way the person danced during the night. When it's a good dance to the dreamer, he jumps from his sleep and gets hold of his boomerangs and begins to clap the boomerang and sings as hard as he can, so not to forget the song. As other old folks hear the singing during their sleep . . . well, the men are up on their feet, and go to the man who had a dream. They all sit round the man's camp fire and sing away. Finally a woman will come along. By hearing the song, she will dance, and that action will be for all women to follow on. Then men will see the action of the woman, and they will find action close by from the woman action. Then the night comes of another day's end. The dream dance is danced by all people who want to dance.

So this feather for the dance, to be given to anyone is real and important to the tribe. It is meant with great interest . . . and to a person who to their eyes is a good dancer. It's a thing, no matter who you are, if you are a good dancer, you are praised by the tribe. The older tribes talk over to each other, and so they decide to whom the feather shall be presented to. As they sing for preparation for the dance, they give three to six people the feather to be the leaders for the show. The old tribes never choose a nice, fat fellow in men to give him the feather, because he is young and you might expect this bloke to be a good dancer, but he is not one of them. To the tribe, they choose the proper people who can dance. During my young woman life, I was often given one of these feathers to join or to be leader of the dance.

Once on a midday, the tribes gathered together for a new dance, to sing and show or give action to the dancers. As one bloke would dance, the others would sing. Then the old people would say, 'That's look good . . . the way the women can dance. The other way, the men can dance that way.' So the show seemed to be Okay to the folks. Then as they sang, each man and woman would be chosen to get up and dance.

On this day I was told to get up and join. Although I never danced before, I had seen many dancing done by others. I was so shy. I really did not know how to take the real style to dance. I said I could not dance, but to the tribes' law . . . you must do it.

So I stood by some middle age women and danced with them, Colin William and myself . . . that's my youngest brother. We both jumped up on our feet the next singing of the song was on. We both danced madly, we put our whole heart into the dance. To us both, we did not fear from anyone. As the singing and clapping of the boomerangs went on, the Spirit of dance was in us, and we just danced. Before the dancing was almost ending, there was a scream of crying from my grandmothers, and tears ran from the eyes of my brothers and other relatives. In their crying they were saying, 'You are a good dancer, just like your mother. Why you dance like that? After all, your mother is dead now.' So they cried bitterly for Colin and me.

Our father was a very proud man on that first day to see us both in action. They got us and kissed us for making a good program of the dance. Gee my heart sank, in sad heaviness, to hear the cry of cheers for we two family. How they really were proud of us. For the first time we showed the people how well we could dance. Once more we made a group circle and finished off by singing. Then the elder of the tribes gave us feathers each, to hold and keep for the dance. That feather represented . . . we must always dance the one dance, everytime this certain dance would be. It meant we were boss or a leader, and we could choose any other to join us. I have never forgotten that day. It was an exciting day . . . the day I learnt the ways of the dance custom and how they treat the dancers with pleasure and proudness.

Also I found out and saw people on the dancing ground . . . any one who puts their whole heart into the dance, and on lookers see the person to their liking and feel that the person is a good dancer, they give cheers of all the nice things about your movements in dancing. They, the on lookers, jump up from where they are sitting and run and grab hold of the dancer, and say any food you hunt for, you must give. Or they say, 'Damper'. . . . you bake a large damper and give it to the one who praised you up. They also say panja, dugong meat, turtle, sugar bag, sugar, curelle, swamp turtle, fish, tobacco, and any such kind. It is the way of the life to carry on, as any dance is held.

So that custom was there to make you always become a good dancer. These food that was mentioned the previous night . . . the dancer goes whenever they go hunting, they must hunt and collect these stuff. Then it's given to the one who asked for it. This certain person must sit on the ground with her or his legs crossed and sit there, as the food is given by the dancer. That squares the whole thing. But to that, no sister or brother, uncles and auntie, mother or father, can eat there of. It's against the law, because it's from the lap leg table of that person. Only grandparents and cousins are allowed to eat the food with the person who has received it. This kind of custom was then called 'Murrandu'. It means . . . ask and give. You feel proud of some one and say she or he is a good dancer . . . 'I like your way, how you dance.' Then the dancer must give you in return for saying something nice. She gives you what you deserve in being interested in her.

So this kind of things went on for so many years, until about 1952 . . . it has vanished away from our midst. All our free life and many happy times we had together died away. Especially when the old tribes were alive, everything was in life with happiness and all its good health. Then as they passed on to the other life, everything went too, with them, left us all with the life of sadness and unhappiness . . . only memories now you can see and think of.

Years went by . . . I was still learning of all I saw, of all I heard, and then one day, after all those years, I went back to dormitory and became one of the leading girl . . . took charges at workers and helped to cook for girls and boys. Meals . . . formed children in lines to say grace before their meals, and helped to wash plates, spoons and dishes. I came to love all that I was able to do. I also did hem stitching on hankies, crocheting edgings on them, fancy work on table cloths, and other crochet works. At the same time, there was more time for other things to do, odds and ends of all kinds for the hands to do.

Things changed a bit in later years. Now again, away from parents and relations, working hard as usual in the hot sun, with gentle breezes blowing, bringing back thoughts of freedom and happiness roaming the bush, thoughts were back again of the way I had been out bush, learning and understanding my tribal people's life. How I missed it all and wished to be out of the missionaries' care, as thoughts came now and then. The only happy times I had were with my only sister May William. We both had many funs and laughs. We were grown ups then, and had to leave Dad and Mum and spend the rest of our times with the other girls in the dormitory.

Everything went on alright again . . . had funs and games, dancing at some time, a tribal dance which we called corroboree. Two of the men would come in for visit in the mission reserve, and sing and clap boomerang for the dance. We girls were eager to dance, and enjoyed ourselves.

How we came back to dormitory . . . most times when the rain had fallen, our old folks didn't have enough good sheltered humpies to keep us dry. So we desired to leave the village camp, and went running in, during the rain, back to the mission. In those days rain had fallen for many days. You could not get anything dry. Half of the time we were hungry. The fire places were soaking in the rain, and there was no other way we could prevent the fire not lighting. So when there was a break from rain, we would quickly make a fire and cook damper and boil tea, before another heavy storm of rain would come. So that was the reason we left our parents and had to go back to the mission. There were only about twelve of us in the dormitory. Then finally the younger ones kept coming in to join us. More came in until all the children had to leave their parents, and the school managed to start all over again.

During that time, before all children came, we had soldiers who came to our island to defend us and our island. They were here for three years. They were very friendly crowd. In 1945 . . . they had to leave the island and went back, to where they came from. Then everything was once more in peace and quietness. But strange things had happened in our midst . . . was more brightness and happiness, your minds seeing things you never thought of or saw the likes. It was new, so many things seemed strange, and it brightened the heart, minds and the whole body with interest to see all what was going on.

During the time the soldiers were here, everything went well, everyone was safe. It was the first time ever we saw soldiers . . . how they were dressed in their uniforms, and how they did everything. It was interesting for we people to learn all about them and their duties. We girls shared concerts along with the soldiers, and other games. During that time, the girls were respectable and polite to the boys. The same respectfulness too, was given back to the girls. That's how everything went well with us here. We were happy to have the soldiers here, and were sorry when they left the island.

On the following year (1946) Dick and I got married. To my surprise, on my wedding day, my father was away in the bush. Therefore my uncle Gully Peters gave me away to Dick. That was the first wedding ever took that custom belongs to white man, of fathers giving their girls away.

Also, I had bride's maid, flower girls, and Dick had a best man. Since then all marriages followed in this way.

We had a nice big party at the back of the mission house on the verandah. There were crowds of friends and relations and other nearby friends. It was a great gathering, one which I shall never forget. How surprised I was to see all kinds of foods, were placed on the tables. It was such a big surprise for me because as I was in the dormitory, I did not hear even a whisper about the wedding feast. I thought I would have a quiet simple marriage on, not knowing there were some good friends who had planned all that did happen to me on that special day.

It was the most exciting day for me. We enjoyed all the funs and jokes while we sat around the table eating. The invitation given to the marriage feast was not by Dick and myself, but by our closest friends, who had gathered up so many crowds to the feast. The ones who took the first tables had to clear out and stand around to let the others come to the tables. We had about three large tables full of all sorts to put on the table to eat at the mission house of the Superintendent. It was the happiest day of my life amongst my relations and friends, thanks to all who made it worth while for the great feast we had, done by our good friends.

I and Dick entered into a large bark hut that was built down the village, by the water front. One thing, it was big, but few months later we left the bark hut. We rather a smaller one instead. So we set to go out bush, two or three miles away, to search stringy bark trees. It was so hot at times and the work was so tough to cut, and build a huge fire to warm the barks . . . then placed logs and rocks to flatten the barks. We would have our lunch and a bit of rest . . . then on our way to our village, with head load stack of barks. By that time we had another small hut to live in. Each day was the same, until finally we had a huge stacks all together.

Our next job was to go out to chop timbers and small pole for battens. We had to carry the timbers on our shoulders. Although the work seemed so tough to handle, but we had to face the task through all its heat and heaviness. Half a mile we would go . . . then another small rest. It was always the same . . . but never gave up.

Then we desired to go bush and cut a dugout, or a canoe. We camped bush for weeks and weeks. One day, as the canoe was almost done, Dick got inside of the canoe and began to chop the inward part at the side in the canoe. He gave a big swing and cut his knee cap almost right off.

I screamed and yelled out to his big brother, Kenny Roughsey, to come at once . . . 'Dick cut his knee with an axe.' So Kenny and Fred came to see what happened. Kenny cried to see the torn flesh of his brother's knee cap. The huge flesh hung down over the bottom top skin. Kenny Roughsey put the skin together, chanted and chanted over the place where it was cut. The blood flowed like water from a running stream, on his leg, everywhere on Kenny's hands, also on my hands and feet. Then Kenny picked up the axe blade and put the blade by the cut knee and chanted, chanted and chanted away. Kenny's mouth was full of blood by then, just to save his brother from dying. As he chanted, holding the axe blade on to Dick's knee, soon the blood stopped flowing badly. That dreadful huge cut was suddenly closed. The flesh, holey skin was not opened, but really was healed back in its place.

Dick managed to walk home, half a mile back to the camping spot. We were far away from the mission. The only help we could get was from his own brother, the tribal man who had the healing chant. So you see there is that great belief. To see Kenny Roughsey, what he did for Dick on that day, I could not believe my eyes to see that. I had no idea how on earth just a song had made Dick better.

Kenny taught Dick to use that song whenever he or his children got hurt or cut on any part of their body . . . to put a tomahawk or knife blade beside the wound and sing the song to heal any sort of cuts. Several times I've heard Dick use the same song when one of his boys got cut with a knife. I got cut once from tomahawk, and the cut closed in that very moment. I believe it can do the job better than if you get stitched up by a Doctor or a Nursing Sister at the hospital. This kind of chant has its own power to heal.

So you see an Aboriginal man has his talent of healing by chanting, whereas a European has Doctors to heal in a different way again. But they both do the same good deeds. One gets no pay for the prize of human life saving . . . that is a black man. He does it because he feels sorry to see anyone in agony. But a European, he gets pay to save life of a human. Of course that's alright because the hospitals have everything good, everyone is kept busy and they do a splendid work. With a black man, it's a most secret living way. It does not apply for all to be treated in the same way, only seldom to few people because those who trust and believe can be healed. Others again do not care or believe.

Days went by. Dick had no more trouble with his knee. So the next was done . . . collecting stringy barks, hunting for fish and crabs, wandering in the bush for goannas, wild honey, wild fruits, etc. The dugout was ready to be dragged in the water. Outriggers were put on, also two side floaters. Then we forced our way towards the sea, dragged it for a mile and half. The tide was very low, so it was a hard day's job to get it down to the sea. Next day we set homeward bounds for the mission or the village camps.

Then Dick started on digging holes for the posts to stand in. Finally all timbers and battens were now ready for a house. Dick and few friends helped him to build the house. It was a very good house for all weathers and for rainy days. It was dry and comfortable. It was hard for other young married couples to get a home for themselves. When it was pouring rain and strong winds, the people used to go to another friend's or relation's house for shelter. Sometimes the rain would come in and wet the whole house. The wind and rain comes from all directions at the same time, with willy winds passing over. Most time, when husbands went out working on Cattle Stations, or crew on different Cargo boats, wives would be left without a decent house. So the men had to find a job on the Mainland, to earn enough money to come home and make a small shack enough to live in. People used to gather bits of iron and stringy barks or ti-tree paper barks to get themselves a small house to keep out of rain and wind. People used to help each other a lot when each woman had no where to live and husbands away working.

I remember how I had to get some mothers who were pregnant . . . really had a hard life to live in a comfortable home. So I brought few mothers along with me to share my apartment, until the arrival of their babies. No hospitals or Nursing Sisters were at the time on the mission. Each women were cared from another woman. Now these women stayed with me. I delivered their babies and attended to them. It was under the small roof of the house made of stringy barks. We worked as hard for that.

But before all that happened, my first born son, Mervyn Roughsey, was born under that roof of that house. The others were born just after I had my other son born to me, Raymond Roughsey. The other children were, Maynard Williams, my brother's wife's child, the next, Betty Roughsey, and Milton Jingles. Opposite to my house were other two couples, Gertie and Sandy Scholes. I delivered their first born daughter, Marleen, also Doreen Scholes . . . now is Mrs Jingles, married to Milton Jingles. Then about thirty foot away was another child. That's Carlton Namie, also Daniel and Bert Namie, Watson Roughsey, Matthew and Calder Peters . . . these, there also were no Nurses at the hospital . . . but down the village . . . also Karen Roberts. But that just gives you an idea how young I was at the time when I had to give some aid to the young mothers, when most of these births were on.

When it was too late for the missionary lady to come to the help of the mothers, also if there were Sisters here for some of these and it was too late to get the women up to the mission hospital in time, the births were entirely under my care and love. Also, there were a number more of births I saw and handled, with children. Mind you, these births never had anything to stand by to be used for that moment. So quickly I would race around to grab hold of a razor or scissors. I hope you don't mind me saying, these things weren't clear but dirty and rusty. So quickly I would make fire, put on a billy can on the fire and pop the rusty razor or scissors in. Then everything would be ready for the birth. I would rush up to my hut and tear up any of my old clothes for the baby's use and wrapping, until help came later on from the mission for both mother and the baby.

I really loved nursing. I felt happy when everything went on so well, especially how carefully I attended to the babies' navels. Nothing went wrong. Three times a day, I made sure to visit the babies, to make sure there was no bleeding on the navels. Each day as the child grew I felt so proud of them, because I was their Nurse. Very few people cared to do these things, not all. Some got very nervous . . . others again so frightened they may not do the right thing, something might go wrong with the mother or the baby. Always death was the trouble, for both.

I remember once when I was helping a white Nurse in the mission, in an old stringy bark hut, one Kaiadilt woman had a baby. I was there when the baby was born lifeless. It was dead on its birth. So the white Sister said, 'Elsie, could you wrap the dead baby while I and Letty Jacob will see about the mother.'

So they did, while I was there with the dead child. I did not wrap the baby, but just put him in the cot, and started rubbing the baby's back. I kept on doing it all the time. Finally the baby was breathing and it gave a little movements. I was amazed to see the movement. The mother was lying in her bed in agony when she saw a strange act on my face. I smiled at her . . . unknown to Sister Creagh. All I said, 'Sister, the baby is not dead but alive.'

So Sister Creagh ran to the cot where I was and said, 'How it happened, Elsie?'

I said, 'I only kept rubbing the child's back until he came back.' So Sister gave the baby a needle and he was able to live on.

But that same child, as he grew up, he was cripple. He could not crawl or walk, but he was a strong healthy boy. I often visited the parents everyday, to see how the child was. I would sit down with them round the fire side and have a chat with them. One night I sat beside the fire, picked up the cripple boy and rubbed my under arm smell on the child legs and placed my hand over the fire to get heat and rubbed

163

my warm hand on the child's knees and legs. Also I pulled each toes on each foot to stretch the foot and legs, so he would be able to walk in a few weeks time. I only did it several times after that. But few days later the parents of that child laughed at me when I arrived at their camp . . . excitingly told me he could pick himself up to stand now. So I thought, Well, the fire heat and pulling his legs and toes did the job alright. So he was able to stand and walk.

That same boy, later on, they sent him to Brisbane hospital where they take care of the cripple children. Few years later they sent a telegram to his parents that the little boy died . . . I suppose fretting for parents. Also, there was another black boy there too. He was Clive Moon. But those two kids died.

Hadn't they gone, they would have been alive, if only they were still here among us. Why? The tribes had a way to cure crippleness with what the tribes had . . . different herbs of grass and leaves of different trees. Also the mothers or really grandparents would pull a child's legs and foot and toes to stretch the tight limbs of the child and even pull the legs to loosen the cripple places. Also they would warm the child by placing the grass and leaf over the fire and warm the child on the spot where the crippleness starts and ends. Even they have this strange noise like kissing, but hard and long the noise are, and at the same time you give this pull to make the flesh stretch . . . repeating for two or three months until finally the child is able to make a first move to the time as it was given.

Each day the child feels that he can move around. Later on he can manage himself by crawling, standing, then walking. It's a fact. I have seen it be done in early life by the tribes. I have seen it often done to any child, whether the child is cripple or not. It was meant to use to any child, to help them to move around a much earlier stage to their right age or month. It was much for growing strengthening movement for a healthy growing of any small, weak and helpless children and this is all it's about . . . something to do with the ones who need help.

Since I was married I had to do lots of odds and ends jobs

in the mission, to help in teaching children in school. As the case . . . some children had difficulties with other younger teachers who were so tough and cruel with their scholars. These children ran away from school and hid under some cliffs by the Church, too frightened to go to school for the same cruel treatment. So the head teacher Margaret Bain asked me if I could come to school and give some kindness to these children that had the hard times. So I agreed to help, just for the children's sake.

1952 . . . I started to work very hard. These children were in Grade 4, but to my surprise when writing words, their words were not spelt right at all. Arithmetic was wrong. Poor little children had a bad start. So they were starting their school lessons all over again. I had a hard time with steadiness and understandings as I worked with them, until finally their lessons were much better to carry on, for the next Grade to continue. So I was happy that all their lessons were correctly, well done. They were no more too hard, for them to carry on. I had lots of fun between times, when other things had to be done . . . in an easy way, how to make them happy and learn to understand and love me. They were bright and clever. If they had teachers who learnt more themselves in the first place, they would have had no trouble in teaching the next ones. But that worked well, ever since I stood over these children as a teacher.

In the other class of children, not far away from where I had my pupils, these were Grade 5, where they had to do their own lessons. That's only as far they could reach the grades . . . then leave school, and go back to the tribal life in the world outside, hunting in the bush for land and sea food. Well, Grade five, when ever they could not understand some of their lessons . . . hard to pick up . . . Eunice, Joyce, would ask me, also Oscar, to help them for their sums, because they were afraid to ask their own teacher of the lessons they could not get along with. One of them, Bobby, who was very clever boy, had everything correct. But one thing about him . . . under the desk he had comic that he always read, after his lessons. Lucky he wasn't caught up to this by his teacher Margaret Bain.

Times passed by when I had to leave my scholars and start off again, now with the smaller ones, Kindergartens. My boy, Mervyn Roughsey, was one of them. I loved teaching Kindies very much, to start them off in counting, to add and take away. I had to send them out of the school house, to bring me certain amount of shells, stones and leaves from trees, and taught them in this way. I knew it would be more easy for the children to understand how to follow the ideas. I had to make the children really understand me. It was no problem in their lessons. Children found it easy now to go on with all their lessons.

Three years I spent in the school, then as I began to have two more children, it was a bit tiresome to carry on the school and attending to babies at the same time. Although it was nice to be a teacher, but walking to school twice a day, back and forward, walking from village to mission school, was hard to keep up with the Summer's heat. Your feet were almost roasted in the hot sands. Then my days of being a teacher were over.

But still, Dick and myself had a place to go on doing work in the mission. Dick was a carpenter. I was a cook for the children and Adults who attended jobs about the mission. We also took children on holidays and for camping out for few days or a month . . . that's school breaks. The missionary man and his wife were nice people, Mr and Mrs McCarthy. We had some happy times with them, although the old man was tough, but fatherly towards everyone.

Going out for the new life

A pregnant woman who never rode a horse before, but galloped away

Then one day Dick was a crew on the Cargo boat *Cora*, owned by the Burke's Company. It was nice for him to be on the sea, doing deck work, taking in turns on the steering wheel, giving hand to the Captain and other blokes who were on board.

He went to Cattle Station on a short period time. He took me too. We had our first baby, three year old. He was a bright, choppy little fellow. All he saw of strange animals and creatures he would say 'It's daddle daddle.' It was a strange word to us, but we gradually knew he meant to say a horse, bull, cow, sheep, goats and different creatures of emu, turkey, lizards, toads or anything that moved before his eyes. Although it took a long time before he could speak in plain english, but he was a smart boy. His father was a Station hand at the time, cutting wood, cleaning up the place, boundary riding and taking care of the sheep. Mervyn Roughsey gave his father hand to round up sheeps in the yard, opened and shut the gate for his father. When resting under a shady tree, Mervyn would creep away and wander round the place. We would miss him and make a search. He would be seen in among the sheep, belting and rounding up the sheep in the corner of the yard.

Then one day the little boy got sick, so we had to go back to Fort Constantine from Fort Williams. On a way back it was long and hot. Dick rode on a horse, in front of him was his son. I walked all the way, as I never rode a horse before and I was scared, so rather walk the way. But it seemed so far for the travel, so Dick asked if I could ride now. He said, 'The horse is very quiet and harmless. That's why the head Stockman gave us to ride this one. It's an old Station hand horse.' I thought for a while . . . really did not want to ride the beast. As for the case, I was eight months pregnant.

Anyway, I put my left foot on the stirrup and swung the other right foot. Then I really was on the horse back, on the saddle. I rode half a mile from where I climbed on the horse before. Then the horse walked and walked . . . and Dick carrying Mervyn on his shoulder just behind me and the horse. I was all right. The aching feet and weariness were going away from my tired feeling.

Then all of a sudden I put my right foot a bit too forward by the horse face. The horse gave a jump. I found myself on the horse galloping away like a wind. The horse did not take a root, or did not buck, but raced away with me. I tried to pull the reins back, but it would not turn to stop, but madly galloped away with me. I just sat on the saddle and let the horse take me wherever it went. Still I tried and tried to put the brakes on the reins. It was of no use. I looked back to Dick, while the horse galloped like mad away in the distance. Very small, there was Dick and baby. I thought I would never see Dick and Mervyn again.

Then a very sharp turn the horse gave. It started galloping on full pace back to the fence, and halted just in front of where Dick and the baby stood. Fearfulness was in the eyes of Dick as the horse stopped. I and Dick just looked at each other with great wonder and surprise. I jumped off and laughed at him . . . although, I did not get hurt at all. It was like a great sport for me, on that special day. I never rode a horse in all my life. That was the only day. If there were others there at the time, they would have classed me to be one of the champion women riders. Never mind how fast it galloped like wind, I did not make a move to slip or fall, but just sat on the saddle and enjoyed the pace of the speed from the horse, as if I was an expert for horse racing.

Going through the fence, the horse reached over the fence to bite me. I hit the horse with the baby's napkin to stop him from reaching to bite. So Dick took the horse and rode it as far as the first windmill. Then we made our camp for the night to sleep. Beside the dam, we both gathered wood and cleared the grass to make our camp. We had a huge fire burning. It was a bit chilly too. During the night one of the toad was saying, 'Old pod, old pod.' It repeated the words over and over again. Then the little boy said, 'Hey Mummy, he's saying my old grandfather, Old Pod.' Why the child thought the toad was calling to his grandfather, because that was the name we often called my father Old Pod. It was a pet name given to him by some Stockmen at the mustering camp, during the time my father spent some of his life in the cattle job at Mornington, and that was the name he loved.

Then next day, we set off once more. This time Dick rode the horse . . . Mervyn in front of the saddle, in front of him, while in the other hand he held a small suitcase that had the baby's clothes. As he rode along, the silly beast rooted with Dick and gave few bucks. I screamed with fear to see the horse bucking with Dick with the baby. So I did not care what may happen to me. I grabbed the baby as the horse bucked. Dick passed the boy to me as the horse was bucking. I stretched my hand to grab the baby, and ran behind a small oak tree and stood there. Then he threw down the suitcase. He managed to control the horse.

So we made another start to the next Station, although the way was long and hot, but we made a slow move. We reached the Cloncurry River. The tide was high and rough. So Dick crossed over by himself, to try how strong the current was for we to cross. It was only chest deep, so we said, 'We both will make it.' Then Dick swam over with our Mervyn first, while me and the horse stood waiting on the bank. Dick crossed the boy on the other side of the bank on his way to the river. Mervyn ran down the bank to follow his father back. I screamed and yelled to Dick to go back quickly. The child was after him. Dick swam back so fast and was in time to grab the child before he reached the edge of the stream. So Dick brought him back with him. Dick pulled the horse in the river . . . put the little boy on the saddle. Dick was swimming and holding the child, while I hung on the horse tail and swam across. Though the day was hot, it was so cooling crossing the river. Some places were very rough and strong, especially near the rocks where the water flows so currently, as if to sweep anything down the stream. So we managed to get to the other side of the bank, and were able to get to the next Station for help.

Next day we made our way to Cloncurry. Dick saw us leave for home to go back to Mornington Island. As we steamed out of the Railway Station on the train, Dick waved Goodbye to me and the baby, Mervyn. It was sad to see him left at the Railway Station. Then he and the boss went back by car to Fort Constantine to carry on with his job. As the train went by, not far away, one lonely house stood. Malbon Station could be seen from the distance. That direction was where Dick had to pass to go out bush again. I felt sad to leave Dick, with the baby, and leave him alone with no other person whom he knew very well.

We arrived about eight o'clock at Kajabbi Station, passing . . . on Quamby Station, then to Dobbyn Railway Station, and then on the mailtruck for Burketown. All night we travelled, just me and the mail man . . . not a word to be said, as we went along. There were no questions and answers to be given to any of we both people, but just travelled on and on. I had a bit of rest on the way, but not a real good one, as I sat with my child, nursing him to sleep. I trusted the mailman. There would be no harm. He was shy and polite. That's why I enjoyed the trip up.

When the first morning Star appeared, we stopped at Nardoo Station. I saw why the mailman stopped. There in the dark by the side of the river, not far away from the mail road, stood four old Station workers. Two hopped on the back of the truck with a small lad. We left Nardoo Station and headed for the rest of the journey. There again, I felt a bit happy to have company on the way. We were strangers to each other, so there was no saying Hello to meet one another.

There was another quietness half the way as we travelled, until we came to Wernadinga letter box. I told the driver I would sit at the back, for much clearer view to see what the country side looked like. I sat beside the little boy, and asked who was he and the other two people. The boy said, 'My name Sydney and that's my parents, Sydney and Mona Webber.' The old man and woman were very happy to see and know I was their niece.

The next Station we passed was four or five hundred miles now, for Burketown. Few days then I got a Cargo boat, *Cora*, to take me back to Mornington Island. On the way I felt sick and vomited. The sea was rough. As for that case, there were no planes to carry people . . . only by boats. It was in the year 1950. We women and children had a hard life travelling on the sea.

It was on the second week in March I came home. Shortly afterwards, I had born to me my second son, Raymond Roughsey, the child that went through all the hardships.

He was later on a very sick child . . . he was six month old. In those times there were no Doctors or Nurses to help us for Medical treatment, only the missionary bit of help. Lucky there was a Flying Doctor came from Melbourne, to see about the Bentinck people on our island, and on his visit he looked into my child Raymond, to find out why he was sick. So all the help I got from the Doctor . . . only to feed the baby with condensed milk, five times a day and night until he was well again.

So Doctor Alram said, 'Elsie, your child's life is not at your hand. If you don't take good care of the child, he'll die, because there's only little hope for him to live. But if you look after him good and feed him well, he probably get strong and live.' Doctor Alram said Goodbye to me and said, 'May God bless you and the baby. If we don't meet and see each other again, we'll meet in Glory. Now take care of the baby, won't you Elsie.' So he left Mornington Island to go back to Melbourne.

Weeks went by. Raymond was able to get strong and big and able to get around, with full of life. So now he is a strong, healthy man. It will be a great pleasure, one day if we could see Doctor Alram again, if he is around, to thank him once more for saving my child's life. And now he is a handsome young fellow of the age of twenty-six.

Memories of an Aboriginal never be forgotten . . . where someone does help to save life and help us. No matter who, in different way . . . is our biggest pride we have towards this one for all he or she had done in the past, is one of the things we never forget. In our heart that person is so often thought of no matter how far away they may be. We highly honour people who do good for us, when we really in need of help.

Just few months after that happenings, one of the earliest friend of Dick Roughsey . . . who of course met each other on Karumba, Keith De Witts, who was the man who piloted the boats out of Karumba River. This man was Dick's best friend at the time when Dick worked as deck hand man on *Cora*, carrying cargo to the Gulf countries. Well, Keith De Witts with his girl friend, Elsie, arrived one day to Mornington Island to get married. Dick was the Groom's best man. It was lovely to see the first white couples to come to our native home to join in hands in marriage. We had a wonderful time with these two people, who are now in Weipa living . . . Mr and Mrs De Witts.

From then on, Dick worked on carrying food suply around the Gulf countries as a crew on the vessel *Cora*. He worked as a carpenter on his own mission. He was a Councillor and policeman. He was a good man on the job, had many friends, as he worked amongst his people. He did many odds and ends job, until he was called to Karumba to work with his friend, brother, Keith De Witts, and there they both worked together. Digger, Shirley our niece, Lindsay's daughter, also Edna and Angus, they all worked there. Week ends these people went out for handcraft and made boomerangs, shields, bullroarers, also painting on barks to help themselves. The girls sat under big shady trees, too, and helped to smooth the wood with bottles and knifes. Just before Christmas they all arrived home to join their families. Dick came home and saw another baby son who was choppy and sweet, and so fat with wrinkles all over his arms, legs, tummy . . . Basil.

Kevin Roughsey was born at the time when Dick was held up in Groote Island. The boat, *Cora*, could not go down the river, because about that time of the weather it was low tide, so they had no hope to get out of the river, until it was a couple of weeks later, they managed to get out and went back to Thursday Island.

Dick has never been much at home. He always kept

himself busy going out on the Mainland, working on Station mustering, fencing, breaking young colts for races, to be ridden at show time. All these jobs he did well. I remember once he worked on Lorraine Station after we got married. He worked so hard until he finally got sick of eating stale food. From the first meal, it was kept for the second meal. This went on for days and days, week after weeks. Then he left the Station with another bloke, Albert.

They footed from there, to return back to Burketown. The Sergeant at the time questioned them both why they left the Station. They gave him full details . . . how hard they worked out in the mustering camp and came back expecting to eat a good fresh meal after a hard day's work, but found they had to eat the same food that was kept from the meal before. So, Dick came home while Albert stayed in Burketown, until he had another job.

Dick then worked on his own mission, for the rest of the years, until he gave up everything. He started doing wood works, carving design on boomerangs, shields, bullroarers, spears and woomeras. Then again, as he worked at Karumba, he sold handcrafts, gave few people for presents, until he met up one day with the Ansett pilot, who was interested in some of the wood work, that hung on the wall of one of the houses at Karumba. They greeted each other with a handshake and good friendly talk and drink, and this is how Percy Trezise and Dick Roughsey promised each other how they could work and help each other. So now, since all those years, they have been working together as brothers, and put themselves in a place in Australia where they were not known to anyone, of the quiet work they both were doing for all those years. Finally Dick's painting were done and sold in cities, with the help of Percy Trezise, to find a place for an exhibition.

Before all these happenings, I can recall of the hard days when we both had to go bush and roamed the bush life, and all the huntings we had to make. Most time during our hunting, the sun was so hot . . . and hardly a food of wild fruits and other roots, also goannas, wild honey and other such food on the land, which we knew were good to eat.

Sometimes we came home so tired and hungry. Dick's other aim was to go down to the sea for fish and crabbing . . . always came home with sea food, stingray, crabs and fish. Dick was a great hunter. He never gave up in doing whatever he had to do.

For keeping up the camp with fire wood, he is the boy. His camp fire never goes out, because there is always a big log burning all the time. In those times hardly matches were bought. We really always depended on firesticks, or made fire with two sticks rubbing together to keep up the bush life fire. I really liked living out bush. You know for why? Well, there are no rules or laws of an European out there in the bush, no policeman or Councillor to order you around, to force you to do anything, but live and hunt, rest in peace and quietness, where there is no worry of all sorts . . . only to take care of yourself and learn the life and culture that belongs to the life of the wild bush life.

Both Dick and myself went through many hardship out in the bush, especially travelling through the bush with huge swag and two babies, and other things to carry, like bag of flour, sugar, tealeaf, milk, rice, frying pan, saucepan, dripping and dish. Mind you, these are put into a kerosene tin and we take in turns to carry all these things in our hand as well as our swag on our heads. I carry baby on my shoulder, the youngest one on my side with a coolamun, besides other small things like billycan of water or some cooked food in a bag, in the same hand that also holds the baby in coolamun, held by string on to my shoulder. That's how we spend most of our life, travelling from place to place out in the bush.

Most time it was hard to go bush. As we travelled, some water bed creeks and lagoon and water holes were dry. That's why we must always carry water . . . to make sure when no water is around, while we are travelling, we have water for the children. Sometimes when Dick carries a large swag on the head, he would carry Mervyn or Raymond on top of the swag and the boys would ride the top of the swag as he walks along. The boys just like it, and would just nicely sit there, as their father tramps along the hard, rough,

stony bush with his family . . . along the scorching sun.
Though it is hot, the boys would pretend they riding a
horse. They laugh and bounce on the swag, up and down
having good fun, not knowing their poor daddy's head or
neck would give him an achingness with pain. Dick would
shout, 'Don't do that. Keep still, or you'll fall.'

But he was such a good father to the children. He did
everything to hunt and help his families to live the bush life.
He did everything to live with his culture. He did what he
saw the elders of the tribes do to live, and he did them all.
That's why, when we speak and write about the bush life,
we really lived with our customs and culture.

As I sit under my new house that I'm renting for twelve
dollars a week, I look into the sky, see the clouds tell of fine
weather . . . or after rain has fallen or the gentle South East
wind is blowing. That hot day and fine sea comes, it tells of
all I've lost. Only, I can see it and feel it by these signs. It
makes me sad to know that all our wonderful ways of life
have been destroyed, and have been taken away from us.
Having most European's way of learning, acting and looking to live forward is not really the stuff we like to live for,
because all our hunting, camping and moving on from place
to place is gone.

Children going to school . . . and there are so much
worries about them to stay home all the time. Two weeks
holiday during school term are more affected, wondering
how to go bush . . . and never make it to go bush. It hurts so
much and that's how children don't understand how much
of their customs are gone. I don't think they would ever
know to live with their culture, customs and laws again. I
mean they won't ever learn to live with them, like I have
faced. I am happy to have understood my parents' way to
live, learnt all their legends, did things of how to act on their
customs and culture, and now gladly able to write a book
about the whole life of my people and all our different ways
of life, living out bush. Now I feel today's life has ruined
everything of the good old days. People of the early tribes
were healthy race . . . no bad sickness, sores, skin rashes,
colds and many other bodily harm illness, they were not

known to have. Besides, they really lived the life that belonged to them, rather than stepping forward so quickly into the European laws and forgetting the way they lived. It was good to know these elders of the tribe were strong in whatever they had to go through, lived to keep all their good ways of life.

I can remember one of those times when Dick and I were out bush, also Phil Jack. It was so dark. It had been raining during the day. The ground was so wet. We hunted for matches in our swag, found nothing dry, all got wet. So Dick and I made a small shelter for the night. Our baby was Mervyn. We did not know what to do because besides we feared there would be another heavy pour down of rain. The shelter was not good at all, so Dick crawled out of the bark and grass shelter and began to feel around for dry creeper sticks to make a fire. We both took turns to rub the stick and before long we soon made fire. We had a drink of tea and prepared for a night travel. Phil Jack took our dugout first, and was told to wait for us . . . the point by the rock on the beach. When we reached the spot the canoe was there alright, but the man was gone. He left for Dugong River, where the other campers were.

So the rest of the journey we had for ourselves through the dark cold night, with us both paddling with a child on our lap, each taking turn in nursing him. Finally we were nearing Dugong River. As we went along, it was so dark. The reefs below the sea looked white, also the sea was starry, like there were lights in the water, everywhere. So we found our way home and the lights helped to lead us the way through. The sky was dark and cloudy, no stars to be seen, but we managed to travel to the next place. Coming near, we could see many camp fires burning, and we were happy to end our long struggle of paddling. It was very cold, and South Westerly wind was blowing hard after the heavy fall of rain. We camped the night there, and left for mission village next day.

Since 1948, we had so many hardships, learning and hunting the life of the tribes, seeing and doing things of our customs and cultures of all sorts. Travelling and hunting in

177

the heat of the day was terrible. Stormy and raining times at nights and days were worse . . . hard to keep dry and not a good rest. But we happily lived in the bush . . . plenty of land and sea food to eat, although the hunting was difficult. It wasn't easy to hunt, it was very hard, but it was a pleasure to roam in the bush.

The night we had travelling together by ourselves in the dugout and met the campers at Dugong River we had a very cold night. As we had a very wet day, it was still looking as we were to have more rain, but during the night the storm cleared away. The next day it was a nice fine weather . . . still rain clouds hanging around. By the time we left Dugong River for home, we had the following day, a big strong South East wind blowing. We felt happy to get most of our wet blankets and clothes dry.

A year later we were appointed to help to take care of some of the work in the mission . . . take children on holidays for camping out. Dick was given a job to be a Councillor. I helped to keep the school children in order and get them together for meals, also took cooking job, gave help to be a teacher for a year and half. Then, having more children of my own, I left teaching and was back again on housewife, taking care of Dick and the children. At the same time, Dick went out mustering camp and really enjoyed the life amongst rounding up cattle with his other mates. When the job was finished he came home. He was a carpenter building houses, and other such jobs that had to be done in the mission.

Times went by. I was learning the European life more closely to understand how to live, also my own tribal life was more important for me to live with. I took so much interest in the life of my people. They had too much good customs and laws. They were the things I really wanted to know and learn from my people. My mother was my best friend, also my mother-in-law, Dick's mother. I spent most of my bush life with them, ran into the real life to roam and hunt with the tribe.

Dick now went mainland for better jobs on Stations, doing different things as he worked. Dick then had to go amongst strangers and seeing strange places. Coming home, back on the island . . . was always happy meeting each other, and more pleasing to be back out in the bush again. We were not much in the village homes, but always had to go bush and enjoyed the life there. It was far more better to be in the bush than staying at the mission village camp. Too much laws and rules of an European, while sticking anywhere in the mission. These laws make a poor black fellow feel miserable and tired and unhappy. You stand by for these laws, you really get yourselves into trouble.

Out bush there is no one to worry you, only the laws and customs you proudly hear, see and learn to do the right thing. If you do the wrong thing, you punish yourself by Mulgree. You forget what you are told when eating anything strange that the salt water disagrees with, you forget to wash before moving into some places you should not go with the certain smell of food . . . well, you get sick or die. These laws have been proved and were passed down to tribes. The tribal culture has been looked carefully through . . . where danger lies and the wrong is done, and where protection must be well guided to all who move around these area. If you are careless and disobey the laws, there is always a trouble in the end . . . the law of creation, Mulgree. I have seen things that happen, I know they were true. I've seen many sacred, dangerous spots. I have seen proved of how it was done, and how a witch Doctor cures a person from being ill, and death . . . also healing touch, the chanting, the brushing of special leaves, by warming on the fire and carefully pressed on the sick person, and very strangely to see, the person is well all of a sudden. Many people may not believe the fact, but it's real and very true.

Times went by. My people were fond of fishing, crabbing, oyster gathering, roots and fruits picking in the bush. On a Saturday and Sunday Dick goes out bush on his own, while I and the two children, Mervyn and Raymond, stay home, working as usual with the house work, washing, working in the garden, planting fruit trees and vegetables, while the children play around the place. As evening comes, me and my two children sit round the camp fire, hoping when Dick will arrive. Poor old fellow, so tired from the day's hunting for wood craft, comes home with a large bent boomerang, piece of wood for a shield and bullroarer. Other people will crack jokes with him and say, 'Hey, your children can't eat wood. Why don't you go for fishing?' But we never took notice of all that was said. We knew what handcraft would be needed one day.

So old Goobalathaldin worked a lot of handcraft, painted them and sold to tourists or to anyone who he met. To my people, they had no idea of handcraft . . . one day will be very important to the people. So when they saw what Dick had done, some people were interested and started going bush and searching for boomerangs, fighting stick, shields, spear heads, woomeras, baskets made of ti-tree barks and many other things.

We worked for a long period of time on our own, on wood works . . . used or mixed for painting different colours from mud for clay. It was hard to find the right thing. We went to water courses, also on the salt pans, to collect the yellow mud. We made fire and put the mud to burn. It turned red. Black, of course, we got from charcoal, mashed that fine . . . while clay was dug from earth beside the rocks or soaks. Gums were found on trees which we collected, cut in small pieces, put in tin to boil to make our glue. That's how we started for all our artifacts, also for painting on barks. It wasn't an easy task. It was very hard for all our plans and ideas, but it was something we could make for our living, just to help ourselves to keep our children going, to feed them. Dick's wages was very little to keep him and the families going, so we were able to do what we have done with our own culture, by making to sell. The tribes only made weapons for fighting and for their own use, but never had an idea to sell what they made. These were nothing they knew of.

After two years from Dick's exhibition in Cairns from bark painting and handcraft, something new and strange came to the feeling of the people here. So they too went bush and collected their stuff of handcraft to work and sell.

Very slowly things worked here. Finally, in another couple of years time, people went crazy on handcraft and sold so many stuff of wood works to the mission. Then it continued to this day. Now Mornington Island handcrafts are being moved out to other places, to people who value these things and buy them now, although it looked silly in the first place, when one man did these things and sold, and saw the beauty of handcraft and the benefit he could get from it. The people only just cannot eat bush food or sea food today. They have found a way to be happy by going bush to search out and cut handcraft and sell. Now they are getting money from handcraft. They never knew the beauty of wood.

Most of our culture, customs, laws and legends were now forgotten. It seemed the European way was much better and we were now looking the future of looking the new life what the missionaries had for us. Our languages were dying out on us, everyone spoke just english . . . customs and culture were nothing also. Legends were still passing around the camp fires at night by the old tribes . . . but since they all died, they were all lost and gone with them. There were some great singers and dancers died, because even the corroborees could no longer go on. These people died by fretting. The young men and women could not co-operate with the tribes for singing and dancing. These were the only real thing that kept up the Spirit of the tribes. Happiness was gone, many troubles took its place.

The reckless life

Forgetting the life they should have, and losing control they should have

Soon the young generation came forward and wanted their own way, and spoilt every customs, culture and laws. They thought these were just foolishness, and would not grasp them. Relationship was cut out of their life. They expected only to love and claim their own parents. But what about the real life that the tribes had . . . the true decent friendship they had for all people, that can make all people love, serve and respect each other as real tribal people, worth while living with the life of the real people who lived to show and teach all they had to pass to us? They were very, very important to look upon and continue living with.

I know that life of my people. I saw the way people lived with all goodness, kindness, helpfulness, lovingness, relationship. People were real to each other. You could not tell who was your near relation to our parents, because everyone was my uncle, auntie, cousin, brother, sister, grandparent. No one I knew was my half relation. They were all my full blooded relation, even to other families because there was that love. Relationship was firm with respectfulness. Everybody was same. No others were different to be known as an outcast. I often longed and hoped that that life may come on again to my people, that happiness we have lost, all fun and laughter may be heard and seen again. I would just think of all those past life . . . makes me sad that no one here can carry on to that life I saw, spoiled and ruined by everyone.

I often wondered why the old people from those early life, I mean the women and men parents of these young generation, why they forgot all the tribal life they lived with, why they threw or gave it away altogether. If they kept the tribal ways they would have been a better, happy people, doing everything right. Now there is more unhappy, sad, tired feeling . . . people don't know how to be happy and be friendly, with no respect or politeness.

I can truthfully say, too much laws of Europeans really scared the people . . . 'You must do this and that. Forget the old ways of your people. Do what we want you to do.' And so they did make the tribes give up everything. They are lost and have been forgotten. Now most Europeans are beginning to really understand the true life of an Aboriginal is good. It's worthy of being understood and should be always kept.

My tribes' laws were so strict. You could not fool around with any of their laws. You interfere wrongly with these tribal life, you have your punishment by threaten with weapons . . . and it is done by a fight. Sometimes you are killed in fight or seriously hurt. But that only helps to keep the law . . . runs straight and good for all to live as one good people on the island.

I have seen many things that were done by this law and customs, saw many good things and few things that were not too good to see, when trouble took place, when I lived with my people. I understood how father and mother-in-law or son-in-law . . . no one could be hurt or in trouble by these people. They looked after each other really good. A son-in-law could not see his father and mother-in-law in the face or go near his in-law's camp . . . only the son-in-law's wife, because she is the daughter to the man or the woman. The woman's husband cannot see or sit by their camp, the man or son-in-law turns his back or puts his hat down on his face, as not to see his wife's parents. This talk be 'shut eye' to his wife's father or mother. Also a woman, the man's wife, cannot talk to her husband's parents. She visits them, but she cannot speak to them or go near . . . only the man who is a child to the father and mother-in-law. These were great laws. They guided the whole family as one.

But then moving slightly, this good laws and custom were giving away with carelessness. People began to speak to each other, although they were little shy whether to speak or answer a sister or brother. Little by little, sisters and brothers wondered if it was a right thing to speak. New race of children came in numbers. Children grew up, did many things that were wrong against other children. Many fights took place. Soon the parents forgot the laws of the tribes and took up fights for their children with other families, and this is what spoiled everything.

Mr Wilson helped to keep these laws, customs and culture going. He did not bother the tribes to give it away. These laws were still in the hands of the tribes. Soon after 1951 all was gone. People were interested most now in the European laws. Things turned out with a feeling . . . let's forget the tribal laws. Others thought the white man's ways were much better, so the people started separating relations and relatives on their own accord . . . not to be near each other.

Especially when school holidays were given, each tribes scattered from each other and the life they had once. We all went to where we belonged to, and took our children to see our home where we belonged to. They had wonderful times together. Children grew up happy, spending holidays with each other . . . spent many happy times. Children were growing up, parents did not want to be together with their own relations. They were more afraid of children . . . may look at each other and, of course, trouble could arise. But why these people did such a thing as that? They should have understood and taught the laws and customs to their children . . . how they lived with it. They followed the same laws and customs. I have seen them live with that tribal life. From then everything was departing of the happy life, of time which they knew could be better, to the life they now entered to follow on.

Now, spending school terms' holiday, people don't go too far away to take children for better holidays. Small groups, about four campers, can be seen at a distance. Most people and children stay home, not enjoying the days out, hunting turtle, dugong, going fishing or crabbing, picking oysters and wandering around in the bush searching for handcrafts.

We have now, at the moment, ten old people from the early tribes, six men . . . one of course, in his latest years,

Dick's uncle. He is very old and is still alive. Three of the oldest tribal women are still alive. Their minds are fading away . . . hardly to remember from the past. After they are gone, we hope that all they gave us may carry on for the rest of our lives, to take over and always use what we have seen and learnt from them. I know it's a thing must be carried on. I feel in me, the way of their life has been one of the important true life of our land, one which most people will never understand how good the laws of a tribal Aboriginal had gifted . . . holding all they had, and were Government to their own laws and people.

But all this has been destroyed, forgotten. European laws have wiped it altogether from my people. My people rather take what the Government laws had for them. Most people thought they could not longer hold on to their own laws. They thought the tribal law was something that was just a waste of life to go on with, just because when they had the missionaries here, when meeting each other in presence of the missionary man or lady. Brother-in-laws could not speak to each other when asking or speaking to each other. They just could not speak, unless there was another person there to explain why they couldn't speak or work together, because the tribal laws had shown them to respect each other. Another times son-in-laws could not see his father and mother-in-laws. They put their hats just below their eyes, not to see. So christianity made the tribes give up all these activities. So the tribal laws had failed with all its goodness, its respects, its true relationships. Laws and customs of the tribes were no more needed, in this new life with the Europeans. They have found hardships, found selfishness, jealousy and other things to make you feel unhappy.

I have seen, met with this strange life amongst my people. Feelings of mixed life have changed into a drifting clouds . . . good and bad laws could not really settle in the hearts and minds of our people. Then for all times we had to cling to the laws of an European.

Recently, a year ago, as we sat speaking together in our villages at different meetings . . . how we could bring up the facts of activities back to our midst, so that the young people could have and understand of the past lifes of our tribes . . . one man made up his mind to try and help the school children in the teaching of our legends. So it did work out.

Children are learning to weave strings from grass on their laps, by rubbing on the lap leg with the palm of their hand. They learn to blow didgeridoo, keeping in time with clap sticks . . . but I did not see any child learn to sing with boomerang in his hand. Also, boys and girls are painting on barks. So they the only ones who are coming back to that past life. Also, corroborees are going on in school.

You can see from them that the culture is slowly working back in our midst. I am just wondering if our laws and customs will be able to come back again from the grown ups. To me it is very hard. They, the people, have stepped too forward to try and look back to the tribal life. Now let's hope the best. It may be done all over again if the people and children are interested. I'd love to see it all happen again. It will make us feel much happier.

The children are getting better Education in school. Fifteen year old children are having a secondary school here now, learning all kinds of trade, ready for different jobs they may take up in future. So I think these children will face two world, old and new, because they are taking up corroborees, and other back ground and also they are learning the European life which we understand it's good for them. Children of today are very lucky. They live with their parents, really under their parents' control. They have all the love and care. They enjoyed recently going out to Mainland to join other children for sports, and seeing some of the activities of the outside life. Others again have been given jobs on Cattle Stations, and it wasn't long before they left the Station and enjoyed life in Mount Isa, before coming home. There you can see many good things are on this mission. Things seem so pleasant. The life is good. Many good things are here to make everyone happy.

I did not have a good schooling. In fact I liked school very much, although I was not too brilliant in lessons. Anyway, I learnt to read and write and that was most important to me.

Other lessons were Okay. I was good at competitions and letter writing, reading tables. Arithmetic often was very hard for me . . . but to get them right, I counted with my fingers and toes, when adding and taking away. But I always got my credit mark, ticket up right.

But now I have a decent understanding. The knowledge of sense of mind I have today I feel so proud of, because what I have seen, learnt and done, as I have been growing up . . . took a big interest, noticed everything. That's why I am able to write a book of my life, the life I went through side by side with my people. It takes a long time before you can understand certain thing. Each day you see it happening. You begin to realize it's good to know how to take it up yourself and you find yourself in the world mixed with many good activities. Many faulty activities are mingled in our lives too.

When the tribal laws were highly claimed and watched, a man could not leave his wife or belt her around. It was against the tribal laws. A grandfather and cousins, uncle and aunties, brother and sister-in-laws know it cannot be treated in this matter. So the man is punished by his relation. A fight takes place. This treatment is only to show him he must take care of his wife and don't hurt her. A man who has children, he is really carefully watched. If he runs away from his wife and children . . . the whole families, relations and countrymen belong to the wife, . . . the man is really in for it, because the children are looked on to have their father to hunt, love and protect and grow up his children always.

Love of children was very important to the tribes. You could not hurt children in any way. The children belonged to all people to take care of. Mother, if she left her man, it was not easy for her to leave. She would be speared or put eight feet below, not for the man's sake, but for the child she ran off and left without a mother's care. That even applied with a man too. You could not spoil any marriages of the tribes.

A marriage way of an European wedding was nice to have, but if the vows of the law of marriage are not carried out properly and are wrecked with human foolishness, in

187

the midst of the tribal circle in camps it is aroused by the relations from both side. Something goes wrong. There is a trouble . . . punishment for either of them, which is the one who did not live rightly, is in a big mess of trouble, and fight takes place.

The tribes looked after all this. They rather man and woman to love each other and not spoil any of these marriage life with carelessness or any trouble . . . to go after another man or woman, go chasing. They taught every young people to live in a friendly way and look after each other. Especially you dare to illtreat a child with neglectfulness, you were in for it. Both side of the families and relations of the man or woman were badly bashed with nulla nulla and boomerang, and that kept them both to be careful . . . to love and take care of their children and to be true to each other, the way the marriage meant to be used.

I've seen many terrible scenes in changes of life what the tribes had done, and I learnt so much with my own eye witness . . . how splendid the tribes kept these laws with great strength of firmness and justices.

Tribal marriages were well secured in the eyes and ideas of the tribes. You could not muck around with a life of two people who had joined as one in the eyes of the tribes. They taught their young and old people how to love one another and to live a happy life. Their laws were strictly watched and protected by the tribes.

The tribes have all died, the laws have been forgotten. Young people are living with each other, not living decently with cleanliness, not bothering to marry in the right way to have love and happiness, also peace and joy. Although, many fights have taken place between children, parents and relation, for the life they expected to win to live with. For short periods of time things of this life went on, until children won the life they'd sooner carry out on against the will of their parents. The young people go on living the way they wish to live, but they are not really safe to protect each other with love and care, to guide against different life they may happen to strike upon one day. They are very sad people. Their real concern is not meant really for each other, but they like the life. Also they fear the seeing . . . moving around as husbands and wifes, and can't be happy about it. They are very quiet and shameful of living with each other. Most of their living with one another is because they have babies to each other.

The young people were looking back from the past, as was told . . . they could be like their father or grandfather who lived and had several wives in their camp. So in the young lad . . . feelings he would like to take up like a tribal relations, to have a woman he can claim too. For this instant a girl would gladly take this step, as no one speaks, whether it's wrong or not. So they live in content and happiness. Most times, things go wrong. The girl is knocked and bashed around. Off she goes, back to her parents, to live for a brief while until the trouble is over. The girl and boy long to be together again, also fights break out from the two sides of the boy's and girl's families and relatives. Although it looks so tough when something goes wrong, after the terrible times they go through, the same life begins all over again.

I often wonder whether the parents are doing wrong with these young people's lives. Did they ever have common sense about this? Does it make the parents feel ashamed of being guilty, along with their children, to live in this manner . . . whether the parents have failed to teach their children to live a true, wonderful, clean life by going to the minister for better support of their marriage? If that was closely guarded by the parents, young people would be far happier, to live as their parents have gone through. But as children grow up, they often say, 'I'm my own boss. I am old enough to take care of myself. I can manage to live to own a marriage life.' But the young people really don't understand they are facing a tough world to place themselves for all the activities of trying to live as man and woman should.

To young people, it's really a strain to become father and mother, to take the real care when having children. They are still childish. They haven't really the life to become mums and dads. It is all sports and pleasure. Then that

189

tiredness, careless neglectfulness is narrowing their life to become useless. All bounds back to grandparents. The children are now placed on their shoulders for care, comfort, health and happiness.

These laws of the tribes have failed. Brothers really don't respect their womanly sisters now. Son-in-law or daughter-in-law is careless about their mother or father-in-laws. Husbands leave their wifes. Wifes leave husbands, all for the love of another lover.

Initiated man is not looked upon as young lurugu. No one has respect on them, which is one of the greatest law of our tribes. People who live in the same land or country with them . . . that very important law has been played too much in our land with no respect amongst the people here. There are dreadful laws of the tribes for punishment against those lurugu . . . that if the man of the tribes still had their own law strictly kept and watched and obeyed. To these young men, it's so sad to think they were not regarded as one of the men who went through the law. They are now not regarded as a big man to their people, but are treated as a child went through the law, unnoticed from the tribes who took part in the ceremony . . . should always protect and take great care of these boys. Everyone should cling to the law and hold it with guidance, interest, love, honour and pride. This is the law of the tribes.

It was not a white man law who gave it to the tribes, but the tribes sought the way . . . how to deal with men to become great men to their own people, and how a man can be healthy and become great leaders to lead this people. If he is worthy to be put in the law of the tribe and live the right way and carry out all its laws, customs and culture, he then can be chosen as one of the elder of the tribe.

Not all men have gone through the law . . . only few, because most of the men weren't allowed by the eldest brother, cousin or uncle, fathers and mothers, when secret gossips have been talked by the tribes. Besides the boy's relation, there was disagreement of no. There was a fight at the very moment with weapons of spears, nulla nulla and boomerangs, and that stopped the initiation being carried out. This meant life and death, and other tribes often went against for the young lad not to enter the law. They never trusted. Probably some have died going through the law, and others became very sick . . . that's if the cutting of the foreskin was not done rightly. And if there was wrong had been done, also a fight would take its place right on the spot. There's many laws, if you want to know of the tribes. Many cannot be passed, or given to anyone who are not of the tribe.

I myself since I got married . . . I have joined in the ceremony when I was so young. I found myself with doubts and fear whether I would be able to do exactly as the tribes would do, although there were many other women who knew the life, and could not join the initiation ceremony. I wondered why I was chosen, as the sister only can dance and do the rest of the activities, with seven of the oldest women of the tribe and three other middle age women.

Recently I also took part in another one of the same ceremony, and from this latest one, which really upsetted me, I saw the failure of the law . . . really did not work out well as the first one many years ago. It took firm step to its law. The only way I saw of this latest ceremony . . . on Sunday morning, show was quite an amazing swiftness . . . activities, that all were over, by then. But their camping away from wife and families was one of the law they had broken . . . and made the initiated lads come back to their family, which of course should not happen. So that's not keeping the law, as it should be. That's why the boys are not regarded by all who should have respect on them.

Now back on the subject of young people . . . I hardly can believe whether two young couples really love each other. All I can see . . . it's only relationship for each other. Although, having babies means that they really love one another, or happy to have a baby, real to become father and mother with understanding. They respond to each other to live real man and woman, to act on that real life, to cling to each other as true two people should be. This is all a play life, it seems, until they can face up to the christian marriage, where it means a big difference. The love really binds up firmly and then they really know they both really belong to each other forever, where only death parts if they have to really care, love and cherish each other with the true love, as husband and wife. People who search the true life of man and woman can see where neglectfulness can creep in and spoil most love affair. You can see most living only meant for sex, and not the true love to help each other to begin the life to carry on for a better life, where you can be happy with future to live and search the world's life with great success . . . land, home and families.

I have seen life that has been wrecked for ages, until the true life has torn apart from one body to another male body. This is not the case of an Aboriginal life. Your punishment is death, because everybody else sees the way the children are treated . . . not with their own fathers or mothers. Father has run off. Also mother has gone the same way. Children are lost and unwanted. Others again, father died . . . mother has no one to take care of her, only her own children.

If the case they have grown up, the grown up son or daughter takes a responsibility to their widow mother. But if this happens, the relatives and all relations find a person who can claim the widow and the children. He must be a great and good hunter, also a protection. So when they have all agreed, the uncle and auntie, grandparents give the man to that woman, so the children may have a father to really care for and love the families. Although, most cases I have seen it took so long for the children to come to like their new father. A child would be afraid to call the man Father, also Uncle, because the child would rather have his mother not with the man. Sometimes if they are only children who are small under age, then perhaps this age would seem right to have a father, also a mother. That can work out well if the bigger sister or brother understands about his mother's feeling to be happy to have a man to take care of.

Well, the grown up ones would tell the small ones not to call the man Father, whenever he or her is speaking to the father, because inside of a children's feeling he thinks of his real father, and not this other man who the eldest of the tribes, relations and country men have chosen. These people look it in a different way for all the needs of widow and children . . . need help so they won't need to worry any more to look after the children, but let the children feel they have a father and mother, always to be responsible for their daily living at all times.

I know it's very hard for a woman to be on her own with a number of children. Children do make you sad when they have no mother or father. It seems rather pleasant when a child has their best friend, a mother. But when in times of trouble, a mother or a widow . . . you really can see where she needs help and mercy, love and care and comfort, because this same woman whose husband has died or left her, she is not noticed by the children's father's relation or friends. Whenever there is that time of trouble, no one looks on that troubled widowed mother, for these reason, to help her understand that she has some people to pity her when she is in need to be protected. That's why I have shared some help in these need to people like these ones. I felt the same pain, if I was one of them.

If that happened to me and my children I know I would seek those same thoughts and feelings . . . where I'll get that love from somebody, who will help me in distress when I'm in trouble? I know I would be really lost and all that I would do is just sit and cry and think of me and my children with no other person to regard us as family to someone as relatives.

It's terrible when you can feel it as I am doing at this moment, writing things and feelings of a widow or father and motherless children. I feel my heart has been pierced with a sharp pain, like knife has gone through my heart for that love from not having anyone to love me, also to care for my children. Some times dreadful things happen to children who have no parents to care for . . . either Dad or Mum has died. That's why when I was speaking of children without fathers . . . meant so much to my people. Woman always needed a man to care for the families. Things like these happenings are in our midsts. It's a hurtfulness. It causes pain and suffering, for love and care.

I am an orphan, both my parents died. I miss them both because I dearly loved them both. Looking many children with both parents alive, they feel safe and happy. We, who have no parents . . . is much hard for us to live like children, because there is no father or mother to watch and care and love us. But when we are older we live as grown ups, live humbly, keep away from troubles and try to live better as we go along, until we get married and we are safe and happy. We have a man to be our husband, to take all the responsibility to love, help guide us. We are no more unhappy children, but pride with love and comfort, to know we have someone as a husband to share the world's life. We are happy and there is not much worry to be unhappy.

The world is full of lovely things to look and taste, and there are so many no good things to see and live along with. But from all these views, you can carefully choose out which are the decent ones to take hold of. Everybody must need to understand to learn more carefully of the deeds of being sensible grown up people . . . learn to do the right things . . . how to help the younger ones, who did not have much of the teaching. Foolish things and careless things children pick up so fast, and act on. Loving, honest, beautiful ways are never noticed much, and these things are wasted and unnoticed to a human life to create a real people.

I know an Aboriginal person has wonderful talent. Why they don't use them to become strong and healthy, to become one of our future greatest learner as hunters, law keeper, protector, great dancer and a teacher . . . for many things we are aiming for, tribal and European activities? The only thing we must understand . . . take great interest and aim to force ourselves . . . how we should live in this island of our own with all sorts of good life. These things are not in our ways here. But it concerns people in other places who have these problems of needs, the love and care towards them . . . who find the situation so discomfort in all the struggles, where others who will never know the need of these people . . . how they live. Very little help they can get from their own people, and homes who they were brought up from.

194

The world is so huge and is surrounded by many pleasures of all sorts of happiness. You are facing the life of what you rather choose for yourself, and in all the good side of things you are receiving with fairness, you are forgetting the others who are poor, unwanted, worried, sad and helpless people, who are not able to speak out for themselves to let the others know of all the need of love, care, happiness and help, they need for them and their families. They are too shy to speak to anyone who may live by their side, and not able to speak, unless they are people who may understand the problems by their quiet life, and maybe hardly seen at all, rather the ones who are really enjoying themselves.

We people from my country, whenever we see anyone in trouble, certain thing has worried them, we go and have a nice talk to them, and then find out why they are quiet or why they are sad, or what's upsetting them. Then, when it has been told, we can help each other. Perhaps the person is hungry, there is no food . . . or perhaps wants to go somewhere and doesn't know where to go, how to get lift or help, or worrying over children who've done wrong and what may happen to the child, or the child is sick, or the passing of death by a loved one. You find people and make them happy.

As I have grown older, I've studied the ways of people, and thought so much of different problems . . . what the world has for different kinds of people each days of their lives. They are too much of careless of love towards each other.

Death custom that has been passed through all ages

I am talking about in writing, but that's just to explain what our customs are all about. They're not just the word 'custom', but it has one of the richest meaning for respect, and be one in the family as a relation. The other thing is also when a European has a tribal name given to him or her by the tribes, you are also in the line of being one of the tribal relation. You don't get your tribal name for fun, or because one of the tribes gives you. You must realise no matter where you are or what family you belong to in your own white race, you still belong to the tribes also.

Not all get tribal names. It's only few who deserve the tribal name, who we tribes think he or her deserves the name, and who shows interest, help and love, and who is friendly. One thing you must understand, you can be friendly, but you cannot receive a tribal name unless the people of the tribes agree whether or not to. It all depends on the way you treat with love and interest towards a black race.

If you find a good friend and later on you become one of them, and he agrees to call you Nephew or Niece, Brother or Sister, or Son or Daughter, you then can be known from an Aboriginal. You are relation to the one who you first were so good and friendly to. Then the rest of the relatives claim you, just for that one black man and woman who claimed you as a friend. I know many white people have someone to call them friend. Some also have a kinship with us. But really, I often thought if the whites really know the love that a black fellow has for them. To me, I think they really don't understand our way. They think we just call them this and that, but really have no idea that my people want to love you as their own.

One thing I have been looking so closely into is this . . .

that whites are afraid to claim us back, because of their colour. Colour makes no difference. The feeling of mankind is within a black person feeling. It's too much of it really to explain to you all . . . heart and the stomach.

There are many meanness and selfishness where someone can get hurt and be murdered, where there is no love at all. Greed and hate is another thing could be done by killing. If where love and happiness is in the hearts and minds of people, nothing like these will happen. It makes people feel awful about such dreadful happenings that often take place. Most time I often wonder why such people like them do the things that are not right, whether they had really not the right care from parents for the start at homes, or could it be they had a heart with no feelings of love?

One thing they often forget before going to action . . . feeling if it should be done to them by someone . . . Wouldn't like this happen to me. Why I must have dreadful things done to someone else like this? Why my hatred feeling drives me madly into all this, to be unfair with the other person to live?

If all this can always be pointed out first before any action takes place, I'm sure the world could have much happy, decent, honest, friendly, loveable people to live with in our midst at all times.

Accident and sickness is far more different to look into, for the passing of death of loved ones, where you may pass through today with sadness and forgetting, has a new life tomorrow. You cannot always hang on to a feelings of being unhappy. Memories are always there but most times you laugh about the happy times you had with your loved ones . . . and that's how we should ever feel their presence by our side, by their memories.

In the early days of the tribes a man who kills another person, either man or woman, he is killed. Also if his or her relations come into taking up for the murder, they too are killed. These lives are destroyed during a big fight, only not done for other reason of just killing a man, but perhaps a mistake done by another bloke at the time of fight. If there is a person which they did not like, gossip is quietly spread

197

how they can attack their enemy. When we have a fight we kill him, but at the same time, when he is killed, the enemies say, 'I did not mean to spear or hit him with nulla nulla or boomerang. It's a mistake. I meant to hit the other one.'

But as I grew up I did not hear or see anybody was killed, as far as I have grown up. Nothing like that ever happens to the people. I know they get hurt, but never really killed in action during the fight. That would be done many, many years ago, when strange people came to their midst from Mainland, to their country. But I am sure my people were people who always liked to live by themselves without trouble . . . only when they could smell that trouble was around at their camps.

When smell of trouble is near at hand, the tribes can smell or feel something is wrong, that the smell of death is also near. No matter where the people are, that feeling of sadness creeps into their body, tells them somewhere something is happening. So they sit round their camp fires waiting to prove what may shortly happen. Sometimes a death has taken place. Often a birth of a child is born, or someone got very sick. Sometimes a fight has taken place and somebody got hurt. Often many things happen in different way, that always warn in a feeling that relations and relatives are in trouble. Most times good news are passed by a messenger from far distances. Often bad news comes and death may be heard, or news of tribal fight will come from the other side of the camp, against the other folks in another camp.

When someone dies, parents and relatives of the dead mourn and weep together with friends. After the burial, or funeral, the people have a great crowd to meet together, to meet the ones whose loved one has died. So when the parents come before the uncles and aunties and grand-parents, they act in throwing boomerangs at the mourners for losing the child, or the husband or wife, whatever it may be. So on the other side . . . have to stand and cry until the last man has thrown a boomerang. Always on the other side where the mourners are, they must be on the alert to keep the boomerang off from them. So they all, on both sides, have weapons to use and for protection. Then all run and grab each other and sit down in large group and cry for each other.

The old tribes, the men cut themselves with the back of the boomerang on their heads until it bleeds. The women also cut themselves with knifes on the head, until blood runs out. Tomahawk is also used on the head, or chest or any part of their body. I've seen broken bottles . . . have been broken in many small pieces. These broken bottles are used by the women of the tribes cutting themselves all over their laps and legs, stomach and arms, to show all the love they had for that death.

After the square up for the dead, they have a great feast, eating and drinking all together to share with everyone. So they sit and yarn and when everything has passed they sing corroborees and have dance. Also, vows are passed from every lips of men and women, that they will help to take care of the parents and relatives of the dead one, help to provide for their needs always. I've seen this important customs of my people, how they share love and sorrow alike to each other when death takes place.

Also, yamma sticks are painted when a person dies. They stand these yamma sticks at their graves. It means so much to the person . . . ones he used in his life time. Also, a bailer shell is taken to the grave, lay with water so he or she may drink the water, and don't go too far to the people's camps to search for water, because they believe when the water is there, the Spirit doesn't move around but just stays there. So each day the loved ones take water and put it in the shell, until the dead is satisfied and remains in the one place, and forgets about everything in the world. If you don't place water at the grave yard for them, they believe the Spirit comes and visits and haunts you.

Whoever dies, they do not belong to their own family, but they belong to everyone. Father of the child is never to be mentioned by name. Father is called, without son and no daughter, gumbingurrida. Mother is called ngamagurrida . . . no son, no daughter. Brother, no father, is called gunthagurrida. Daughter is also called gunthagurrida. Son and daughter, no mother, are called ngamagurrida. Also

199

uncle to a dead girl's mother's sister's daughter is called gardugurrida (niece). Auntie is also called the same as the child's father because she is the father's sister. Brother and sister of the mother is called the same way as the mother.

To the others of the tribe the dead is spoken of as Yalbudd, where a certain creature unknown, or is known, is called. Well, the simple way I can pronounce . . . a snake, rat or bird. These are also spoken as Yalbudd. So the tribes always use Yalbudd as for an older person who died.

Grandfathers and grandmothers of each sides of grandchildren from the father or mother are called gangugurrida, for grandfather's dead grandchildren's sake. Grandmother is called bubbigurrida for losing her daughter's child, either a girl or boy. We call the grandmother bubbigurrida . . . no grandchildren. To a brother, maybe eldest brother is called for his small brother's sake, is called gungugurrida . . . no small brother. For small brother, to a big brother is called thabugurrida. Big sister died of a small sister is called yagoogurrida. Big sister is called goonoogurrida. Goonoogurrida means small sister has no big sister. Your uncle is called jumbagurrida . . . means no niece or nephew. Auntie is called marrkagurrida. Gandagurrida is a person with no husband. Yugudbagurrida is a man who has no wife . . . who died.

So that's how everybody showed love and respect to everybody's loved ones who died and who are left to be honoured by the tribal folks. Sometimes without first thinking of speaking to these people who should be respected by these above customs, you call them by their english name. There's always a trouble. You not supposed to call these people by their names at anytime, until the dead is really forgotten by families and relatives. Everybody shares the loss of the dead, no matter who they are. Even everybody puts hands to take care of the ones who are the families still with us. People share with whatever food stuff they have, visit their camps to comfort them, also to show their love to these people.

These customs went on each at a time when some one died. These were part of the law as also a strict customs. The tribes have done so much good to their people, to show how love can be shown. With that love you must care for those who need that comfort . . . love and share to those who cannot get from those who have gone and died. My people were very careful about people who needed love and care, especially to them at the time when hunger, longing and loss of parents and other families and relatives. You could not hurt each other by nasty way, by speech or action, or even walk past by without speaking to the ones to make them happy. If, when passing by certain camp of families who recently lost their loved ones, you take no notice of the sad families, the tribes look the passers by who just went by without thinking of these unhappy ones . . . the old folks say, 'You don't care, you too flash. You just walk pass, because it's not your people or countrymen.' You either got to go back and visit these people . . . if you don't bother to go back, you fall in a trouble that teaches you lesson . . . don't be unkind towards others who are sad and lonely. Before you know where you are, you in a tribal fight.

All laws and customs of the tribes were carefully watched. All show offs, unkindness, no love, no care, no respect were so strictly watched. The tribes were highly proud of their own ways of life before the white man came. Most people think my people were taught by a white man or missionaries the way . . . when you might think how. When I write about my people everything was their own life, the way they looked upon one and all to be equal . . . no one better than the other. Everybody had to live the way how the tribes figured it for all to live. It's all right a white man and woman brought love and care, things from the bible to teach people, but these things came too late to my people. They already lived with their own life, their own laws and customs. Although white man came to teach to write and read in their way, but still my people already wrote letters and spoke to each other by message stick. They, the tribes, had schools out bush . . they did and showed and taught by the elders of the tribes. They also had different games that everyone joined in. Lots of laughs and fun they enjoyed

201

My one and only daughter Eleanor.

202

Legends of our country are true. Where legends have been seen and told of the happenings, how certain creation was done by certain man or creatures . . . are true, and you can still see what was left of it. Today all this is a warning . . . you must not touch or don't disobey. You must learn the good things to obey, to protect others if they are careless. You must tell and show them where danger lies, learn to sing songs, so whenever a person falls sick, has black outs or takes fits, you can help others again to become well and get better. There is also another of its sort. You sing a love song if you want to be in love and get married. Shortly afterwards, it does work. I have proved all this. I've seen them and heard the songs and seen how things did work, and for sure they are true. So the tribes had so much wonderful and interested world's talent that they had to help each other for the welfare, for health, strength and happiness for their own people.

One, who they did not know of Him as God, even by their own way of looking upward to help, give and answer for their need, was a Spirit of someone who they knew could be perhaps one of them who died, and could give them all they want. But there was another of the kind they called upon. To them, there was this other person who was greater. But the dead ones were always who they really depended on after death. But God has given us such interesting life . . . its laws, customs, culture and legends. Dark man had his ten commandments long before a white man came with his gospel and bible. They believed of one Spirit, but they knew not of His name as God. But still in all, they knew that same person was there, above their life. He was there. He was the One whom my people knew of, for all their life, help and protection. Only the bible came and they

203

knew . . . yes, He is the One, whom my people had faith on. So the tribes knew Him a mighty long time before the gospel came to them.

We also have heard that there were many people of the past, some of whom lived here long before our grandparents were born . . . were great, tall men and women, and from these my father and mother would not know their great, great parents, only the one great would be their father and mother's parents and great parents. Then from there, they would and will never know the second grandparents. That's only far their minds and their relations can go.

But only three years ago up at the top end of the island, some huge bones about six feet in height or more . . . bones after bones have been found. The heads were so huge, thigh bone legs were so long that it still covers the tallest man here. So those people were great men of that time. South East wind blew so much earth sands away from the grave holes, and that's how these bones were found. It amazed the ones who found the bones, to see huge long bones of a man. So these were the first people of whom our parents did not know of . . . could have been their great, great grandparents. Only their bones have been recently discovered.

From them could have been descendants who came after Marnbill and Gin Gin, and probably they were the ones who passed the legends of their time, and lived and saw the travels and work on the island of these first settlers of the first man. From them could have been the great, great grandparents of my parents, because only their memories could look back to two of the families of whom they knew of . . . my father's father's father, the same as my mother's mother's mother. That's all. From then on my parents would not have known of the rest of the families . . . who they were or who they should have known. So the early tribes died long before they saw their great, great grandchildren. So they, the poor souls, could not tell where they first came to this island, where they could be one of the tribes who saw and knew of the travels of our early men and women . . . Marnbill, his wife Gin Gin and her Uncle Dewaliwall.

Anyway, we have heard the legends so we know they could be our descendants for start. What strikes me more . . . when the legend first reminded some of the folks of the early people from the Mainland. As they travelled, they were only strangers travelling from place to place. No one knew of them until they came to Goonanamanda, a tribal name which means . . . here on Mornington Island. So any people believe they have created all things, as the story tells us all here.

So way back, in those thousands of years back, we know of how God Almighty created all things that move and creep upon the earth, and how he visited Adam and Eve every cool evenings and walked and talked with them. And Eve did wrong. Both of them were driven out of the garden, and were placed in another world again. Now God was left alone in another or the same place or elsewhere, not too far away from the garden of Eden. So I suppose God is still there, and there He waits for all who love and serve Him in this world. So the Sun that shines all day shining brightly is the flaming sword which turned every way of the tree of life. Where Adam and Eve lived, He placed them at the East of the garden of Eden Cherubims. So no one can tell or say, could God be in Heaven beyond the blue sky? So what I think . . . it's somewhere on this great vast of the earth, far East of the garden of Eden Cherubim, only what blocks us from God is unseen, unknown of this world . . . is the flaming sword that cuts us out of Him.

So strange people travel and wander all over the place. Half of the time you cannot find the real truth of their life, who they are and where they really came from. Could be God the Spirit who moves around and helps mankind to create the life of all creation. So the tribal man in his darken points of view can look the way he thinks of all, that God can help a black man to understand Him.

In a rather different view of point, white man can look in His way of all creation by writing books called bible, that has been passed from man to man to keep up the things which once had been seen and told by people who lived in those thousand and thousands of years. So if anyone wants us to believe that the bible says, and has and can teach us today, why doesn't any one or some one believe we tribes . . . of all we lived with and what has been done, and how we look and believe how things have happened and were done in the past, where a tribe has known and understood of certain creation . . . has formed before their eyes, how legends after legends have been handed down from fathers to sons, mothers to daughters?

My tribes never did write books, because they never could understand any of the kind, but only sit in circles around about the bush or camps and yarn about which is a right way to keep all their laws to be carried out, and how to be kept . . . same with customs, legends and cultures. But a white man keeps all their past life of their heroes . . . are kept in books to make a history of the adventures of great men of the past, scenes of the past and the last words that he spoke.

But my point of view is to look both people who have been placed in the world. One has much greater knowledge of doing different things by writing, reading and explaining, than for the other one, who lives wild and free in the bush, who has no Education comparing to the other bloke. But they, both race, have the same life to live to find differences in the way they live, look and use for everyday life. So both of the race can be ignorant against the laws and customs which on both sides . . . cannot know or see. But still, each sides of both people should see very closely and carefully at each other, and give each other a chance to get around, sit, hear and all to obey one another's laws, customs . . . how to see it, how to use it, then put it together and work together.

All our males and females and children will have to learn two kinds of laws and customs, abiding in both. Make one. You find that Australia and other continents will be a happy people, and our friendship towards our kinship would and can be a successful life to live with. Then we can be one big families, as sisters and brothers, father and mother, uncles and auntie and all in-laws . . . can be a lovely race of people, everyone understanding each other very well, especially where only love and interest can be made. I know everyone needs each other's help and understanding. We never can do anything without one another's love, help, guidance, understanding, advices, controlling. We cannot do it by ourselves as one or two, but by many people, as all in one. Bad things can become good, good can become bad, but to put one of these out of our lives, we can be wonderful, uniting together with love, friendship and happiness. You find it could be a better world to live.

Before Dick took up the job painting, having exhibitions, travelling everywhere, working up at Laura, searching primitive cave painting in rocks and shelters, being the first Australian Aboriginal Arts Board Chairman of Council of Arts, he was a great leader of our Church. He was one of our elders. He was ordained by the minister Rev. Douglas Belcher. He stood at times on the pulpit and preached to his people. Sometimes in the past, and recently, I have stood up in Church, air open meetings, and preached to my people, about God's love.

So we do not only do things of our tribal ways. Also we do what the Europeans have given us and showed us to do, and also have taught us. You only can be a teacher and preacher if you are not afraid to serve and love God and able to do, willing the things the world can allow you to do. For these things you allow God's power to move you with the strength He has given you. And you can gladly obey to do His will. I know it's a sure thing, because the bible tells us all power is given to us on earth and in heaven.

As I have learnt and found out of human likeness of life, some people have that feeling of longingness of some thing to hold on to . . . 'I want this. How can I get hold of it? Is it fair for me to do it against another person who would not want to be hurt in a serious way? Will I hurt him or her by killing, stealing, teasing, hating by selfishness?'

There is that power of self controlling yourself before you are able to do them. You may answer these questions, before anything can be forced to happen . . . 'How I like this to happen to me? I would not like this happen to me. I hate to be hurt or killed, steal, tell lies, be selfish. I rather toss all this aside.' You find there is no need to, but live with your families, how the way God has planned it all for us to do so.

I can truthfully say, as I write I think so much of tribal laws and customs. They are really the life I rather grab hold on to . . . because you know why? Where there is punishment there is love. But the laws of a European are fearing. You are punished where there is no love. Faults and lies are taken up to be the truth. But still it's unworthy to be swallowed up for penalty. You must always be sure . . . never do the wrong things, unless you are an eye witness. Bodily harm and killing, stealing . . . when that happens it is fair to strike upon the ones who did that. All my desire is what I am trying to press forward, is the life we are circled with, right on my very own home. It impresses me very much the way so many things are happening here.

For instance I do a thing, fight my people. I get hurt. I get cuts and bruises and bleeding. I get punished just as actually as the other person who I did not hurt. The other person who cruelly hurt me has a very light fine. But there you can see I've been bashed and bruised and chopped. I receive punishment just as much as the other person, although I am suffering with bodily harm. As for the case, the other bloke is friend or relation to the one who has taken up laws into his name. There you see the unfairness. When can we meet up with someone who can judge rightly where there is fairness?

If I was in their place working with the law, I'd do the right thing . . . one to be punished because he already did bodily harm. If he tells lies, that's too bad. He puts double on the one already was harmed. So the other fellow gets away with all. His fine is light, also he is happy about it. But the most importantness of all, you forget the One with seeing eyes is watching and hearing to all the lies. But He is there, waiting for the limited time when He will allow punishment to revenge. Earthly laws don't tell us that, the bible tells us that. I don't say that because I am a good christian, but I believe what I read or hear, teach and learn myself reading from the book. Really my feeling lies towards others, who feel miserable or being blamed for the other crook . . . humble ones in the families, often choked down with harsh words. Finally the crook wins with lies. He bears it no more, so no matter how hard the other bloke can speak for himself, he is no good, because he is just a member of the public.

Uniforms within the law is where they can hide and be unfair with justices. If the law wants everybody to like those who have the protection for the need of their people as whole, you do the right thing. You and your law will be loved by all who look upon you as their man or woman. Another case is . . . when a trouble is on, you make friends. It is already forgiven and forgotten. Police visit comes over from Burketown. A month after, everything is Okay. The lawmen keep what has happened before their visit over certain trouble, in their note books and hold it there for the European police to read, and then all from the past are undone again, to refresh the whole thing to become new as the day it happened.

Well to all this, a black man doesn't like to be reminded over troubles again. Because he was taught by a tribal man . . . at the very moment you had your quarrel and fight . . .

no more, you must be careful. Next time don't do it or someone else of the tribes will fight you the next time. So that what I've learnt . . . forget and forgive, no more trouble.

But concerning this other method . . . Sergeant comes over, looks up troubles, warns the people, then Councillors make the decision and fine people or send them to another place to be watched and for their good behaviour. Well, that's alright in doing things like that, but couldn't they fix the trouble once and for all while it's fresh, and punish from the day or the moment it happened? Because keeping or wrapping up trouble in a bundle, for later month, gets people worried. Then all dislike and hate starts all over again. Best everyone keeps quiet with anger boiling until the Sergeant's visit turns up, then speak to him all over again. But why bother him? Can the law manage themselves? Small things should not hurt anyone to fix up.

Alright, we don't mind any European police can come to attend to very badly bodily harm case, because we know for sure that's where they step in for protection and where punishment is to be given to anyone. But black people like having their quarrels and fights. We like to forgive and forget it at the same time, because most times we are not really serious. We like to forget and become friends again.

If you drop the whole thing you are safe, and you are one in the family again. But there it is. These things got to be understood through Aboriginal tribal laws, and feeling against the law of Government.

If we carefully understand each other's feelings we could be right and helpful to each other, as the days and years come and go by. It's not the meaning we are trying to get away from, being treated for the wrong we have done, but we ourselves as black always like to forget and be friends at the few moments when things go wrong.

Sure we understand when doing wrong . . . is fair to punish, but always be sure it's the right one, not the other person who did not expect the trouble. Everyone must realize, the fault of one is not the other poor fellow. We must always speak the truth after doing a wrong. Don't throw it bounding back at the other one, because we must place him also to say up truth for his right. Bad habit with lies is terrible, because when we do wrong, there is One who is mightier than us, sees all the happenings and lies, and He knows who are choked down by laws of unfairness.

As I live with my people here I hardly can feel myself to be happy to see how my people live towards one another. It's sad to know people don't understand at all . . . and where no understanding is in our midst, there is always a mistake with trouble, or this ungood feeling towards another who tries hard to give small portion the meaning of how to get about to live, to do things rightly, and more to understand right from wrong. Most people prove themselves the European ways . . . act and laws are good, but when it comes to the point where the law strikes upon anyone, they find it difficult to go along with, to manage with the law. It's a bit on the bitter side of things, where the law deals tough, because there you can see two sides of people . . . really don't know each other's lifes and ways. They don't know each other's feelings, feelings of white and black. They count much differences.

But if a white man or woman wants to really know the truth of each race, the best place is to visit, or holidaying, or camping, or being one of each other blood relation. That's the most interesting sight you can believe . . . the truth of yourselves where two people meet to understand each other. Then our feelings, helping love of friendship will go along side by side in knowing to understand the both man's laws. I think everybody will be a fine, healthy, happy people to live each day as the life goes on. There's more in life to do than just depending on one to give and support for everyday's earnings, with nothing to give back. But work and play always meets happiness. If we can only closely study ourselves and see what we can do for all we can get. Give back rather a better way to work. Live wisely. Obey rules, orders and laws. Then we will find all our laws will not worry too much, for the things we are able to do ourselves . . . how to keep off all the police's books as to be closely watched.

211

I myself hate to be watched at all times by the police. Although it's a fearing thing . . . that's why I myself try my hard not to get entangled with them in the laws. I feel so timid with the unlawful thing. If I had to do, I would feel so guilty or would not even hold my head high to try and trick the law with lies. I'd sooner get away from all that and live as a sensible and happy person.

Some people say, 'I don't mind going to jail as long as I get my feed and be away from home.' They only say when they feel after . . . 'I've done a thing. I don't care what happens to me. I'll be away from home and everybody.' But the truth is, is not really he means that, because we often told these ones jail is not good. It takes your happiness and you are not happy at all away from home and families. It's shamefulness to the other families who love them and would not like to see them pushed off their homes. After all, jail was really never known to them amongst the circles of their background.

Now things have changed and that's where we must be very careful about doing things which are not right and good towards our fellowmen . . . but live as our fathers and mothers have taught us, and how they lived in the past. In those many years our folks lived with not too much of these stuff. They rather lived in the bush, and took care of themselves, roaming the bush, collecting all the food from sea and land without bothering about laws and missionaries. They were too happy to be away from all the life we are going through today.

Days are all gone now . . . when everything the tribes claimed are not more to ever be used again. The bringing of new life, new ways, new everything has really torn the roots out of their tribal life. Only remembrances are now. To look back to those times it makes one think so much of the times when people were free and happy. It sounds . . . everything is lost and is not needed again. Feeling of sadness creeps in to the ones who found and knew what belonged to them . . . is no more interested to the people of this land. I often wondered how in the life, ever it could come forth again. To me it is very hard to hope for the same life to be once more in our hands again.

Truly, as I write, I just can only see the life as a picture . . . never would appear to try and carry on again. Besides, with all this new stuff my people are on their way to take a poor step forward. Even the new modern life seems reckless, careless, being looked at with no interest. Although to many, everything seems a way of happiness. It sounds so pleasing. Everyone wishes to have a go at all that is pressed to their minds, when it is read or told to them or explained . . . but whether can it be done, or how long it can be done, when someone chooses the future aim to step on.

I like taking forward step with different activities if I have the chance to do them. I like to do and know something new too. It can make me happy to get to have them done, because it is something new that I did not know of at one time. As I was growing up, there was no chance in the world of my life to become one of them. There was only the limit to go, and a limit to learn, and that was all enough.

But look at today's life . . . is rather a great step forward to gain. It's there, but who shall tackle the future that lies before our eyes, with all that what the whites expect the people to offer themselves to take up, as they are doing today? They are offering part of their lives with all the different activities they have and what they have for their living. The needs for all are this . . . where can we find them from, who can help to see the needs, that should be responsible in giving us, or teaching?

But things for the future sound so tough, that in that case we must have a European to stand side by side along with us, to advise us with all our problems in entering this new business, or new life, that we never dreamed of, that will come to our land one day, as it is now knocking at each of our doors of our life. Each year things change a bit, whether it's for good or worse, or for better. But it's hard to kick a brick against it. We just don't know when to put our feet to stand on the right way of life. How can we do it? When will be the day or time? What shall we do to start ourselves? How to get away from the old ways? There are so many questions to answer.

We will find Aboriginals can do anything if they can have chance of being interested, or sticking on jobs that can be shown, or teaching. But the most important is . . . life away from home for year or more, that black people can go a long way to do the things, work amongst people from other places. You find a lot of big differences in a person, because he also can live, work, play, enjoy life like any other Europeans can do. Living in one area on the island is not enough to see, hear or learn to find the real true life that we need to do for life and health. Travelling and scattering ourselves among other folks is needed to be done, and that's how people to people are learning from each other and living decently all together as one happy big families.

I envy the life of today where there is much to look upon to be able to do. I wish I could do this, and tackle everything what Europeans are doing. My young life never meant much to me because those years were . . . never could be told or do to become one of those today people. I could not do the things of today . . . all freedom and happiness that one can do today. Many good things that are happening today never happened to my time . . . richness of jobs on better wages, training different activities for a better life to become of, softness of the laws. Whenever actions are being done, there is no hardness to deal with. Rules and laws are being broken and are not firmly being noticed by the ones who should be responsible to stand over. But to these, people are different from my life time as a young woman.

I think of these times . . . are much pleasant. Everything is good and satisfying. You get too much for nothing you give back for. You take and give nothing for the benefit of your being alive to live each day with so much food, clothes, and pleasures. But look at what's offering to we Aboriginals today. There are so much thoughts for planning for work to do, to take different patterns of activities that have and can be given to us, if we only can possibly do, if we only step forward for that aim.

It is so sad when different new changes are stepping in our midst, such as why an Aboriginal is just beginning to come to know that he must be in a place to stand to be chosen as a boss of certain jobs of controlling what he is appointed to do. He feels so happy, so he starts off good. He may be nice to someone, then he gets so used to his job he is a different person. He gets proud of his Australian European idea of how he can get around. Although he is just a learner, but he lives himself too much. He gets careless to work, and to treat his fellowmen and women, so he becomes more useless in his ways.

I am now a boss. I have been chosen to take over certain jobs. I'm a Councillor, I'm policeman, I'm manager, I'm head Stockman, I'm school teacher . . . helps in the school, helps in garage fixing vehicles and motors. So he is a nice bloke.

Then that day comes. There is neglectfulness of not too much bothering how to be careful, how to love and treat your people. This is how many bosses all over the States, and in our own midst . . . people are cheating one another because they stand high above the other poor fellow as a leader or a boss. If you look closely being one of these, you can be Okay, nice boss, friendly, smiling, but never cheat, be nasty, be selfish, to hate, to be careless, love yourself too much . . . then do all this, it will never help you to do the right thing. You will be unhappy because you have the differences of treating your fellowmen the wrong way.

But to be a good boss or a leader you must always share the happiness of your people, who you have responsibility over. Always be one of them. You find your work will never be upset with joy and pride of thinking about yourself. Always think for awhile before you can hurt your people for faultyness of mistake of some other person. Right thing is to always be ever ready to hear reasons, before you hurt the other bloke for her or his rights.

One fault is here today . . . concern myself as a pattern . . . 'I can do this or that. I feel I give myself for the activity for what I can do or learn to do. I say I'm willing to do that.'

Then some one else says, who has not my will, goes against me. Well, to these people, they say, 'She's not fit to do it, send some one else, find another person.' So it's done by others for the other person, who did not care to plan that.

215

So poor me, desired for my own liking, I go without that job. So somebody else has the privilege of having pleasure to do, and not me. So then I'll be buggered up. So this is the life of what's happening today.

Many strange things are happening like this. People are suffering for what they can do and cannot have it being done, because somebody behind the corner is not bothering. Ideas of the other person work out well for the other bloke, not for the one who thought and brought it forward. He is right out of it. Things have been going on like this for years and years. Jealousy is so in a high position at the standard of the people on this place. But everyone has talent. In fact you get more from people who are not known, or who you think are dull, or in another word stupid.

But he is the fellow who is able to do so . . . to the ones who they think. Or this fellow he is able to do that, so give him to do it. He wastes Government's money, goes for a course. They go for a conference meeting, have a nice trips to help their island. He is happy. Then the time comes for him or her to be home again. What happens after then? Well, he plays hop, step and jump on a different job. Not for long . . . he walks off the job and hopes for the best to be treated by parents. He once more gains laziness or doesn't bother about anything. But there you can see two different kinds of people . . . wish, hope, go nowhere . . . don't bother about anything, get somewhere. This is life of today.

Like wise, many went out to study, or college training for better life of learning, which of course made no headway for their mission. Some got married and forgot about their head way, which meant so much for them and their people. To these children, things could have worked, if their parents in the first place did not utter a word to them . . . 'Don't come back and work here for Mornington people. You'll get all the cheek and swearing.'

But these children would not say, 'No I'll do the work, because I went to this reason to help my people.' The parents and children did not realize how important one day for all, this sort of life we are now putting our foot on to. There was no interest in those back years. They thought we would always live the same as we went through . . . learn enough and that's all.

So we all live most of our lives at home. People say we lazy, could not get a job anywhere, depend on social benefit. But that's all we can do. Of course plenty of jobs right enough, but no money to pay. Of course one time many long years ago, I worked very hard, never left undone jobs for another day. But I worked so hard. I did not get money to be paid off. Only meals were supplied to me. I was contented. I was happy, but that's how I lived and worked. But today's young people have too much money for really not a proper task they do. But gee, they get too much money.

Still today, my life is still the same . . . hardly any money. Only my greatest supporter is my husband. We only have money when he sells his painting and books. But we don't have it ourselves. We still share it out to other relatives and friends. Also, when my husband works hard doing painting he has an exhibition, we have money. Some of it goes for the gallery, and the rest for us.

We both depend on ourselves and children. That's the only way I get my support from the only man and no other way. When Dick is away from home, I do handcraft and keep myself going. So Dick and myself are still working hard to keep ourselves up. Very seldom one of my boys gets job, when no money around, just to help the families while their dad's away. But we are contented and happy until Daddy comes home again. Most time of my life I stay home, care for the children.

Sometimes Dick takes me on holidays for a change to see Cairns, Sydney, Canberra once, Melbourne once, also Mount Isa when passing for Sydney. But I've enjoyed my trips.

Up to Laura . . . I saw the shelters with engravings on them. They were exciting and interested. Not much people live at Laura, about thirteen children attend school there . . . so sad when I saw there were only few amongst the many people who lived there long ago. Only with Percy Trezise, who cared to work and live among them . . . is now helping to keep them up to live on their land. But people like them up at Laura could be neglected, unknown for their wants and needs, if there weren't a man like Percy Trezise to care for their welfare of their need. No other person will care to take much of the responsibility to help them. Others would only take them to be just a wild mob, taking care of themselves as bush people. But you always find only half of the people in the world who care to help and find these kind of people, who live alone out in the bush. They rather the bush life. But also, the children side is where the supported can be taken notice and cared for, because children must grow up to learn to know and understand the other life . . . what the missions, towns and city life children are having today.

While my short stay with them at Laura last year . . . Dick and I explained raw materials, how and what to collect for handcrafts, showed them the stringy barks . . . were good for making small huts for shelter, also for painting. We went out with them one day to help them cut, and how to cut didgeridoo, to work and blow them. The only handcraft one or two men only could do was to make spears and woomeras. But these were men from Mitchell River, not from that country, so the only thing we knew . . . they only

218

lived there and did not know anything about handcraft or their background.

Jimmy Archer and his families, halfcaste, lived there also. Young Jimmy had learnt to do handcraft from Percy and Dick. They were nice people, so friendly. Once I asked Jimmy's mother if she could recall any background from the past from Laura. All she said . . . she can't remember nothing, because they only recently had gone to Laura to live and work among the people because her son had gone there to live. But the poor old lady's mind could not think anything. She did not hear anybody talk from the past. The only thing she said . . . they went to the city life when they were young and lost all the background, legends, customs and laws.

I've been to Mitchell. There were only couple of hand bags been made by cabbages' leaf, few mats and spears . . . just began. So they too, by the looks of things, they have not their background with them.

Next to Edward R. . . . we went around and had a look around the place. The mission is not far away, feeling the lovely sea breeze and looking at the sea. We went to see the place where they have their handcraft. I was surprised when I went with a young man to his home. On the one end room he showed Dick and myself one fighting stick, nulla nulla, and three small spears with wire prong. It was so sad to see that. I felt so very upset of this young man and his wife . . . how they tried to help the people there to make handcraft and how low it was to see what was all they had. But we only hope there are more now to make and sell out, since we last saw them. They had a meeting there about handcraft, and how they will work and make more handcraft.

To Aurukun M. . . . we landed there. There was no one came out to meet us there, only few children who came to see the arrival of the plane. Although they knew we'd come, but no one wanted to receive us because at the time we went around these places . . . when for the election for Independent for Leichardt. So we found ourselves in bit of stir by the missionaries there, who did not want to have anything to do with us. Also, at the same time, we had a look around for other needs too . . . how we could help them and how the handcraft and art were like.

But anyway, we were there . . . saw the handcrafts. There was a big collection right enough, but when we asked them, do they sell their stuff anywhere? . . . all they said, 'We sell them here. They buy the stuff here only.'

The lady who bought the stuff said, 'They have no place to send, or no market place anywhere to send the handcraft . . . only sell the stuff to anyone who wants to buy handcraft here.' We saw few of them and talked to them . . . how they can get lot of help if they need, is Council of the Arts in Sydney.

So we sat under a mango tree and explained things to them. They even agreed to work together in small group or team of men and women, and do more and send it away. Also we told them good stuff cannot only be in Aurukun. Plenty of people like Aboriginal handcraft and would like to see their work, also buy them. So we hope they did send most of them away to Cairns and Sydney.

Next, our visit to Weipa . . . we waited there after we landed at the airport almost two hours. So our customs belongs to black fellow . . . when we send word first or telegram, we expect big boss belongs to that place, come meet us, and welcome us to their country, whether they agree with us or not. But all the same, we know that kind of fashion. White man behind it all . . . make 'nother black fellow not like us too. But we did not care. We weren't gladly welcome. Everywhere we arrived was the same. Still, we met up with some good people. There was no handcraft there at the time. So we left a word with Kitty, as she was a member of the Council's board.

Then next, to the last settlement up at Cape York, Bamaga . . . the day we got there, it was raining heavily. We could not see the place to land, so we went across to Horn Island. Flying towards Horn Island . . . saw many small islands. On one island there was a house built. So that fellow is lucky to have an island to himself. Looking towards Horn Island, then to the wharf . . . the wharf was so beautiful from the air . . . and circled round. Finally we straightened for the airport and landed. So we three of us, at the edge of the bush, gathered wood and made fire and put the billy can on the fire and had our lunch, waiting for the storm to clear up. We had water alright, but no tea and sugar. A bloke from the airport gave us some, so we were alright. We put the fire out and made our way for Bamaga.

Now it was rather clear, so we managed to land. We got out, it was clear. Then the rain started falling, so we waited there another almost two hours again. Started to get late, so Percy and Dick started to rig up a small tarpaulin on the plane wing for me and Dick to sleep for the night, if there was no one to come and take us into the mission. At last a tractor came, so three of us were happy to be taken in. The way was long and now we were able to settle down.

While staying there, it was nice to get around and make few friends. The Chairman's families were so friendly, especially the few children who were there . . . asked all kinds of questions. I answered them all . . . wondered where I came from. I told them from Mornington Island. And now I am with you, here at Bamaga. So they said they would like to come over, and see my home. I said, 'Perhaps one day, if everything goes well, one day.'

Saw the store there, with few food stuff and clothing in at the same time. So small, the store . . . I could not believe my eyes to see that, although it's a very big place with so many houses and people. I was wondering if there were more shops there besides the one I saw. Went to see New Mapoon and saw the people there, talked with couple of them and had a walk down the beach. By the beach there were places where they, the people, do all their covermarie meat, dugong, fish and turtle. It really surprised me very much to see that all food were cooked in the one place all the time. So here you see where the covermarie ground is highly kept all together and where customs are kept still. Also wallaby and pigs are cooked there. Only no one spoke to us about the cooking place, but our eyes told us the story of their law and customs. I only wished . . . I would have liked to speak to them and ask question. But strangers meet strangers . . . there is only a glance and each person's afraid to speak to each other, and that's where the problems . . . don't understand each other at all.

Then the next day, we did nothing. There was a ship in trouble or a barge . . . was washed off its course and capsized, and Percy Trezise had to stay for the day to get further news if they wanted help for the search by a plane. So everything was Okay. Next day we left back for Cairns. On our way we flew almost over Cape York, to the tip of Australia. I really enjoyed the flight, seeing for the first time up across there with a good friend Captain Percy Trezise.

Also as I am writing, I think . . . the day we landed at the airport at Lockhart. No one was there. It was on a Sunday. No one was anywhere, only few boys who went for walk about a half mile away. We could see figures like post standing, just standing without moving. They were some boys. Percy and Dick looked across and said they were straight sticks of post, been put up there. I told them both, 'They not sticks, they are children.' So I waved hands to them to see if we could see a movements. I waved and waved, and the children came running up towards us. So we asked, 'Where are the people?'

But the kids told us, 'They have all gone out fishing.'

We had no one to refuel the plane, so we did it by ourselves . . . left a note on the drum of petrol, and money. I wrote a note to one of the boys who was my brother, Jackie Clarke . . . told him Dick and I were here at the airport and could he help the people for election. We gave the boys couple of tin meat and fruits and some peanuts and sweets I had. We said Goodbye to them and lifted for our journey, looking down below. The kids were waving madly, although it was only a moment with them to speak and have fun with them. They also sang songs for us while we were filling the plane. Another moment we were gone and could see them in the distance racing back to the village into their mission.

Although, not much cared to come and meet us at all airports. I wondered why they all turned us down. Only Mitchell River and Edward River ones came down to meet us. But anyway we were not really welcomed to their missions. Everywhere we went and landed we were just taken in to the reserves, not in a friendly manners. Why should they have turned us down? After all, everyone of these people on these missions knew Captain Percy Trezise very well. He'd been their first white man friend, better than the ones who worked among them in their country. Percy flew many times backwards and forwards landing at the airports, caring and working for them, making special friendship and liking to them. Percy heard all their complaints and helped them in many thousands of ways to make them happy.

I know for sure, how an Aboriginal can be noticed by a protector in any states . . . is always one white man who is a friend and one they can expect to get help from, and who can speak for better advancement. He makes a black people be recognized to the ones who should have recognized them from the word their settlements or the missions had been claimed. But no, it always takes one person out of the law circles to do all that with love and mercy, so they can have and face the standard for a better life, to go equal as black and white, or I should say white and blacks to be equal to work and play and live always alike.

For sure everyone of these people knew Dick Roughsey. What he had, he also shared to them. He made a very good relationship with most who saw him and heard of him. But that did not work out well . . . to be pleased to see him, but it did not matter the two blokes, anyway. But I was the one who really felt miserable and unhappy. After so many years I heard these two men have often spoken many friendly talks of these people in these areas.

Why I say and write this, of this visits or trips I had . . . made me think right back to my own background. My parents never taught me to turn down anyone, but always to meet, talk and welcome anyone who was a friend or a stranger. My tribes were loving tribes. My parents were loveable and kind. I feel so proud of them, because they taught me the way of their humble life, which meant so much to me. That's why I don't like the idea . . . Aboriginals have the taste of turning another stranger black

223

fellow down, because they have some one in the same ground to give them the feeling of don't care at all. I know if a stranger, whether they are white or black, call anywhere around my way and come to my home Mornington Island, I would be pleased to speak to get to know them and have lots of fun and laughs. I would make them welcome at home, because I like people. I like friends, and that's how I feel happy and safe.

Why I feel different from others . . . it's the background which I am proud of, also European life is a view of my point to press on to. I have sought . . . is good to live with. So I should feel I am in two world, which I have found both world of life is so real and wonderful to me to live each day. It's only I feel low at times, when my children make mistakes and upset me. I love my children very much. I like them to be like Dad and Mum. My children don't realise they have happy, friendly Dad and Mum. They should be proud of, and become like me and my husband. I cannot express a feeling we parents have been blessed by. I often wonder why our children don't take our footsteps. I know my children are friendly, loving, but they are too shy. They have more chance in life to come yet. As they grow older perhaps they become wiser, and will understand what the life, the world has for them to seek out.

One thing I have felt sad about and wondered how can it be . . . say I take these two men as an example. Dick Roughsey and Percy Trezise are blood brothers, so the wifes of them, we are sisters. Our children should, or are brothers and sisters. Then many would say also the white children of Percy's will say, 'How can that be? We have different fathers and mothers. We are different in colour and we have no relationship with them. We only can be friends and that's all.'

But no, that's not all. I must explain to both race . . . one's white and one is black. They are brothers. They are true brothers because now the white man has joined in that real relationship in blood line. So why then Mrs Trezise is afraid to call me Sister? Percy should call me Sister-in-law. Mrs Trezise calls Dick Roughsey Brother-in-law. Percy's children are afraid to call me Auntie, and Dick, Uncle. Why is that? Because we are not their race . . . or they have no idea. They call us both by our names. That's not right.

If you are proud of our love, relationship and our customs, we would like you white children to call us Uncle or Auntie. I teach my children . . . say Uncle or Auntie, or the more respect, to call Mr and Mrs Trezise, Dad and Mum. That seems more to show and do to respect these two couples. If we use these terms, the strength of our love and relationship grows more strongly towards each other. This is the proper way.

I know as I am writing this, there are more whites who already have made relationship with an Aboriginal man and woman. But the only importantness is that we must speak hard to our white children to give that same respect to our black children.

I think some of you Europeans already know what is the big secret of this softness feeling to my race. It is in us. It grows up inside and stays to keep us alive to our health and happiness. I don't know much how white people could understand our feeling, because there's rather a different taste to their kind of love. I have been to some places, where of course I did not hear a white girl or boy, man or woman called each other Sister or Brother, Uncle or Auntie . . . cousins or in-laws. Never. They just call each other by their names. The relationship is really not what they claim. No custom is there. But if you look carefully and notice our way, you'll be surprised how we love each other and own everybody, although they out of our family circle.

There's times to learn of the laws, and how to respect too . . . binding love, respect, obedience, be careful of doing harm to each other, guiding our foreground for the future. We can all work and help each other and live as a decent people should, both with the law inside and to our people. I'm sure we can always be happy.

What I have written is all my interest. Things of each day life. No matter where I've gone to, I have found differences of nature of mankind. Some is not pleasant, most were exciting.

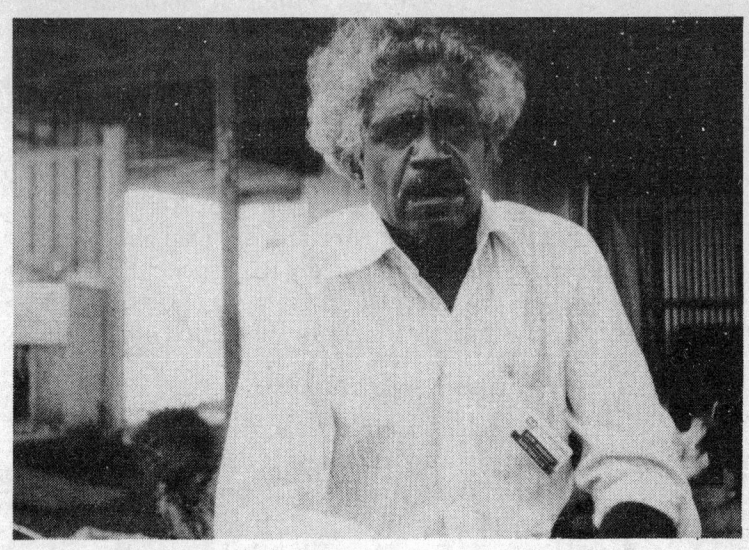

My husband Dick Roughsey.

My sister and myself with my sister's daughter and son with
grandchildren.

Within the days of my life I've spent, I've found myself learning and understanding, being so interested . . . what everyday life meant to me. Closely and carefully I watched nature of my people . . . how we treated our laws, customs and culture and they were almost wiped out. It is sad to know we haven't carried out all that was best for us. Now few things are coming back slowly, such as teaching children in school of their language. Legends are told to them, hand craft are being shown and taught, but are not really interested for children to grip hold of them yet.

Now we are walking into life to be independent people, so we are able to start all over again to understand, to work and take control of what the Government is passing on to us to live for. The difficulty in my people here is that they do not really understand the meaning of many talks, ideas explaining of the future that lies ahead of us. Everything is a misunderstanding by hearing . . . how or what can be rightly worked. Some have a good idea or reasons, then believe it or not . . . whether what has been talked about, whether it can be worked. Who shall respond to act on?

To see the life here among my people, you can see where they would like to go forward and be independent people. But to my people, it takes a mighty long time before they can stand or place themselves as European, because looking into the European work and life has been their life from child hood . . . and had all given to him or her, and what they took after their parents, and they carefully worked and lived together through all ages, and had a different life to learn and understand, differently from the Aboriginal. They lived only what they could get, how to learn and live very simple, so little, and that was quite enough for us to go. So you see it's a tough world of life for us to grip hold

227

of, something that never, never has been showed, or we live with to handle right at this moment. So there is a struggle of life.

So now the Government expects us to take over to be independent, but my people never heard of being independent before, because they never heard or knew the word or what it all means. It's just lucky few of us understand, and had to explain the word 'independent'. Means . . . help yourself to all living in life. 'Depend' is the word we knew of, because I cannot depend on you or you don't depend on me, but not this other one. That 'independent' was a European's act and life. He only knew. Aboriginal could never in the past years be equal as European. It was never meant to give to all my people here and in all parts of Australia.

There was only a small limit to know and learn, especially to read and write and other small jobs like cutting and carrying wood for cooking, working and watering in the garden, cleaning around the house, and tidying up, washing and drying up the dishes. Stock jobs were done by Aboriginal men for the start here on the island. Men and boys had to help till the ground in the garden for all plants and fruit trees and vegetables. They were taught to help build houses with the missionaries and were able to work and build houses themselves. Then to thirty to forty years back, changes had come . . . rather different.

Times like at present are beginning of a new life of living and understanding to look into it. It's tough. We really cannot think how one thing to another can be handled by the Aboriginals. It's easy to say or talk about business, how we can go about, but we know it's difficult . . . of how to co-operate on materials, how to order such and such articles to do the jobs. I cannot see if there is a head way to get a help from anyone who can help we Aboriginals to give us the idea where to order anything that a man can do . . . and be able to begin certain jobs, say to make motorcars, motor bikes, tanks for water, to make push bikes, to be plumbers, to build a boat, to make all kinds of articles. But where are the materials? On an island . . . is so very hard to equal as European, to work and live to their standard. Mainland is far more better because you can learn and work to live with the people who can do all things, to have to do the jobs and business as they free to do, and travel around where ever they wish to do. And with these Aboriginals . . . are in fact much better learner and trainer than we on an island like Mornington Island.

If anyone wants to look into this, can they imagine how unlearned people we are . . . even had not the chance of life as most other Aboriginals can get. Here on the island you are able to do a small effect to reach, to become somewhere in a small way . . . of what is shown to simple jobs of life is good. But we like to learn more and more of how to increase our understanding, whereby we can be able to live for ourselves. I know we are unlucky tribes. There is no other way I possibly can make the readers, who will read my book, try to understand the poor, hard, reckless life we have . . . unlearned, uncared life of knowledge was wasted.

Although the talent and knowledge of my tribe is in amongst us, but how shall we feel to be interested and try to uplift ourselves for the future that we are about to aim to go through? A new life . . . which means we don't know how to start to take it, which of course we never knew of, never lived to become like European. So where we are now, it means we got to start all over again to enter into the new way of life . . . how to work, how to understand, how to live by it, and still to learn to have responsibilities for all activities we about to face. I really feel dismayed of how to explain about the need of my tribes. It wasn't meant for us in the first place to know many things that we have missed and would never mention to know. So that's why we Aboriginals have been far back from every way of life that we should have known, before anything like this what they expect of we Aboriginals to do so.

I feel sad about my tribes, of the life we went through, as most life was not granted for us. It wasn't allowed to be given to us. We learnt few thing that were simple, just enough and no more to go. I could stretch out my thoughts . . . all living here, most benefits are not ours. So we remain still in the same place, because we are black. We must not know too much of the European ways of life. That was meant from the start, when I was young and went to school. Now the opportunity of a new different life is on its way. But we have a poor mind to understand small ideas . . . weak, faint glimpse of looking for better way of going about to live. Now it's all coming to our hands. We wonder about with wonderingness . . . how things will work out? When will we start? How can we do to prove ourselves without a good neighbour to be our best friend, to help us in all we would like to do?

My people in Australia have been forgotten people, disliked, uncared, unloved, neglected for the way of life to be equal. We lived low and sad, calm people, but we were contented how we lived. The thing I am speaking about . . . it's the life of Education. From that, we only got reading and writing and could not get hundreds of other benefits in life, which could have been our big support today. If only it was given to us those many years back. Today we feel, stepping into the future of better way . . . how to live. That's Europeans' life, which of course will mean so many hardships against our tribal life. That's why we feel to live normal and simple . . . not too much of a white man's life in us. Your ways can steal, wreck . . . and lose all our humble culture, customs and laws.

These laws of having our own tribal Government, policeman, as men of peacemakers, have led their people to a very careful high standard, especially on care for others, as well as love everybody and also obey the laws of the land. Our way of the tribes meant so much to us, because everything was good, came out of the wild life. This life was the tribes . . . how to be careful about everything. You could not go wrong or do wrong and spoil things, and life that belonged to the tribes and the life they had from the start was the life they chose to have and own.

Long before the white man found my people this was all they had and that's why our tribal life is so important for us not to forget and step away from it. If we take no notice our back ground of our descendants, of our forefathers, we never can walk too far to face the new life that recently has been sought for us to take up. Then we can say that we have started to live, and what was for us to live with, can be well covered over with all its European's life and all its ways. It's alright to learn and live some part of the European's ways, but how to come to know, how to live and work like them, but we don't expect too much from them, because it means that all the good we have had from the tribes, can really be nothing. No one of us will have the feelings for others, with love and kindness, respect and to be respectable towards each other. These will be outnumbered of the history of the Lardil tribes, then there will be nothing to be remembered and passed down to the children to claim.

The times of years, months and days are now almost to say our tribes shall be forgotten. The older tribal people seem to put everything behind their backs and don't want it no more. They have broken many of the Lardil laws, customs and culture. It seems to the people of the tribes that they ran too far forward of the European ways, and the christianity has let down all the good the tribes had. Once they knew of the christian life, seemed to make the tribes live different according to all its ways, but the same life can be both at once.

Our tribal life meant so much to us, because our way had a powerful and richer meanings. Christianity is a rather different form of life. It concerns somehow to be kind and helpful, loving and understanding of everything, to obey the laws that were given so many hundreds of years, to know of the first Governors and rulers, of how God showed Himself to man so we may know all His works. Then the Son of man from Him came to show and teach us more of His Coming, and how They both became One person in Spirit. Then also how the Lord has lived amongst man of human flesh. Men could not live well enough to know the truth. Man was still hard hearted towards each other . . . bitterness, self pride, murder, stealing, cheating, insulting their neighbours, greed of all life of whatever may be . . . they also never changed a man to become good.

So what is today, it is still a hard world of man to understand and they still have their own way of life to live

231

with. But still you get from the people of christians, they are still mixed with all this and with things of its life that are good and evil. So from where a tribe had before . . . still belongs to us and it should never be taken from our way of life. We must hang on to the tribal life, because the Almighty has given the life to us, to know of and understand how to live to ourselves as people of the tribes. Something of the tribes should not be wrecked, taken, forgotten or stolen. It leads to nothing, only to take up what has already come in our hand at the present time. It makes us wonder how now we can live with all its European's life, because it means much hardness to know how to live as real Europeans, because it's not ours to live really with and stand the woes and strifes of labours and all sorts of difficulties that we never were able to do from the start . . . early stage of life.

A European could not live like the tribes . . . hunt, roam the bush, have corroborees and do what we can live today. A tribe could not get and have what the Europeans had, because it was not meant for us to live with. Those times and years were like two different kinds of people. Tribes were outcast, or never being taken much notice . . . because we were black, wild savages, living our normal life as savages, living in the wild life, with all its beauties around. So this is where the life of whites is rather difficult for us to really understand yet, although we are beginning to operate with the Europeans in understanding all their ways of life, how to live with.

Many readers may take up reading this book. Only the eyes of witness and minds of understanding have seen many different life of two kinds of people. White and black . . . we could not gain from each other too much to be given to each of these two races. There were limits for sharing, how to live. Not too much to give away, too. But from my point of view I have closely studied the life of two races. I cannot show and give a white person too much of my tribal life. What I have been able to do . . . because it was not supposed to give strangers something which I own and have. That was the custom and laws of the tribes . . . same as a white man could not give too much of what they had and what they knew, because it was their way to live with them. Now today, at present we realize to give each other and share the same customs and laws to each other, which at one time we were not allowed to share. But man must live to share now to understand and work together as real Australians should live from the start of our founding.

Black people don't like to live any more better than the way they love best. It's so hard. It is so strange to come forward as Europeans. Although there are many good ways of life to look upon and learn, but an Aboriginal has to look far back behind to all its life. They feel ashamed to live in higher standard. It gives them a feeling . . . 'I'm black. I rather be left alone and live the way I was brought up.' It's not because a black wants to be white, but we Aboriginals feel different to the liking of where a European stands. We like to live normal and do the things in life in our own liking. Although young people, as well as Adults, care so much to become a learner and a worker in different way like the Europeans and begin to live somewhere to acknowledge themselves, but they will miss so much of their land and people. Soon, in later years, they fret for home and parents and wish to be back to the land where they belong to, where the home life is so free, and not much of the strict laws of an European can fear them.

I have known of most people throughout Australia. I can say I wish I never become civilized of the fact of science, methods, of Government morales. They are very carefully and strictly kept in highness to try and live up to it. We folks rather live by our own tribal laws. In some parts of Australia, especially where customs and laws cannot be broken and most carefully are watched, I can say these people care not about civilization. They love the bush and its wild life. They become strong healthy people and live without sickness and disease. Bush food also is so pleasant. You can eat all kinds of sea food and land food without being sick. You eat too much of white man's food, you can be sick. Tummy ache you have and get very ill, then most time you die because you not allowed to eat the food that has caused you to be sick. Your tummy cannot hold the food you have eaten because it is not the food your parents and their parents ate, before the time of white man's ration. Food your parents and grandparents ate, you can eat . . . never can be sick, because it's in our blood and this is why any bush food, it belongs to the Aboriginal to hunt and eat and live that way. Entering civilization has caused many infection to the tribes.

They made us throw up all our tribal ways, kept us away from our hunting grounds, made us give up our sacred grounds and sacred laws. The white man, like missionaries, said they were no longer to have and hold on to. So going to school and living apart from parents and tribal laws can change the life of the tribes . . . and live by their ways. But to look at that, is far more to stand and hold to what the early tribes had found to live alive with. It should not be taken or forgotten by any other people who are not of our race.

Before the changes of white man came to our midst, my people were so happy and healthy. You can hear the sounds of laughing. They have their own sports of dancing, singing with clap sticks and boomerangs. Everyone is really enjoying themselves. After hunting they are happy, sharing all what they have hunted for. During the time of cooking and eating there is funs of all activities . . . are happening to keep their health going.

Finally, since twenty-six years ago, the happiness of the tribes was vanishing. It was not a time now . . . how to go forward, or look still to the way the tribes had it going. Missionaries wanted a different methods, of their way of teaching and to know of their life. That's how our laws, customs and cultures, also legends, were soon left far behind for anyone to look to carry on. We thought we were aiming for a better life to be treated fairly and equally. But as years were going out on us in our lifes, we soon found we were rounded by wire nettings and fences, and we found living in this modern life, we had lost.

That really cost our life to live on the good laws, customs and our cultures . . . are no more in our hands. We could find some goodness of the present life and bad and tough ones to go any further. We feel it's too much harder to live this way, because we are only poor black fellows. We like to live our own life, so we may not forget of the past, especially our back grounds . . . are so important to live by them.

As often I sit and write I cannot really express the good old times of the tribes. These were many exciting happenings. We were surrounded by laws and customs. They were a real stuff of great protection, its needfulness was well watched and guided. Respectableness was strictly held and commanded by the tribes. We were punished by the tribal laws in a different manner . . . never to do it again. Other laws that were broken, by sacred waters and ground . . . well the great Spirit of the sea fixed that part. For even that, we still had good men of the tribes to chant to drive away the evil Spirit. Many were cured instantly.

I love my native home, I pride all that I have seen and learnt. It's too hard for me to forget them all. My people were great men of power. They were heroes, hunters, leading Government. Tribal men were wonderful people, as well as leading women, who guided their own people and their country. We have drifted so far away from that life, and have gladly marched forward into the life that really is hurting us, to care not to go any further.

This is the life of my people, and with the Europeans. I feel that people may understand what I have written about. I have thought I didn't want to lose all that I have learnt. I knew it could have been lost for most people would have never known how we lived on this island if there was no one like me to put my thoughts together, to write about all that belonged to me. Now I'm looking forward to see this book being published.

Although it was hard for me to get a help, because I didn't know anyone to pass my manuscript, so I decided to get help from Paul Memmott and other good friends who helped to typewrite my manuscript and made it to make something come worthwhile for the book. My biggest regards to the ones who were richly interested to give an Aboriginal woman a chance in life with her book.

So now you can read with the most interest and learn from it, so we may closely contact with love, relation and friendship and all unite as one in God's big vast of land. That's why God has sent His Son . . . to teach us all to live the same as my people of Lardil, with happy smiling faces, and a most gifted people of my country. So there it is for the Year 1982.

I thought and thought for many days should I write a book of my laws and customs and culture and legends, because ancestors that lived in the past passed all their good living all through the ages. It has been passed on so that we could live by it. My parents were middle age people, never spoke english but language. But the years I lived with them made me proud of them. They are both dead. I wish they could be alive and be young to understand what their daughter has done. I am proud of myself . . . I was their daughter and could write and understand that I have already come to the time that I am able to write and bring it to the life, that some other people may understand and realize what the life of an Aboriginal people had to go through.

You will read all that I have written . . . is the true life, all I've seen of different people I'm writing of. The fact is really true. You may not believe it all, but come and live among my people, you'll be able to believe . . . two kinds of Doctors, native and a European, work together to heal the sick, the Mulgree Spirit, chanting a baby to be strong and healthy, also to give strength to a sick person, bush medicines, leaves and grass to give healingness to the body. The handcraft wasn't known to be made by a person, only boomerangs, spears and nulla nulla were made for weapons for fight and hunting. Now the handcrafts are being sold and now it's worth a price. So already that handcraft is so important that my people still continue selling.

Another of these . . . we have many corroborees. The man dreams at night. When he dreams this dream he gets up at nights or during the day time showing other men the action to the dream dance, and that's how we get all our corroborees done. The recent years, Dance Festival was not known to we Aboriginals. Then it was explained what the Festival meant . . . was to get other race of people to come together and join in the dancing to show how their way of dancing. Everyone works at it to make our community a very happy and interesting one. Some people found relations from wherever they came, made a very exciting crowd and all became wonderful friends.

At the present time Moyenda elders made a step forward to work equally with Government Councillors. Moyenda elders are bringing their laws and custom to give the background laws a different act against the European law. So the Moyenda law was accepted by the Queensland Government, that some of their good act could work together with some of the Queensland Government's act. Presently it's working out well. There's another thing . . . the Moyendas brought forth some of our young men to become initiated men. And now we already have quite a number of the boys here are men that are known as lurugu.

Now we have our Shire Clerk here. He's a guard and a protection to the people and business. We haven't had a Shire Clerk here before. Already two were here but they resigned. We have still another one. We already have a Council Chairwoman. We have nominated many women. I was one of them but failed in voting so I collected my twenty dollars back, and the other rest who failed. Our Chairwoman now has lived with us for so many years. 1942 . . . we were evacuated from the dormitory, she still remained with us here. She was voted in for three years. She's a good and a faithful one who loves to help her people. It makes worth life going on to make her people happy.

These life with all its [Government] act, it's new and strange to us now, although some act fears my people. So the new act really makes us . . . is a warning to control ourselves, not to do the things that can hurt our own people, to live as brothers and sisters. Although you may think many law should not be here, but it is the best way to live with the law. There's love, sympathy and kindness that we should well regard to the ones who are carefully keeping the law to make us live better people. There are lot of different acts now. Sometimes it's hard to co-operate with laws of this time, for my people are really not understandable person to know many ways that we believe. Sometimes the act are so strong that people feel the new laws are bit too firm. They rather live simple without too many act, and they feel free to live the same life they had lived in many passed years. Some day they gradually will think that these times will find themselves to understand that the future lies for the good of them to inherit the days and years to come, and make it better for the two kinds of laws that are now right in the door of our life, to live with what we know is safe and good and obey all laws that have been given to us for a better use.

When I sit and think of all I have done, what I have written, it was a pleasure of me writing the things that I've seen. I can remember the times when I sat and just wrote, everything came afresh in me. Everything came into my mind as I was writing. It was one of a thing that gave me an idea that my customs, culture, laws and legends will never be forgotten. That's why I began to write. When I looked into the background of my dreamtime I knew everything was good to be known so that my dreamtime life will never be forgotten. I only hope now that people who read this book will take some lesson and understanding to be one of my people and take up the life that should always belong to them too.

Often in the time when I got well stuck into the writing the days were beautiful, and most the wind came blowing from the North East, brought back many memories of the days of the past . . . refresh my minds, knowing so much, thinking a lot of the happy times, when I can see the folks far behind of the dreamtime now.

How good it all meant to me. I could not hold myself back from doing the things I was about to do . . . writing so nothing can be lost or unknown and forgotten. I thought of the many good life, of all I saw of all its background . . . how wonderful the way people lived towards each other, and how the elders of the tribes kept their people in perfectness, to guide and protect the land with all its laws, customs, culture, legends. I wondered many times who taught them the laws of the dreamtime and how they gathered the laws together and made them, and it was wisely attended by the great men of our land.

I will always remember the tribal people, who have given and taught us, so many tribal laws to have. They loved the hunting grounds, sharing all alike. Most of all they had their fun and games. Laughing was also heard, clapping of the boomerangs was heard. They were always happy.

As I close the writing of my wonderful people, I feel sad to know they are gone now. Only memories last forever.

23 August 1982

A note on the editing process

The manuscript of this book was completed by Elsie Roughsey in 1972. It survived a ferocious cyclone on Mornington Island which destroyed all of the community's buildings, and then it was in the hands of several roaming custodians in North Queensland. Fearing for its safety and future, Elsie eventually asked us to help her with its publication, and so it came to rest in our office at the University of Queensland for another five years whilst we negotiated with publishers, sought grants for editing and resolved our editing policy. The idea of publishing Elsie's manuscript in its unedited form was discussed with several publishers. It became apparent that some editing would be required in order for it to be acceptable for commercial publication, and accessible to the average white Australian reader. This presented something of a dilemma in view of our desire to retain the work's individuality and resist any directive to rewrite it in standard English. However, Elsie makes it clear in her book that she is addressing the non-Aboriginal world, those who she describes as being 'in the outside part of the world', overseas from Mornington Island and its community.

The manuscript was first typed exactly as it was written. It was proof-read to ensure that this was the case. Non-standard spelling and grammar were retained. This was to provide a faithful copy for use when editing.

Undertaking the editing was an enormous challenge. The flow and expression in manuscript were unusual and very individual. It became obvious that if changes were to be made they had to be sensitive to, and match with, the rare qualities of the work, and done in such a way as to be perfectly consistent throughout.

Thus we felt it essential to develop a clear editing policy. This policy, and accordingly the text, was revised continually as we experimented with change and non-change, and questioned our results. At first we tended to 'over-standardize' which meant a great deal of change, but eventually a limited number of change policies were devised that aimed at preserving Elsie's unique Aboriginal style but which would, at the same time, make easy the reading of the text for the non-Aboriginal reader.

In addition we had to deal with the problems of Elsie's presentation of the traditional oral style of story telling, in a written form.

The changes made were largely as follows.

The text was divided into paragraphs and chapters. This was relatively easy because Elsie told her story somewhat sequentially moving from moment to moment, and from theme to theme. As a result very few parts of the original manuscript have been repositioned. Where repositioning of some minor parts did occur, it was done so with Elsie's consent. Similarly, in a few cases where material was repetitive, these sections were edited out with the author's approval. All chapters were named by the author.

A second change was that of standardizing tense. Elsie's verb tenses were often influenced by her traditional language, Lardil, and Aboriginal English, which divides tense differently to standard English. In Lardil, for example, there is no language distinction between past and present. The difference is expressed using other language 'markers'. In many instances throughout the text Elsie demonstrated that she was familiar with the tense usage of standard English, involving past, present and future. Thus we felt justified in standardizing verbs in other parts of the text that could have presented the reader with tense confusion and prevented ease of comprehension throughout the progression of the prose.

Variant spellings of English words were standardized and additional punctuation was introduced in order to structure the text clearly into sentences. We felt this would make reading easier for those unaccustomed to non-standard modes of expression. When sudden changes in the thought process occurred in mid-sentence, or when vital linking phrases or words were missing in the original, an elipsis was used.

There are a few comments inserted in the text to qualify meaning. These are all contained in square brackets. Geographical locations are provided on a map at the beginning of the book. The inclusion of these was with the author's approval.

Whenever meaning was in doubt Elsie was consulted. She also reviewed the editing as it progressed, and approved the final manuscript.

Despite the changes to the text, we feel that we have preserved the flavour and flow of Elsie's work. It remains comprehensible to her fellow Mornington Islanders, and will be of interest, no doubt, to many Aboriginal readers, as well as to the white audience. For those who wish to examine the hand written manuscript, the typescript of this manuscript, the final edited typescript and the editing policy, they are lodged in the Fryer Library of the

An Aboriginal Mother Tells of the Old and the New

University of Queensland.

Paul Memmott and Robyn Horsman
Aboriginal Data Archive
May 1983

Glossary of Aboriginal and non-standard words that appear in the text

Most of the Aboriginal words are from the Lardil language. Elsie's spelling of each word is followed by the phonetic spelling that appears in the dictionary of Lardil prepared by the linguist Kenneth Hale and his colleagues at the Massachussetts Institute of Technology.

*The non–Lardil words are marked with an asterisk and consist of a mixture of Aboriginal English and colloquial terms used by Mornington Islanders.

banner (bena).   A plant that grows in swamps, part of which is edible.
* *Bentinck*.   Bentinck Island is one of the South Wellesley Islands which was occupied by the Kaiadilt tribe, and was named by Mathew Flinders in 1802. The word 'Bentinck' is also used to refer to the Kaiadilt people, hence 'Bentinck people'.
Billmaree.   To cause someone to get sick due to failure in observing certain taboos.
Booralungie (burrarangi).   One of eight social classes used by the Mornington Island Aborigines as well as elsewhere in Aboriginal Australia. Each individual belongs to one of these classes which is determined from the class of one's mother and father.
bubbi (babe, babi).   Paternal grandmother, sibling of paternal grandmother.
bubbigurrida.   See 'bubbi' and 'gurrida'.
Bulletgear (bululkiya).   A place at the eastern end of Mornington Island, said to be inhabited by the 'unseen people' — people who are rarely seen but at times heard, and who are believed to belong to a spiritual dimension.
Bulletgearmanda (bululkiyamenda).   The people from bululkiya, i.e. the 'unseen people'.
Bullimbanda (balumbenda).   Westerner, person from the west, member of western division of the Lardil tribe.
burrumbad (barrambarr).   Hairstring, hairstring belt, worn by initiated men.

conborras.   An edible native vegetable, wild cucumber.

* *coolamun (coolamun)*.   A multipurpose container and carrier. The Mornington Islanders used two types: one manufactured from bark in a trough shape, and one made of timber in a shallow dish shape.

* *covermarie*.   An oven-type method of cooking, similar to the Maori 'hangi' or the Torres Strait 'kup-mari', involving the placing of food in a pre-heated hole and covering it with bark.

cumbered (kamburr, kambuda).   Pandanus nut.

curelle (kuriyal).   The edible 'flesh' or 'meat' part of the pandanus nut.

Damen (demiin).   A special auxillary vocabulary taught secretly to male novices of the second degree initiation, or subincision.

Dewaliwall (diwaliwal).   One of the first three people to come to Mornington Island, when it was still a peninsula of the mainland, over 6,000 years ago. They are said to have made many resource places and their adventures are recorded in Aboriginal legend. The other two people were Gin Gin, Dewaliwall's niece, and her husband Marnbill.

dulnu (dulnhu).   A fish known today on Mornington Island as the 'month fish' because it runs in schools during only one lunar month of the year, about the time of August or September.

dunarga (danaka).   A knife made from the bailer shell, used for cutting meat and string, scraping wood, etc.

dunga (dadngka, danka).   Barracuda.

galgar (kelngka).   A species of grass used for making string.

ganda (kernda).   Wife, wife's sister, brother's wife.

gandagurrida.   See 'ganda' and 'gurrida'.

gangu (kankar, kangkari).   Grandfather (on father's side), sibling of paternal grandfather.

gangugurrida.   See 'gangu' and 'gurrida'.

gardu (karda, kardu).   Son, daughter, woman's child; nephew, niece (of man), man's sister's child.

gardugurrida.   See 'gardu' and 'gurrida'.

* *gigjie (gidgea)*.   Lancewood, a species of Acacia called kurrburu in Lardil, used for manufacturing a variety of artifacts due to its hardness, e.g. boomerangs, spearheads, digging sticks.

Gin Gin (jin jin).   One of the first three people to come to Mornington Island, when it was still a peninsula of the mainland, over 6,000 years ago. They are said to have made many resource places and their adventures are recorded in Aboriginal legend. The other two people were Marnbill, Gin Gin's husband, and her uncle Dewaliwall.

Goonana (Kunhanhaa).   The Lardil name for Mornington Island. (Now that the old mission settlement has become a township it has also been given this name, simplified to Gununa.)

Goonanamanda (kunhanhaamenda).   The people of Mornington Island.

goonoo (kunu).   A form of the word 'gungu' (which see) used as a term of address.

goonoogurrida. See 'gungu' and 'gurrida'.

Gooroodmanda. A mysterious fearful person believed to inhabit mangroves on Mornington Island and referred to as the 'mudshell man'.

gumbin (kambin). Son, daughter (man speaking); brother's son, brother's daughter.

gumbingurrida. See 'gumbin' and 'gurrida'.

gungu (kungku, kungung). Younger brother (of man), brother (of woman); younger sister (of woman).

gungugurrida. See 'gungu' and 'gurrida'.

guntha (kantha). Father, father's brother.

gunthagurrida. See 'guntha' and 'gurrida'.

gurrida (kurirr, kurirru). Dead (of person, animal or plant).

Guthan-Guthan (kathankathan). Someone who takes on the regular role of being a funny person or comic.

guyil (kayal). White pipe clay; white paint.

jaet (jeyirr). Grass skirt worn by women.

jumba (jembe). Maternal grandfather; sibling of maternal grandfather.

jumbagurrida. See 'jumba' and 'gurrida'.

* *Kaiadilt.* The Aboriginal people who occupied the South Wellesley Islands, i.e. Bentinck and Sweer's Islands. It is also the name for their language, as well as their tribe.

labumore. A native fruit like a wild fig indigenous to the Wellesley Islands.

Lardil. The Aboriginal people who lived in the North Wellesley Islands — on Mornington, Sydney and Wallaby Islands. It is also the name for their language as well as their tribe.

* *Lewit.* An Aboriginal form of the word 'leeward', referring to the north-west side of Mornington Island which is protected from the strong winter south-easterly winds.

lowalen (lewalan). Large bailer shell, used for carrying water.

lurugu (luruku). A male who has undergone first degree initiation which involves the circumcision ceremony.

maga (meka). A fire torch made from tightly wrapped Melaleuca bark.

Marnbill (maarnbil). One of the first three people to come to Mornington Island, when it was still a peninsula of the mainland over 6,000 years ago. They are said to have made many resource places and their adventures are recorded in Aboriginal legend. The other two people were Gin Gin, Marnbill's wife, and her uncle Dewaliwall.

marrka (merrka). Aunt, father's sister.

marrkagurrida. See 'marrka' and 'gurrida'.

mejeal (mijil). A small handnet for catching fish and also used for carrying things.

mooru. Ball of grass string.

Moyenda.   Aboriginal elder.

mulgan (malkam).   Deceased person, dead person. The spirit or ghost of a deceased person.

Mulgree (markirri).   n. A sickness imposed by the Rainbow Serpent for violation of rules mainly concerning eating behaviour.
        v. to incur the mulgree sickness.

Mungada (mangarda).   Child, young person, youth (before initiation).

Murrandu.   To give gifts in return for other favours, to 'square-up' over a debt, to give food as a token of thanks for privileges received in a dance.

* *myall*.   A derogatory and racist term referring to traditionally-living Aborigines who allegedly are 'uncivilized' because they do not recognize or prescribe to Western customs and Christian beliefs.

ngama (ngama).   Mother, mother's sister, son's wife (of a man), brother's son's wife.

ngamagurrida.   See 'ngama' and 'gurrida'.

* *nulla nulla*.   Fighting stick.

panja (benja, kurka).   Edible root or corm of a swamp rush.

* *sugarbag*.   Wild bee honey.

thabu (thabu, thabuji).   Older brother (of a man).

thabugurrida.   See 'thabu' and 'gurrida'.

thubun (thubun).   Timber pestle — used for pounding foods.

thundamalmal (thandamalmal).   Male pubic tassle, used in dancing attached to a hairstring belt.

walpa (walba).   A V-shaped raft made of buoyant timbers lashed together with rope made from Hibiscus bark.

weeare (wiya).   A poker stick used while cooking, for pushing ashes and coals, and moving food in the fire.

* *Winded*.   An Aboriginal form of the word 'windward', referring to the south-east side of Mornington Island which is exposed to strong south-easterly winds in winter.

yagoo (yaku, yakuku).   Sister (of man), elder sister (of a woman).

yagoogurrida.   See 'yagoo' and 'gurrida'.

Yalbudd (yarburr, yarbud).   1. bird, snake, noxious insect.
             2. person who is dead.

yamma stick.   Women's fighting and digging stick.

Youngul.   Cave.

Youngulmanda.   People who belong to a spirit world who live in caves and are not seen by humans, but are sometimes heard; often referred to as the 'unseen people'.

yugudba (yukarr, yukarrba).   Husband, husband's brother, woman's sister's husband.

yugudbagurrida.   See 'yugudba' and 'gurrida'.